. . . .

Naming the Enemy: Anti-corporate movements confront globalization

Amory Starr

. . . .

Pluto Press
AUSTRALIA

Zed Books
LONDON AND NEW YORK

Naming the Enemy: Anti-corporate movements confront globalization was first published by Zed Books Ltd, 7 Cynthia Street, London N1 9JF, UK and Room 400, 175 Fifth Avenue, New York, NY 10010, USA in 2000.

Distributed in the USA exclusively by St Martin's Press, Inc., 175 Fifth Avenue, New York, NY 10010, USA

Published in Australia and New Zealand by Pluto Press Australia, Locked Bag 199, Annandale NSW 2038, Australia tel: 61 2 9692 5111; fax: 61 2 9692 5192 website: www.plutoaustralia.com

Cover designed by Andrew Corbett
Set in Monotype Dante by Ewan Smith, London
Printed and bound in the United Kingdom by Biddles Ltd, Guildford and King's Lynn

A catalogue record for this book is available from the British Library.

US CIP data has been applied for.

ISBN 1 85649 764 x cased
ISBN 1 85649 765 8 limp

Australian ISBN 1 86403 138 7 pb

Contents

Abbreviations

APEC	Asia Pacific Economic Cooperation
CSA	Community Supported Agriculture
EBRD	European Bank for Reconstruction and Development
FTA	free trade agreement
GATT	General Agreement on Tariffs and Trade
HIPC	heavily indebted poor country
IMF	International Monetary Fund
LETS	Local Exchange Trading System
MAI	Multilateral Agreement on Investments
NAFTA	North American Free Trade Agreement
NGO	non-governmental organization
NIC	newly industrializing country
OECD	Organization for Economic Cooperation and Development
WB	World Bank
WTO	World Trade Organization

Introduction

> What an astounding thing it is to watch a civilisation des-
> troy itself because it is unable to re-examine the validity
> under totally new circumstances of an economic ideology.
> *Sir James Goldsmith*[1]

§ THE 1994 Uruguay Round of GATT (the General Agreement on
Tariffs and Trade) institutionalized 'the right to free trade' as having
precedence over human, civil, environmental, workers' and governmental rights. GATT's new standing enforcement body, the World
Trade Organization (WTO), unelected and meeting in secret, can
demand repeal of member nations' laws. Corporations are now
protected by binding and enforceable international agreements whose
powers far outstrip (while contradicting) the United Nations' International Declaration of Human Rights, which celebrated its fiftieth
birthday in 1998, still non-binding and unenforced. Corporations now
have global rights. People still do not.

An example: the French government had imposed an import ban
on US beef because it contains residues of drugs and growth hor-
mones. Recently the US government took the French government to
the WTO, complaining that the French ban was a 'barrier to free
trade'. The court agreed, warning France to repeal the ban or face
trade sanctions in an amount equivalent to lost sales claimed by the
US beef industry. France conformed. When outraged French citizens
demanded a strict labelling law so that they could still avoid buying US
beef, the USA took France back to court, now insisting that the
labelling interfered in the industry's ability to compete in the French
market, another 'barrier to free trade'. Again, the court agreed, denying
French citizens' right to know what they are eating. Now the entire
European Union is repeating this battle, struggling for the rights to
decide what is safe and to choose what to eat. The chief US negotiator
at the Rio Earth Summit announced that 80 per cent of US
environmental law is subject to challenge through the WTO. To

arbitrate science and safety, trade agreements refer only to industry-dominated bodies, like Codex Alimentaris.

The US state of Massachusetts' ban on products made in Myanmar/Burma, like other legislation against products made with child, slave or prison labour, can be challenged on the basis that it makes an illegal 'process distinction', a distinction based on an aspect of production that cannot be discerned in the quality of the end product. The continuation of such challenges will make it impossible to use economic pressure to deal with countries committing human rights violations. In cases like these, the language of 'discrimination' can be invoked legally by corporations as the basis for challenging laws that affect their competitive status in the market. Multinational corporations will not hesitate to challenge any law that restricts their profit in any country. Bans on carcinogens in food, lead and asbestos are on deck for repeal.

The WTO has no mechanisms for 'harmonizing' regulations upwards, since suits are brought on the basis of hardships caused by higher regulations that restrict market access or increase the costs of doing business. Thus WTO member nations no longer have the right to enact the wills of their citizens into law as sovereign nations. Existing laws must be rescinded if they are shown to be 'barriers', and member nations have agreed not to implement any new legislation that could conflict with free trade. Under this logic, civil and human rights (which often conflict with market freedoms) are not defensible. Citizens, towns and nations will not have the right to decide what can be done with land and natural resources or to regulate working conditions within their borders. Lawyer Richard Grossman summarizes this shift simply as 'the legalization of corporate authority over everything that counts'. Citizens' rights are being downgraded to consumer opportunities – what more could we want, anyway? Corporatized 'consumer choice', however, often entails the destruction of choice, substituting product diversity for diversity of economic enterprises. Much of what is defended in the name of consumers actually serves corporations. As US Congressman David Bonier points out, free trade agreements (FTAs) provide 'no sanctions and enforcements for labor and environmental infractions, but criminal sanctions against pirated compact disks'.[2]

Free trade is enforced by other international agencies, such as the World Bank, and by regional trade agreements in addition to the

WTO. Free trade is one of the most significant components of globalization. In the third world, globalization is devastating as it empowers corporations to drive local businesses out and to move production operations constantly, leaving behind economic devastation. Deregulation, privatization and investment liberalization hand the economy over to multinational corporations.

As Sivanandan has argued since 1989, globalization particularly brutalizes people of colour. It is racism that allows the toxic, low-wage conditions of the border Maquilladoras and the petro-chemical industries to be both imposed and hidden.[3] Corporations are taking every advantage of this free input. Internationally, lands that are the habitat of people of colour are stolen by (or handed over by comprador governments to) multinational corporations. Low-skilled industrial workers are easily replaced if they exercise their right to refuse dangerous work.[4] Corporations' ability to externalize the costs of workers' health means that these expendable workers become unemployable after three to four years of work.

Workers of colour are subject to a range of subtle forms of corporate exploitation, invisible to the public eye. With capital freed to set up production facilities anywhere in the world (and with corporations possessing the technology to manage them), workers have little power to make demands for adequate wages and working conditions. One of the most vivid examples of this crisis is the anencephalic babies (born without brains) in the Maquilladora towns toxified by the electronics assembly plants celebrated for bringing needed jobs to the Mexican economy. Another example is corporate biopiracy of indigenous peoples' genetic resources and science. Undaunted, modernization theory and the neoliberal economic model insist that unfettered and constantly expanding productive capacity and trade will somehow deliver all other needed social goods, despite 50 years (or two or five centuries, depending on your analysis) of evidence to the contrary.

Scholarship on globalization provides a description of these historically specific conditions, of global corporate hegemony as a moment in capitalist progression. This book is a study of the corresponding response from current social movements, which are beginning to organize against corporate domination. It makes sense that there *should* be an anti-corporate movement, but is there one? Anti-corporate discourses are emerging in many places and in a variety of quite different ideological approaches: left and right, first and third world, workers and petit bourgeois, urban and rural.

The existence of such movements is also confirmed by the use of the phrase 'anti-corporate' by corporate personnel who find themselves under attack. One of the earliest such recognitions was the 1972 annual meeting of the Council of the Americas, a group of 200 US-based corporations doing business in Latin America, which addressed the theme of 'anticorporatism and how business must "explain itself" better' (Barnet and Müller 1974: 23). Likewise, an editorial in the *International Herald Tribune* quoted the head of the World Economic Forum as saying 'Corporations should start taking the backlash against globalization seriously',[5] confirming that corporations know that *they* are the enemies of movements against globalization. The public relations firm Mongoven, Biscoe and Duchin warns corporate leaders that activists

> want to change the system; they have underlying socio-economic/ political motives; [are] anti-corporate – see the multinationals as inherently evil; winning is unimportant on a specific issue; [they] can be extremist/violent ... These organizations do not trust the ... federal, state and local governments to protect them and to safeguard the environment. They believe, rather, that individuals and local groups should have direct power over industry ... their principal aims ... social justice and political empowerment.[6]

Beyond documenting deductively that such movements exist, this book focuses on two crucial aspects of the movements' discourses: how they understand their enemy, and how they envision rebuilding the world. As social movements research, such work is both old and new. It is old in its interest in the movements' critical ideology, a concern that has been eclipsed by attempts to understand *how* movements mobilize, under what particular circumstances they manage to do so, and why individuals participate. Analysing ideology (particularly intentions for the future) can also be understood as a new project, in so far as theorists of new social movements have argued that in the face of postmodernity what we really need are 'new cultures' and 'new consciousness' (Melucci 1989). So, rather than trying to 'account for collective action' (McAdam et al. 1996: 5), this book focuses on the movements' substantive projects, the content of the 'frame' (Snow et al. 1986). I therefore do not evaluate the movements' size, scope, practices or chances for success.

The three central chapters of this book describe, perhaps relentlessly, a wide variety of movements that are naming corporations as their enemies and working to envision alternative political economies that meet their goals without empowering corporations. Chapters 2, 3, and 4 each present a mode of anti-corporate ideology.

The first mode is contestation and reform, which is where the most explicit forms of anti-corporatism appear. Peace and human rights movements have long criticized the behaviours of multinational corporations. They are joined by movements fighting structural adjustment and seeking land reform, cyberpunks, and some movements that describe themselves explicitly as 'anti-corporate'. Most projects of this mode attempt to recover the authority of the state to regulate corporations, constrain their abuses and deliver social benefits.

The second mode, 'globalization from below' (Falk 1993), refers to the development of a people's internationalist populism. This is 'workers of the world' uniting in a widened framework of dispossession that includes multiple sites of oppression. Articulating this approach are environmental movements, socialist movements, labour movements, movements fighting free trade agreements (anti-FTA), and the Zapatistas. Movements of this mode plan to supersede existing governance bodies.

The third mode is 'delinking' (Amin 1985). Also taking the forms of relocalization and sovereignty, it proposes a radical restructuring of the globalized political economy as localities voluntarily cut themselves off from the global market and its denizens. This is perhaps the least familiar mode, yet I have found its goals and its anti-corporatism articulated by an astonishing array of movements, including anarchists, movements in defence of small business, sustainable development movements, sovereignty movements and religious nationalist movements. This mode is less interested in governance, and is busy instead spawning vivacious alternatives.

While these groupings mirror traditional responses to industrialization, the categories were constructed inductively from analysis of the movements. Several months after the analysis was completed, John Cavanagh gave a speech in which he named three critical responses to globalization: restrained globalization, democratized globalization, and localization – closely matching the three modes.[7] Remember that the modes are actually archetypes; no movement or its members work exclusively in one mode.

As I was making the final revisions to this book in February 2000 I worked to update the data on the various movements. It took me several days to realize that what was overwhelming me in my capacity as a researcher was the success of the movement I set out to trace the first glimmers of in 1995. At this, I experienced a great rush of joy that *this* book is outdated before its publication. Vandana Shiva announced in Seattle that although the first attempt at globalization, colonialism, lasted 500 years, and the second, so-called 'development', lasted 50 years, the third one, 'free trade', lasted only five years (IFG 1999). I am pleased to announce that the movements I analysed in 1997 as 'implicitly' anti-corporate are now actively so and that youth and anarchist movements that I worried were being seen as marginal to the struggles have been recognized by more elite sectors as valued partners. Two of the movements, the struggle against genetic engineering and the struggle against the WTO, are now shared struggles by nearly all the movements I so carefully assembled as potentially anti-corporate. It doesn't seem quite fair to describe the movements as if they are discrete, when they overlap so much now. But the three modes of response described in the book represent distinct options and there is a great deal at stake in the differences between them.

In keeping with the goal of collecting all available ideological strategies for dismantling corporate power, the movements studied were not restricted to those arising from the left. In addition, the descriptions of the movements focus on their construction of anti-corporateness, not on their relationship to established left-wing political expectations. The brief concluding sections of each chapter begin to explore the movements' implications for left-wing principles among other things, which are explored more thoroughly in the final chapter of the book.

Method

This is, admittedly, a broad and shallow study, a shape formed at the intersection of determined internationalism and something less than a living wage. This is an attempt to document, from the United States, an international movement, using sources available in English that have been transferred to electronic media and coincidentally match my conceptual encodings. I am quite sure that it is intermittently both ethnocentric (surely it is irrelevant to separate culture and structure in discussions of the fourth world)[8] and colonial (to some extent I am using third and fourth world data to elaborate a study in terms appropriate for first worlders). This is a story from the first world for the first world about things a first worlder can see from the USA, which may well be the worst spot from which to make such an attempt.

The data are drawn from the alternative press, organizational documents, the world wide web, and participant observation. One way of thinking about the data collection is that I wasn't sampling. I was looking for the population – all anti-corporate movements. I was interested both in commonalities among movements and in extreme and unusual forms of anti-corporatism (outliers).

I have no interest in defending the world wide web as a research device. I used it as a way to expand my search for anti-corporate movements, not in the hope of getting a representatively accurate slice of the world, or even of the webbed world. The web provided a *glimpse* of this emerging movement in its institutionalized, technology-wielding instances (those who have the resources to present themselves on the web) and who appeared through some happy coincidence of their and my articulations. I've come to think that the most accurate way to describe the web is as an extension of the alternative press.

The unit of analysis is an organization or movement, but this is not pursued with textbook consistency. Eventually, I stopped trying to sort by unit of analysis, except that I was consistent about ignoring anything that was clearly an individual rant. Each of the three central chapters discusses five movements. These 15 movements are quite different as units of analysis. One has recently emerged from a single point of origin (Zapatismo). Others are fairly coherent but multiply institutionalized and ideologically heterogeneous (Peace and Human Rights, Cyberpunk, Environmentalism, Labour, Anti-Free Trade Agreement, Socialism, Anarchy, and Sustainable Development). Some are my constructs, movements I have grouped together on the basis of similarity of political economic ideology (Land Reform, Anti-Structural

Adjustment, the Explicit Anti-Corporate Movements, Small Business, Sovereignty, and Religious Nationalism).

In this work 'corporation' refers not to any legally incorporated enterprise but to those that exceed a certain scale, surpassing dependence on their original locality. 'Corporate' as an adjective refers to the operating principles typical of such enterprises, such as prioritizing profit and growth over all other values; profiting on uncosted externalities, such as the environment, quality of life, environment, workers' health, stable jobs, and community; and pursuing the homogenization and increase of consumption in order to maximize markets. Some of these principles may be held by small-scale enterprises, but they have far less power (via market share, advertising budget, etc.) to pursue them as rapaciously as do corporations. Corporate principles can be enforced by the demands of shareholder profitability and they can also be held voluntarily by privately held companies.

In this light, there is no meaningful difference between 'transnational' and 'multinational' corporations; these terms are used interchangeably herein. Likewise, although movements of the 'globalization from below' mode do define themselves as global or postnational, most of the movements studied are operating within nations, making links across national borders, but both aware of and constrained by national culture, political knowledge, and context. Thus I describe the emergent anti-corporate movement as 'international' rather than 'global' or 'transnational'.

Acknowledgements

Tony Samara's encouragement of this work was solid and precious and life-giving. Dick Flacks, John Mohr and Mark Juergensmeyer were respectful and supportive from the beginning. Aimée Shreck's diligence and extraordinary mind made an enormous contribution to the international breadth of the data collection – the book was fortunate to cross her path. Robert Molteno of Zed Books was simultaneously sharply engaged and honouring of what I was up to. A contentious dialogue with Gord Laxer has been one of the most pleasurable parts of analysing this material. Pete Taylor not only generously read and edited the manuscript, but also patiently worried political economy with me.

The original idea for this project was developed in dialogue with John Rodgers, who has lent constant encouragement, reflection and books. Grandma Georgia Starr's legacy of stubbornness and unfailing support must be credited for the similarity between the initial ambition and the final project. Sean Robin, Chris McAuley, John Nemec, Rachel Luft, Huda Jadallah, Matt Mutchler and Jane Ward have shaped my thought in ways that cannot be tracked in citations. The 1990–91 Indigenous Planning Group at MIT laboriously inducted me into the intellectual and political tradition of community self-determination that informs how I have related to many of the movements discussed herein. My students are the spark of every careful explanation and most insights. I must especially thank Sabrina Kwist, Mutindi Kisini, Juventino Gutierrez, Benjamin Aparicio, Lupe Marquez, Sam McCoy, Jack Zedlitz, Seth Roberts and Adam Bishop in this regard. Patty, Don, Rick and Cindy, Shu, the Kendricks, Chris Cadwell, John, Richard and other farmers of the Santa Barbara Farmers' Market Association first showed me the complex wealth of local economies. My union, the Associated Student Employees, provided a patient site where I finally learned the hard and necessary work of organizing, without which I ought not dare to write about social movements. Lou and Eric of d'Angelo's baked the bread that nourished this work in many ways. The Department of Sociology at Colorado State University provided support during completion of the book. Brian Cairns and Andy Griguhn cheerfully pitched in to furious last-minute data collection.

Also visible in this work and how I did it are the living commitments of my teachers. I was fortunate to learn algebra (and thus analysis) from Tom Fandall. Jeanne Lister imbued us with a vision of relentless and rigorous inquiry. Jim Mohan and Jim Durham gave me the gift and task of honest writing. Two art teachers, Patrick Collins and Otto Piene, convinced me that my vision was worth something, an enduring message and one of the few that penetrated a decade of anorexia. Dwight Johnson and Mel King challenged me to embark on a path of compassionate action in community and Marie Kennedy provided a model of how to do praxis. Lenny Clapp insisted that scholarship was indeed a thing I could do. Avery Gordon patiently encouraged my belated entrée into theory. It was Sheila Starr who taught me how to work.

Finally, I have recently been honoured by inclusion in several communities: the Ward Valley Van Crew, the 1997 Political Economy of Food Seminar, the Santa Barbara Community Currency Organizing Committee, the Student Sustainable Development Group, and the Seattle '99 'Don't be a tourist!' group transformed theory into reality and, thereby, critique to commitment.

Notes

1. Goldsmith was said to be the richest man in Europe at the time of this quote, which was published in 'Free trade, up to a point', *The Times*, 5 March 1994, p. 8.

2. Grossman and Bonier quote this paragraph from the International Forum on Globalization, *Teach in 3*, 1997. Hereafter 'IFG 1997'.

3. The Maquilladora factories along the US–Mexican border were the prototype for 'Export Processing Zones', in which national labour, environment and tax regulations were weakened or suspended to facilitate foreign factory operations.

4. See the Justice for Rodrigo Cruz Campaign, Santa Clara Center for Occupational Safety and Health.

5. In Elisabet Sahtouris, 'The biology of globalisation', *Perspectives in Business and Social Change*, September 1997.

6. All unattributed quotes are from primary data collection.

7. At IFG 1997.

8. Definition of 'fourth world': 'Nations forcefully incorporated into states which maintain a distinct political culture but are internationally unrecognized ... These are the 5,000 to 6,000 nations representing a third of the world's population whose descendants maintain a distinct political culture within the states which claim their territories. In all cases the Fourth World nation is engaged in a struggle to maintain or gain some degree of sovereignty over their national homeland' (Griggs 1992). Term popularized in 1974 by Shuswap Chief George Manuel's *The Fourth World: An Indian Reality* (New York: Free Press).

this work is dedicated
to my students,
for whom I learn

to the teachers,
who taught me to teach

&
to the elders,
for their fearlessness, forthrightness,
and precious countermemories

. . . .

CHAPTER I

Structure and Anti-Structure in the Face of Globalization

> GDP growth is the rate at which the powerful are expropriating the resources of the weak to create garbage.
> *Edward Goldsmith*

§ THIS chapter situates a study of anti-corporate social movements among the relevant intellectual discussions that pre-date it. It first reviews the debate over the existence of structure and the related debate over how to conceptualize globalization. It then theorizes and describes globalization. Finally, it explores the basis for agency in the face of globalization, laying a theoretical foundation for anti-corporatism.

The phrase 'naming the enemy' asserts both that an enemy exists and that it is recognizable. Many cosmopolitan academics would describe this claim as outmoded 'structuralism', an epistemological position that is, at the moment, in a state of considerable torpor among first world intelligentsia. At about the same time as academic leftists took up poststructural mudwrestling, first world nations started dismantling the social contract and third world elites were wooed into levels of debt that have locked them in dependency relations for the foreseeable future. So now poststructuralists and neoliberals speak resonantly, denying that market structure is determining. Structuralists conceive of a discrete set of forces (probably capitalist) having some kind of (complex but specific) international system set up through which, in short, they can efficiently get what they want (whatever that is) from people and nature, incurring minimal inconvenience to themselves. This system is sufficiently powerful that it works as intended nearly all of the time. It is a major factor in determining the conditions of life for most people.

One set of issues under dispute is organized around the intentionality of the system and systematicity of the structure. These issues will be addressed as relevant to this study in the discussion below on globalization. A second set of more philosophical issues inquires into whether we are capable of knowing and specifying the system. In its extreme form, this approach wonders if the system has an existence prior to our discourse about it. In its more mundane form, it questions our ability, as unwilling participants in a system, to think independently of it. I will refer to these questions as issues of consciousness and knowledge. A third set of issues explores to what extent the system determines outcomes, what sorts of events are part of the system, and which others might have slipped beyond its grasp. These are questions about agency and the possibility of it, and will be addressed later in this chapter. The rest of this section presents and wrestles with the issues of consciousness that frustrate the possibility of knowing the structure.

In 1922 Lukács proposed that without Marxist categories as mediating interpretive tools, it would be hard for people ever to recognize the enemy clearly. Critical theorists in the Frankfurt School took on the task of explaining the perplexing non-emergence of the revolution and began to wrestle with the complexities of ideological hegemony, culture, and civilizational narratives like rationality. Foucault's findings were consistent with but went beyond the projects of the Frankfurt School. His studies of imprisonment, asylums and sexuality revealed the incredible accomplishments of oppression as it is incorporated into categories of thought and implemented through self-surveillance. The Foucauldian tug-of-war positions his recognitions alternately as liberatory rupture of the idea that political economy structures the rest of our social institutions, or as merely adding, along the lines of the Frankfurt School, further useful analyses of exactly how the structure structures.

Another theoretical pressure towards poststructuralism is the epistemological strategy of multiple truths, developed by marginalized peoples, women, queers and people of colour, as a means of confronting hegemonic knowledge and entering the canon (without having completely to refute colonial knowledges first, itself still a vigorous project). In part this was necessary because the data available for refutation were not always from admissible sources. In part it was a way of revaluing the skills and knowledge of oppressed peoples. There is no point in asking now whether these goals could have been achieved without making the epistemological move to multiple truths.

Building on the legacy of the critical school and incorporating subaltern specificities, structuralists could sophisticate the perhaps simplistic claim that a structure exists and is knowable by recognizing how it is many-tentacled, disguised and beguiling. Concerned about the structure's ability to turn us into its creatures, poststructuralists take their Foucaudtian inheritance as a total rupture, which demands problematizing every perspective, every 'truth', and every liberatory narrative. (Recent events in the former Yugoslavia excellently support the postmodern position as doubts emerge as to the facticity of 'ethnic cleansing' – a term that effectively muted and divided potential opposition while the war machinery swung into action.) From a post-structural perspective, the attempt to name an enemy ironically becomes a new form of false consciousness that distorts the reality in which the enemy has become the fabric of our lives and thought. Haraway (1983) argues that the enemy is us, not merely by invasion, but through our own processes of survival and pleasure. Steven Pfohl (1992) would warn us that once we play with the machine (or the 'master's tool') it has us: we cannot think outside of it. Butler (1990) would point out that the enemy is different everywhere. How would we recognize her? Any kind of pointing to an enemy risks dishonest or inaccurate categorizations. A single name could obscure the iterations (what does women's access to corporate individualism portend? [Spivak 1989: 225]), internalizations (Said 1978), and horizontal integrations (Mills 1951; Marcuse 1964; Althusser 1970) of the named object. As a result, only quite modest claims about particular circumstances, acknowledging the multiplicity of even local meanings, are valid.

The resulting popular focus on local, particular experience as a basis of knowledge can slide into the supposition that the enemy can *only* be named personally and momentarily. But Marcuse (1964) and Pfohl (1992) reject quite conveniently the value of the everyday world as a source of truth. Marxists from Lukács to Althusser and beyond have been willing to acknowledge capitalism's obscurities and have worked continually to articulate them. Even powerful critics of the limits of structuralism, like Adorno in his study of fascism (1951), eventually position culture within the purview of structure. Published in the same year was C. W. Mills' discovery of 'white-collar' culture as a new product of capitalism. Marcuse (1964) goes on to elaborate how capitalism invades our identity, beguiles us to identify with our consumption of it and our meaningless roles within it, and even remobilizes us around its own meanings – 'freedom' as the freedom to consume, 'peace' as the repudiation of enmity.

> *I stand in a beautiful field of vegetables with a soft-spoken organic farmer (white, early 40s, frequently surfs with his teenage sons) who sells vegetables at the farmers' market because he 'loves diversity' and 'enjoys sharing different vegetables with people'. I ask him if he feels that he has any enemies. 'No. I don't really think about things that way.' I tell him that I'm worried about corporations. 'Yeah, but we can't reject them so generally.' Moments later he tells me a story:*
>
> 'So one day I came out here and there were these two suits standing in my field and they said they were from Motel 6, like that one right next door, and they told me they're wanting to build their corporate headquarters here on my field. And the mini-storage company on the other side also wants to expand over here.'
>
> *The farmer lost his lease. The owners sold the land to the mini-storage company two years ago and what was a local source of organic food, farm stand and field, sits idle, covered with weeds, awaiting its service to global capital.*
>
> *Do you have any enemies?*

Laclau and Mouffe (1985) agree that it is only in the development of a relationship of antagonism that situations of subordination and domination become understood as situations of oppression. Despite the particularities of racial formations (Omi and Winant 1986) and its seeming lack of rationalized centre, race is a world-historic, systemic phenomenon that is enforced internationally and certainly can be named (DuBois 1940). Gandhians and Freireans insist that there are truths about oppression, that ordinary people can see them, and that it is collectivity, grounded in historical culture, that enables them to do so. According to John Langston Gwaltney's research, African American folks don't think there are many truths about the structure; they think they have the truth and that sociologists and other elite knowledge dealers are self-interested liars, 'that phalanx of fatuous hucksters and junketing assessors who prey or groove upon us'

(Gwaltney 1980: xxiv; Starr 1994). The critique here is not of the possibility of an accurate centralized process of naming, but of peoples' dependence on such a process as the *only* access to truth. The form of structuralism articulated by Gwaltney and others is one that may not be immediately recognized by the intelligentsia. It involves the kind of data that poststructuralism claims to be better at seeing, but the data themselves refuse poststructural conceptions of the world.

Foucault's warning that we must be careful that we have really got the right monster in the bag does not render structure irrelevant, just makes it more complicated. Structure works not only through political economy, but also through culture, basic and sophisticated social institutions, technology, and political theory. Wallerstein's (1976) theory of world systems and Fanon's (1961) analysis of colonialism are structuralist documents of how a racialized capitalist world system is more than a set of institutions, it is clearly also a Foucauldian 'episteme', an entire (and culturalized) system of power and knowledge. No such recognitions of complexity dissolve the enemy or its enmity.

Naming 'Globalization'

Theoretical sport has, of course, emerged in debates over the meaning of the term 'globalization'. To some, globalization is the now nearly omnipresent technological web that at least elites all over the world can connect to and into which more and more economic processes are drawn. Others use it to refer to 'global culture', which is defined on the one hand as the 'hegemony of the mass media in the realm of human consciousness' (Nyang 1998) and on the other as the creole incorporation/appropriation thereof and the resulting proliferation of new cultural formations. Political economists variously view it as delivery of the best goods to the most people; as entirely consistent with capitalism (more of the same); as a qualitative shift in efficacy (or thoroughness) of exploitation; or as part of the constantly shifting world-systemic order (Schwartzman 1998). Political scientists variously see it as the triumph of secular human rights; a rigid 'new world order'; a frightening post-Cold War multilateral scramble; or a neutral 'multilayered global governance' which is 'reilluminating and reinvigorating the contemporary political terrain' (Held and McGrew 1998: 242–3).

In my view each of these usages refers to something rather different and all are, more or less, happening. But what do we think of these happenings? What does global technology do to the quality of human life? Is it neutral? Does it homogenize? To whom does it deliver global connectivity and what is that valuable for? How is global culture different from what happened along ancient trade routes? From empire? At what cultural cost are 'new cultures' emerging? Can we compare substantively the capacities and messages of new and old cultures? Do economies of scale, comparative advantages, industrialization of the workforce, or new products enhance quality of life? Add to human meaning? Establish social justice? Increase the peace? Respond to disasters? Are secular human rights multicultural? Are they centrally enforceable? Are they liberatory?[1] Who fears international mayhem? For whom has international law delivered at all? For whom has the international order suddenly become violently unpredictable?

Is the pernicious and fickle global assembly line in its productive activity the most important force in restructuring life on earth because for an unimaginable proportion of people life is now about a *job*? Is it instead at the other end of the line, consumption (including consumption of media and advertising), where the real action of globalization is taking place, as new global cultures define themselves? Is the hegemonic political order (the nation-state) subservient to economic powers or do these powers wheel drunkenly around each other (one moment sparring, the next arm-in-arm)? And which of these happenings is the *process* of globalization and which are the conditions, or outcomes, of that process?

Postmodernists and neoliberals both emphasize globalization's 'incompleteness' and 'partiality'. They come to this conclusion by quite different paths. Postmodernists are concerned that totalized views of the world are inaccurate and disempowering. Neoliberals see the globalization project as being, as yet, incomplete, and are concerned about potential obstacles. Mark Rupert points out that the theme of the 1996 Davos World Economic forum was 'sustaining globalization' – as if those present were by no means assured of hegemony (1997: 107). Held and McGrew agree that globalization is not 'by any means fully secure' (1998: 242). Neoliberals wield their nervousness as apologism, denying that globalization really has superseded the nation-state as a base of authority, harmonized standards downwards, or disempowered unions and people's organizations. At the same time, they present globalization as 'natural', 'evolutionary', and 'inevitable'.

Neoliberal disbelievers and apologists argue that international trade today barely equals that of 1913 (Cable 1995) and that corporations are not as 'footloose' as they seem (stuck with fixed assets at home and doing much of their trading regionally). Such arguments hardly disrupt the reality of the corporate globalization project, which is clearly proceeding apace. Corporations are busy dismantling economic boundaries to their operations, busting open new markets (which may not require moving fixed assets), homogenizing consumer tastes, and harmonizing civic standards downwards – while persuading citizens to interiorize their necessary flexibilization, abandon social goals in pursuit of 'international competitiveness', and reorganize their human aspirations into something called 'consumer choice'. These projects are indeed incomplete, but that fails to render them trivial.

It seems clear that its reality and its name are in part being sold to us in advertisements; we are supposed to believe in the inevitability and universal beneficence of globalization – and this rightly arouses critical suspicion (Amoore et al. 1997). But this single insight is in-conclusive: are we being indoctrinated into a corporate project or are corporations struggling for hegemony over a concept (and process) that has long had well-informed critics (who also, dangerously, wrote well)? (Barnet and Müller 1974; Sklar 1980). Should we, then, imagine that refusing the reality of globalization is a way to fight it? Or should we acknowledge the corporate intention to globalize and critique it?

Edward Herman describes globalization as an 'active process of corporate expansion across borders ... also an ideology, whose function is to reduce any resistance to the process by making it seem both highly beneficent and unstoppable' (1999: 40). Understanding global-ization as a process accounts for its incompletion while acknowledging its dangers. Concern with these dangers is less capitulation to the neoliberal 'inevitability' narrative than a recognition that globalizing economic processes increasingly infringe upon nationalities and localities in colonial fashion, with devastating effects. From the point of view of multinational corporations, globalization means opening up the whole world to their incursions as rapidly as possible. The fact that Pepsi still has most of its fixed assets in the USA tells us nothing about the number of local drinks manufacturers they have put out of business or the ways in which they are modifying culture. The fact that globalization has yet to reach every place on earth is not reassuring. Clearly it would be absurd to decry critical analysis of biotechnology simply because it is 'incomplete' and 'partial' – observations that apply to many corporate projects.

For the purposes of this book, let me propose that we accept the existence of globalization as a process and also as an emerging condition, a (quite consistent) pattern of outcomes – what Chakravarthi Raghavan (1990) presciently named 'recolonization'. Keeping in mind the questions raised about what it is as a process and about its incompletion, I shall also insist that it does have agents. Leslie Sklair can document that transnational corporations 'do work, quite deliberately and often rather covertly, as political actors, and often have direct access to those at the highest levels of formal political and administrative power with considerable success' (1998: 286). Even conservative commentators agree that 'Multinational corporations ... are the linchpins of the contemporary global economy ... qualitatively and quantitatively more extensive in their operations and more intensive in their importance than their predecessors ... more significant economic and political actors ... this, if nothing else, distinguishes the current epoch from the gold-standard era' (Goldblatt et al. 1997: 277).

There has been a conspiracy. But to trace the corporate interests of the political and economic elites who crafted the free trade agreements and to note that they did so deceitfully is not to claim that the problem is individuals rather than systemic operations. They are part of the system, their craft is consistent with it, and their story is a genealogy of its historic development. I suspect that for first world citizens it is the *deceit*, not the self-interest of the conspirators, that arouses ire. (Such deceit is, of course, old news in the third world.)

One of the most contentious of the globalization debates regards the relationship between globalization and nation-states. While some structuralists sound the alarm on globalization's threat to national sovereignty, a range of other folks (including, oddly, Marxists, postmodernists, and neo/liberals) dismiss this concern as absurd, insisting that the power of nations will not so easily go away. These perspectives ignore the factoid that this project is the avowed agenda of globalization. It is certainly worth pointing out that this is to some extent a consensual project on the part of nation-states, and theoretically consent could be revoked.

Analyses that doubt the loss of state power tend to see globalization as a diffuse, agentless situation. They under-emphasize both the structural change wrought by such agencies as the WTO and the ideological impact of neoliberalism on statist projects from public education to economic protectionism. Ian Douglas (1997), invoking Foucault rather usefully, proffers an alternate explanation of the globalization campaign and its relationship to state power. Rather than overwhelming the political order, globalization as a disciplinary reality is its current embodiment. The 'crisis' of international competitiveness rationalizes the 'hollowing out' of the state (Strange 1996), legitimizing conditions of exploitation and insecurity and state non-interference and non-amelioration. Workers 'interiorize' this particular political order and rationalize their self-discipline and self-monitoring to its performance specifications, relieving the state of its enforcement duties (except, of course, among the unemployed, who must be rounded up, imprisoned, and made to work for their supper). In 1995 Susan Strange argued that 'authority once exercised by states is now exercised by no one'. In the sense of authority accountable to people, she is correct. But there certainly are sources of unaccountable authority that are exercising power. The World Bank and IMF structural adjustment programmes have been asserting ideological and governance authority for decades, and in 1994 the GATT determined that the WTO shall have the ultimate authority to define reasonable laws and sound sciences. Douglas' contribution is to show how, even on the much smaller scale of a community, neoliberal authority speaks without the state.

Charting the path of its destruction

> Monsanto should not have to vouchsafe the safety of biotech food. Our interest is in selling as much of it as possible. Assuring its safety is the FDA's job. (Phil Angell, Director of Corporate Communications, Monsanto, *New York Times*, 25 October 1998).

Things economic include a variety of different functions. The economy includes the production and distribution of basic needs such as food, clothing and shelter. In pre-capitalist societies, these functions were accomplished using a range of social systems, including many forms of collectivity as well as various forms of private ownership and systems of markets and trading. Today's global economy includes a large amount of speculative trading (what Marx described as M-C-M'), in which trading participants are not interested in the intrinsic use-value of the traded goods (Commodities) at all, but only in their ability to expand investment from M (Money before trading) to M' ([more] Money after trading).

International agribusiness reduces formerly independent farmers to agricultural workers, or simply dominates purchase of export crops, reducing farmers to serfs on their own land.[2] The requirements of capital-intensive production systems cause many farmers to lose their land to debt. Formerly self-sufficient rural people flood urban areas in search of wage labour, suddenly dependent on corporate jobs for their basic needs. According to Helena Norberg-Hodge, urbanization is a function of the 'destruction of economic possibilities in rural areas'.[3] Torn from traditional communities and livelihoods, people around the world accept consumer culture as the definition of the good life (what John Tomlinson [1991] calls 'cultural imperialism'), which increases their dependency on cash wages and urban economies.

In almost every locality, small businesses now face competition from powerful multinational corporations, who use huge advertising budgets to homogenize preferences (in the guise of 'choice'), cut prices based on their socially costly comparative advantage, eliminate inconvenient regulations and protectionist policies of all kinds, and now have the very definition of competition legally defined in their interest. New legal instruments include free trade agreements, which do not actually defend 'free trade'. Instead, they strengthen the powers of corporations against other actors in the economy, such as states and small producers. Recently, under corporate pressure, the Indian government passed a packaging law for cooking-oil, immediately putting out of business millions of tiny oilseed operations.[4] Simultaneously, WalMart is driving out small retailers in several sectors every day. Thus the situations faced by farmers, small business-owners, workers, consumers, and those needing assistance from the state in first and third world countries, in urban and rural areas, are increasingly similar (Starr and Rodgers 1995).

This discourse is a distorted version of free-market capitalism that, according to David Korten, ignores basic components of its own theoretical foundations, the work of Adam Smith and David Ricardo, both of whom are often cited as authorities by neoliberals. Smith's free market, described in *The Wealth of Nations* (1776), was one in which small-scale buyers and sellers used the market to distribute goods optimally for the well-being of society. The market could produce beneficial results when capital was 'rooted in place in the locality where its owner lived' and when owners were motivated to provide for themselves and their families. Only under these conditions could 'the invisible hand of the market translate the pursuit of self-interest into optimal public benefit' (Korten 1995: 77). This delimited self-interest did not allow any corporation to become very powerful. Smith emphasized that this optimal outcome could only exist when 'no buyer or seller is sufficiently large to influence the market price' (ibid.: 74). Smith is well known for disliking government intervention in the market, but his reasons for this position are less well known: he disapproved of governments' tendency to intervene in order to subsidize economic elites and to defend the rich and propertied against the poor.

In total contradiction of Smith's principles, international trade and investment policy, from the 1944 formation of the IMF and World Bank to the 1994 Uruguay Round of GATT, which created the WTO, are organized to facilitate and subsidize transnational corporate activities, giving corporations advantages over small-scale, locally based, owner-managed enterprises in every country of the world and forcing those economies open, which is a huge subsidy to corporations. Smith's market theories are used to legitimate policies that defy his most basic principles.

The misuse of David Ricardo's 1817 theory of 'free trade' is even more blatant. His idea was that *under specific conditions*, trade between two countries could be mutually beneficial. *If* the participating countries both have full employment, *if* the total trade is balanced, *if* capital is prohibited from travelling between high- and low-wage countries, and *if* under these conditions the countries could each produce an item at comparative advantage, *then* trade would be mutually beneficial (Korten 1995: 78). But 'free trade' as defined and enforced by the recent FTAs ignores the need for such conditions. The computer simulations designed by economists in support of the North American Free Trade Agreement (NAFTA), which predicted fabulously positive results, were based on Ricardian assumptions such as full employment, immobility of capital, and cross-border wage equivalence, conditions far from the truth (ibid.: 82). The simulations also failed to include China, which is providing the (prison) labour for 'US exports' to Mexico (ibid.: 236). Under FTAs, 'comparative advantage' is the ability to produce a good at a lower cost *by any means necessary*. The use of unemployment and wage differentials to achieve lower wages is endorsed and protected. Not only is trade balance not a goal, but trade advantages are awarded to the victors in trade disputes. As Korten articulated most informally, 'free trade is the right to go anywhere and make a quick buck'⁵ – quite a different goal from meeting needs efficiently through comparative advantage. Who has the capital resources to 'go anywhere' to take advantage of this set-up? Only corporations.

Where did FTAs come from? The use of legal institutions to pursue the corporate agenda scored its first major victory in 1886, when the US Supreme Court gave corporations the rights of persons. Until that point, and for a few decades afterwards, popular public opinion differentiated between corporate interests and those of smallholders (Williams 1988; Grossman and Adams 1996). Korten explains the importance of the USA as progenitor of the corporate order. In the late 1800s and early 1900s:

> A conservative court system that was consistently responsive to the appeals and arguments of corporate lawyers steadily chipped away at the restraints that a wary citizenry had carefully placed on corporate powers. Step-by-step, the court system put in place new precedents that made the protection of corporations and corporate property a centerpiece of constitutional law. These precedents eliminated the use of juries to decide fault and assess damages in cases involving corporate caused harm ... ruled that workers were responsible for causing their own injuries on the job, limited the liability of corporations for damages they might cause ... interpreted the common good to mean maximum production – no matter what was produced or who it harmed. (Korten 1995: 59)

Corporations benefit from possessing a two-fold legal character. First, their supposed service to 'common good' trumps any accused social costs or harms; this legal character derives from their original status as entities temporarily chartered by the government to serve public purposes. Second, they can claim rights and protections due to citizens. These two ideological/juridical characters have been internationalized in economic theory and international legal instruments.

Since the Second World War, the USA has played a leading role in defining economic means and ends internationally, and most of the world has come into line with the visions and strategies put forth. This leadership has been accomplished through private and secretive domestic and international organizations that have built consensus among economic elites and indoctrinated political leaders to assure their cooperation. These organizations include the US Council on Foreign Relations (founded in 1918), the US–European Bilderberg (founded in 1954), the US Business Roundtable (founded in 1972), and the US–European–Japanese Trilateral Commission (founded in 1973) (see Sklar 1980). The World Economic Forum is a private institution that hosts an annual conference of corporate leaders in Davos, Switzerland. La Conférence de Montréal is similar, but also involves a lot of government officials. The Transatlantic Business Dialogue was founded in 1995 to identify barriers to US–EU business activities. Its purpose is to converge conflicting priorities before they emerge as visible trade conflicts. It includes 120 industry leaders and key US and EU ministers, as well as the director-general of the WTO.

While none of these organizations has jurisdiction or authority to make policy, many of their members do, so the consensus achieved within the ranks of the organizations has been effectively transferred into consistent domestic and international policies. It is through these organizations, according to Korten, that 'economic globalisation has been crafted and carried forward as a policy agenda largely outside the public discourse' (1995: 133). Five hundred corporations were official advisers to the US negotiation of the 1994 round of GATT.[6] As Lori Wallach emphasizes, 'it took a lot of planning' and is now being promoted as evolutionary and 'inevitable'. In fact, it took seven years to negotiate the creation of the World Trade Organization.[7] Catherine Caufield (1997) argues that free trade/liberalization policies were developed experimentally by the IMF and World Bank, paving the way for the ever-wider institutionalization of corporate priorities.

The postcolonial third world has been invaded ideologically with a theory and practice of national economic development called 'modernization'. This 1950s theory proposes that first world countries could assist the nations of the rest of the world to become democratic and modern by transferring the infrastructure, capital, technology and expertise needed to get each country's industrial economy built. This theory insists that standard 'indicators' of modernity, such as health care, higher wages and labour safety regulations, environmental regulations, product safety, democracy, and other benefits enjoyed by first world citizens would soon appear in third world nations if they pursued economic growth.

Since the 1960s, critics of modernization theory have been analysing how hierarchical political economic relations can never deliver truly independent development. For this reason, they called modernization-style development 'dependent'. Export-based economies remain dependent on first world nations and global market prices for their well-being and often for imports of basic needs (Gunder-Frank 1967; Cardoso and Faletto 1979). Growth as the definition of development has failed utterly. Martin Khor explains that export-based development results in 'continuous fall in the terms of trade, with a disastrous growth in poverty (and) acceleration in the depletion of natural resources ... and the transfer to the South of polluting industries' (1993: 165).

A group of 'newly industrialized countries' (NICs) are cited as having escaped the cycle of dependency. They are developing independently and are finally achieving the social promises of modernization theory as measured by increased standards of living – even, in South Korea, a democratic political system. But analysts reveal the costs of this industrial development. In *Dragons in Distress* (1990), Walden Bello and Stephanie Rosenfeld document that the change from agricultural to industrial economies required land appropriation and permitted factories to engage in direct environmental degradation. The investment of national resources (land, labour and environment) in 'modernization' resulted in a *loss* of national food self-sufficiency, loss of safe air, water and soil, loss of agricultural livelihoods, and the devotion of labour resources to production for first world uses.

In the 1970s private banks flush with oil industry deposits made generous loans to developing nations with very little or no oversight. The banks believed in modernization theory and assumed the countries would have no problem paying the money back. Much of the money was spent not on economic enterprises that would produce revenue to pay back the loans or on social programmes that benefited the people, but on the military, 'symbols of modernity' like airports and hotels, and sometimes on dictators' personal projects. Many of these loans were taken on by undemocratic regimes. World Bank projects tend to be huge infrastructure projects (such as dams), which are essentially subsidy to industrial development. These projects do not deliver services to the poor or to rural areas, and in many cases displace or degrade the environments of the rural poor (Bello 1993).

In the early 1980s, international interest rates skyrocketed and export markets collapsed, so that third world countries that had been making their payments got less for their exports and were faced with higher interest rates. When third world countries started defaulting on loans (Mexico was one of the first in 1982), the IMF and the World Bank (WB) stepped in and gave loans to repay the private banks. These institutions then held the debts of the third world. In the 1980s, the IMF and WB started imposing 'structural adjustment condition-alitics' on loans, which include: freezing the minimum wage at current levels (and sometimes cutting wages), repressing labour organizing, cutting social services (education, health, and food assistance to the poor), devaluing the currency (this makes labour cheaper for foreign corporations, but makes any imported items more expensive for consumers), privatizing any state-owned industries and state services like transportation, and enacting free trade policies.

Basically, structural adjustment demands that countries devote more and more of their total economy to debt payments. Debt payments are devastating the third world in two ways. First, structural adjustment programmes are brutal. Seven million children are dying of preventable diseases and malnutrition annually because healthcare has been cut.[8] Second, countries are putting too much of their total gross national product (which means devoting too much of their arable lands, fisheries, forests and productive capacity) towards debt service, which means that there is just not enough left to have a decent society. Many of these countries spend twice or more as much on debt service as they spend on education and healthcare combined. There is now a net outflow of *capital* as well as natural resources from the third world to the first world.

According to Caufield, the World Bank has become a 'global overseer', which has the power to enforce its economic opinions through the promises (and potential withholding) of money. Since it is self-financing, it has autonomy from any existing governmental authority. It has been able to enforce the economic ideologies that international trade brings 'prosperity and peace'; that there is such a thing as 'under-development' (and that most third world countries suffer from it); that loans are charitable aid (evidence of first world generosity); that corporations deserve 'aid' backed by the taxpayers of the world; and that the 'overseer' should have the right to require changes in sovereign nations' laws. John Mihevc proposes that the World Bank not only is theologically Christian in its salvific assumption of 'the inherent right and duty to change the world' (1995: 22–3), but also fundamentalist in its denial of 'the legitimacy of alternatives' and its active work 'to ensure that all of the options available to developing countries have been narrowed down to one' (ibid.: 16).

Walden Bello has been arguing for years that the first world is also undergoing structural adjustment. In the name of 'international com-petitiveness', wealthy first world nations are cutting social spending, privatizing government services to save costs (supposedly in the interest of 'efficiency'), rolling back regulations and their enforcement, and undermining wage rates and other labour gains (Bello et al. 1994). European economic integration legitimates austerity programmes, many of which result in corporate subsidies. In June 1997, 331 European economists collectively opposed the European Monetary Union on the basis that it does not 'serve the interests of human beings'.[9] A gruesome paradox completes the story. Economic global-ization is destroying consumer purchasing power, the Fordist bargain that mollifies workers. The Organization for Economic Cooperation and Development (OECD) actually commissioned a 'Jobs Study' in 1994, but ignored this issue (Hines and Lang 1996: 486). Service-sector employment (the growth of which was supposed to compensate for loss of manufacturing jobs in the first world) is already being cut back.

Neoliberalism, which was made hegemonic in the 1980s, is the political discourse/ideology that recommends deregulation, privat-ization, and the dismantling of the social contract. The political leaderships of so-called democracies have been convinced, and have in turn convinced their constituents, to accept corporate hegemony as the best way of organizing the economy. Nations (and localities) can increasingly be counted on to subsidize the costs of corporate projects. Neoliberalism advertises the market as a space of freedom, which is compared favourably with formal political processes, and promises that free markets will do best at supporting the productivist social contract and procuring the maximum goods for consumption. 'Consumer choice' replaces citizenship as the pre-eminent right. Once forced to implement neoliberal policies, even the Dragon economies faltered and are now facing structural adjustment, sale of assets to the first world, and a future of indefinite debt.

Elites use the desperation of the poor to justify any form of economic activity, no matter how unsafe, as providing people with needed 'opportunities'. With nations (and localities) convinced that they must compete for the privilege of production facilities, labour, safety and environmental regulations are relaxed or eliminated and massive public subsidies (including infrastructure provision) are given to corporate projects instead of to social services, sanitation, public housing and other basic needs. The US state of South Carolina has given a total of $300 million in subsidy to BMW to woo a production facility to the state (Brecher and Costello 1994: 16). Northern Irish workers are advertised as 'Smart. Young. And affordable.' Companies are promised 'a supportive, pro-business environment and excellent transportation links'.[10]

Corporate ideology continues to promise the end of poverty and the emergence of democracy while enacting policies that undermine social welfare, workers' rights, and citizens' and national sovereignty. Free trade is really forced trade, in which local control over economies is superseded by the most powerful global interests and subjected to their law. Barnet and Müller (1974) summarized the concerns of the business world as the need for 'acceptance of the global corporation as the most effective and rational force to develop and distribute the resources of the world. In short, political legitimacy.' They concluded that the coming crisis of globalization was a crisis of 'political authority'. Twenty years later, Barnet and Cavanagh find that 'there appears to be a direct connection between economic integration and political dissolution' (1994: 421).

In 1969, Jacques Maisonrouge, a corporate leader from IBM, articulated 'the critical issue of our time' as the 'conceptual conflict between the search for global optimization of resources and the independence of nation-states' (in Barnet and Müller 1974: 19). After decades of highly organized effort, 'corporations have emerged as the dominant governance institutions on the planet' and now wield the state: 'the corporate interest rather than the human interest defines the policy agendas of states and international bodies' (Korten 1995: 54). The new international legal institutions use the carrot of capital investment as the enforcement mechanism to create a new *international* juris-diction in which corporations make the law and reshape their very purposes. Corporations have defined 'free trade' in ways that resemble the rights of citizens, yet unlike citizens, corporations are not subject to extradition, imprisonment or criminal law. Signatories to GATT and other FTAs have agreed to design all new public policy to be 'least trade restrictive', which narrowly restricts how governments can pursue democratic public concerns. In March 1998, the US State Department successfully pressured the Maryland state assembly not to pass a bill (ban on government procurement from Nigeria) because it would be a WTO violation.

By 1995, it was a *fait accompli* that industry (and its public relations agents) had 'convinced the public that the corporate interest *is* the public interest' (ibid.: 143) and public problems and solutions are defined in ways that 'support corporate objectives' (ibid.: 149). Cor-porate leaders acknowledge their accomplishments. Asked what had changed in the last 25 years, David Rockefeller replied: 'Corporations were just standing on the sidelines then. Now we're in the driver's seat.'[11] At the 1997 Food Summit in Rome, the corporate-influenced US delegation insisted that 'there is no right to food security', contradicting the International Declaration of Human Rights and the concerns of most other participants.[12]

Certainly, this qualitatively new situation of corporate dominance is made possible in part by the quantitative situation in which half of the world's one hundred largest economies are corporations. By mani-pulating and hegemonizing a narrow economic theory that prioritizes 'free trade' over all other economic issues (such as employment, domestic production, income generation, fulfilment of human needs), corporations have produced legal devices that enable them to strike down government regulations that annoy them – in their own words, to create 'a worldwide business environment that's unfettered by government interference'.[13] United Nations conventions are not legally binding, which clarifies why the WTO is now the multinational corporations' 'vehicle of choice for global governance' and why they can violate with impunity conventions like the Declaration of Human Rights and labour conventions.[14]

Brecher and Costello call FTAs part of a 'corporate agenda', a planned international project to achieve 'downward leveling', not only by pitting workers against each other and driving all wages down, but also through 'harmonization' of pollution, product safety and labour regulations (1994: 4–5). The problem with 'harmonization' is not the idea of worldwide standards, but the *process* through which FTAs produce harmonization. Nations may bring suit against one another's laws before the WTO Dispute Resolution court on the basis that any given law constitutes a discriminatory barrier to doing business. If a law is ruled to be 'unfair' to plaintiff traders, the losing country will have to repeal the law or face trade sanctions to match the trade 'loss' caused by the law.

Of course, there could be a positive form of 'harmonization', such as one that established a worldwide 'living wage' (with benefits) or internationalized strict pollution controls by simultaneously upgrading all nations' environmental laws. Such an approach would increase the responsibilities of corporations and limit their skyrocketing profits by forcing them to internalize costs currently paid by poverty, public health crises and the permanent loss of environmental resources. But this would require a different legal structure and different adjudicators.

The WTO Dispute Resolution Court is composed of three unelected pro-trade officials, meets in secret, and does not accept unsolicited documentation. The court's policies do not require members to be disinterested in the issues they adjudicate. There is no media or citizen participation. No unsolicited submissions of evidence are accepted. Decisions are binding and enforceable (with fines and trade sanctions). Appeal is virtually impossible. This process of harmonization is designed to enable corporations to leverage the permissive regulatory structures of structurally adjusted and/or third world countries against the regulations enacted by wealthy democratic nations. The free trade priority undermines first world purchasing power as a basis for leveraging improvements in third world regulations. It can also be used against progressive legislation in less powerful countries whose economies are highly export-dependent. FTAs provide no mechanisms to harmonize standards upwards.

Researchers now have sufficient evidence to give a distinct image of the pattern of effects produced by this structure. Taking the North American FTA as an example, the Mexican government's own figures on the percentage of the population categorized as 'extremely poor' rose from 32 per cent to 54 per cent in the first few years following the passage of NAFTA. Rather than increasing the quality of Mexican jobs, NAFTA has mostly increased investment in the Maquilladora sector, where wages and working conditions are worse than in the rest of Mexico.[15] The US Department of Labor commissioned a Cornell University study of US companies' intentions with regard to using NAFTA as a threat to drive down wages and break unions. The findings showed that NAFTA would exert downward pressure on wages. The department then refused to release the study. According to the Institute for Policy Studies, US job loss has mostly affected women and rural people. Data from Canada document that it is not the less profitable companies that are taking advantage of NAFTA. The NAFTA 'side agreements' intended to strengthen Mexican labour law have been completely ineffective. 'Mexicans' attempts to unionize have been routinely and systematically crushed, and petitions to get the side agreement's governing body, the National Administrative Office, to take action against these violations have yielded little to nothing.'[16] International trade volume is up, but so is inequality, both within and between countries, and even the United Nations attributes this to trade rules. Developing countries are getting a smaller share of trade. Consumer prices have not come down.[17]

As Lori Wallach points out, if the WTO were about free trade it would not need 900 pages of rules.[18] The global free market is a free competition only between multinational corporations, which are increasingly able to monopolize it and prohibit entry. It enables the privatization, commodification and corporatization of public domain resources such as seed, which reinforces dependency while destroying alternatives (King and Stabinsky 1998–99). Martin Khor of the Third World Network summarizes the real meaning of free trade: 'free trade always benefits the stronger partner'.[19] The global economy is not a free market of innovative entrepreneurs.

Describing corporate political economy

> The global corporation is the most powerful human organization yet devised for colonizing the future. (Barnet and Müller 1974: 363)

What is the foundational logic of this system? Marxists would say 'capitalism'. But critical globalization scholars disagree. They focus on five analytic categories of political economy, which they see as particularly important to understanding economic globalization and corporate domination of the economy. These are growth, enclosure, dependency, colonialism, anti-democracy and consumption.

Growth is a supra-capitalist creed, which claims to be the only way to ease poverty and save the environment. This premise has been debated since the late 1960s on the basis of its ecological impossibility and social undesirability (Michan 1967). Barry Commoner's 1971 *The Closing Circle* argued that post-Second World War US growth had not contributed to quality of life. Logan and Molotch (1987: 34) argue that urban 'growth machines' (Molotch 1976) pursue value-free development that has no concern for what is produced or under what conditions and 'does not *necessarily* promote the public good' (original emphasis). Richard Douthwaite's *The Growth Illusion* traces the history of the growth idea and its results, concluding that 'economic growth has made life considerably worse for people' (1993: 3). Douthwaite argues that 'the groups that make the investments that generate growth are getting good returns – although at the expense of everyone else'. While European citizens rarely list growth-related accomplishments (increased consumption) among the most important factors in 'satisfaction' or 'quality of life', the things they do list are adversely affected by processes of growth. Contrary to promises, growth damages employment rather than enhancing it (ibid.: 305).

> The great, centralized economic entities of our time do not come into rural places in order to improve them by 'creating jobs'. They come to take as much of value as they can take, as cheaply and as quickly as they can take it. They are interested in 'job creation' only so long as the jobs can be done more cheaply by humans than machines. They are not interested in the good health – economic, natural, or human – of any place on this earth … They have said repeatedly that the failure of farm families, rural businesses, and rural communities is merely

the result of progress, and such efficiency is good for everybody. (Berry 1996: 409–10)

Enclosure of the commons resources on which people depend privatizes community goods so that they can be commodified and sold. Such commodification is the core of the capitalist process (Marx 1867, Ch. XXVII) Corporate cost-externalization amounts to enclosure of public resources. Vandana Shiva describes genetically modified seed as a form of enclosure that dispossesses the farmer of seed as a means of production and dispossesses communities of seed as a means of survival. Corporate seeds neither produce on their own (they require costly chemicals and excessive water) nor reproduce themselves, completing the corporate invasion into and commodification of every step of the agricultural process (Shiva 1991; King and Stabinsky 1998–99).

The notion of *dependency* relations articulated by Cardoso and Faletto (1979) to describe nations is extended by critical globalization scholars to describe the economic conditions of workers, households and communities. Separating (enclosing) natural elements like water and social processes like childcare from their complex environments creates producers and consumers who are dependent on the global economic system and on sellers (now corporations) for their basic needs. Enclosure destroys independent, non-monetarized and informal economic systems and replaces them with dependent ones (*The Ecologist* 1993).

Jane Ann Morris teaches American audiences about dependency by explaining how European colonists cultivated dependency among Native Americans. Before long, those who survived outright genocide were getting their food and some new thing called 'employment' from the settlers. As native economics increasingly revolved around the trading post, independent capacities were weakened and cultural values were partly abandoned. That particular invasion was so brutal that native peoples were all but destroyed (Morris 1996). First world peoples have a hard time even seeing our dependency, so accustomed are we to interiorizing the disciplines of work, pseudo-democracy and corporate rationalization, such as the necessary poisoning of the food system in service of 'feeding the world'. Third world nations that succeeded in throwing off colonial rule only to embrace colonizers' values soon find themselves hanging around the trading post. Dependency on export earnings and imported goods is a problem not only because the centre's profit relies on the underdevelopment of the periphery, but also because of its absolute effects on the possibility of autonomy (not just on the ability to 'catch up').

Colonialism is a system of economic, political, social, cultural and ideological domination. Powerful external agents use enclosure to extract natural and human resources from a locality while transforming its people into dependent consumers (Rodney 1972). Using a colonial analysis to understand the activities of corporations clarifies the political effects alongside the economic ones. In the 1960s and 1970s, rural sociologists and racial liberation movements tried using these concepts in the first world. They concluded that the concepts did not quite apply (Buttel 1980; Omi and Winant 1986). As used by current scholars and social movements, the terms explain the processes by which both resources and political control are alienated from a people. As early as 1990, Chakravarthi Raghavan began to use the term 'recolonization' to describe the economic relations that were being forged through the emerging Uruguay Round of GATT.

The difference between postmodern corporate colonialism and modern European colonialism is that corporations have slipped their moorings and are no longer responsible to nations. They have advanced from being agents of the sovereign to being sovereign agents accountable to no political entity. Yet corporate colonialism has all of the elements of the eighteenth- and nineteenth-century nationalist version: it demands political modifications from the colonized country (structural adjustment, FTA compliance), it involves ideological and cultural invasion, imposes particular economic structures, influences social values, and may involve military force.

Neoliberal reforms and corporate operations must be *antidemocratic*. Corporations are anti-democratic organizations, within which freedom of information and freedom of speech may not be exercised. They are perfectly happy to operate in non-democratic environments and, when necessary, do their best to manipulate democratic processes in their benefit. One of the ways in which they have done this is to reduce the notion of citizen to that of consumer, whose rights are narrowed to the right to consume; thus the only task for the public sphere is facilitating maximum consumer choice. According to McKinsey & Co. Japan's Kenichi Ohmae, the only role left for 'obsolete' governments is 'ensuring that their people have the widest range of choice among the best and the cheapest goods and services from around the world' (in Korten 1995: 127).

Shiva claims that because it needs dependent consumers, corporate economics actually 'requires totalitarianism' because it must 'deny the right to know and to choose'.[20] The citizen-consumer's 'right to product choice' is limited to the corporate product lines and may *not* include 'process distinctions'. Choices between 15 varieties of genetically engineered processed corn cereal owned by the same corporation is an illusion of choice and an elision of knowledge. Illusory product diversity replaces the right to know, to participate, to regulate, to govern. In order to control the definition of science, the WTO must bar the doors to public scrutiny and democratic participation. Under cover of rationalizing trade policy, the WTO has overridden the powers of other democratic governing bodies including other international treaties.

> The World Trade Organization is, in effect, a global parliament composed of unelected bureaucrats with the power to amend its own charter without referral to national legislative bodies ... Under the WTO, a group of unelected trade representatives will become the world's highest court and most powerful legislative body, to which the judgments and authority of all other courts and legislatures will be subordinated. (ibid.: 177)

Consumption is critiqued as a false basis for economic prosperity because it is ecologically unsustainable (or suicidal) and because it is based on incessant pillage of resources from the third and fourth worlds. Scholars who also write about the psycho-spiritual aspects of capitalism and postmodernity explain how consumer culture evacuates meaning and community. 'By marketing the myth that the pleasures of consumption can be the basis of community, the global corporation helps to destroy the possibilities of real community' (Barnet and Müller 1974: 365; Mander 1978). Not only community, but culture itself is destroyed. Corporations would prefer to sell standardized products, and in that context cultural diversity becomes a 'problem of efficiency'.[21] European citizens' preference for non-chemical beef is referred to as 'historical culture', which must be set aside as 'science prevails'.[22]

Instead of capitalism, the enemy named by critical globalization scholarship is usually 'economic globalization'. (The word 'economic' distinguishes this globalization from humanitarian peoples' internationalism.) Frequently the enemies are corporations. This literature is documenting the fact that quantitative shifts (accelerating size, concentration and penetration of corporate capital) are producing qualitative shifts in political jurisdiction and authority, livelihood, access to resources, forms of communication and culture. These scholars propose that there is a qualitatively new dimension to this moment in capitalist progression, the planned and intentional construction of international legal institutions that protect and prioritize corporate rights. New legal mechanisms such as FTAs impose global governance with far greater scope and enforcement powers than the United Nations. Their rule will affect everyone whose livelihood or basic needs are in any way connected to the global market and they include mechanisms (such as biotechnology patenting) to force more and more people into that connection.

Marxist method proposes that 'the mode of production of material life' structures social, political and cultural aspects of society (Marx 1859). If the dominant relations of production change, this indicates a significant shift in the structuring force. If corporations have taken a place in the relations of production, we could be experiencing a significant change in 'the relations of economic control (legally manifested as property ownership) that govern access to the forces and products of production' (Bottomore 1983: 207). Lenin foresaw this in *Imperialism* (1916). By 'imperialism' he meant not only colonial 'territorial division of the whole world among the greatest capitalist powers', but also monopoly and finance capital, 'the merging of bank capital with industrial capital' resulting in 'financial oligarchy' (1916: 89). He called this a 'stage' in capitalism.

To some extent, Marxists can say that corporate domination is consistent with the systemic development of capitalism and that the new institutions of the global economy are just part of it. Corporations are just the interests of a capitalist class. However, the composition of this ownership class has changed in three ways. First, it excludes many owners of capital (owners of Smith's preferred small-scale, local, owner-managed enterprises). A divergence of interests is emerging between smaller-scale more C-M-C businesses attached to locality and large-scale locality-surpassing M-C-M' ones.[23] Whether this divergence holds and produces a politics remains to be seen.

Second, it is changing from family- or partner-ownership to ownership based on stock. This enables sudden shifts in the qualities of ownership: it becomes indirect, unattached and fickle, and has narrower priorities. The rules of the financial casino subject all productive activity to the high stakes of short-sighted gambling so widely dispersed and carried on so rapidly that it can no longer be controlled by humans, however agentic. Since corporations are primarily accountable to the financial markets, corporate leaders have little choice in the setting of goals and policy. Human beings may still sit on boards of directors, but they cannot change the rules of the global financial casino or its systematic pursuit of ever-increasing growth. Even stockholders are barred from making decisions about working conditions on the basis that 'working conditions, wages, benefits, respect for human rights fall under "ordinary business operations"' and are therefore not in shareholder jurisdiction.[24] Recent crises within financial institutions have made it clear that the 'system (is) so out of control that its best and soundest institutions cannot protect themselves from flagrant fraud and abuse by their own staff' (Korten 1995: 205). The system is even moving out of human control as computers are used to make split-second decisions buying and selling investment portfolios. Corporations become agentic.

Third, when corporations buy their own stock and own themselves, they become the capitalist class. Surely a change from human to non-human ownership signifies a shift in the mode of production. The 1994 Kathmandu Declaration of an International Trade Union Conference stated that the 'basic economic unit' of capitalism is transnational corporations.[25] Monopoly corporations have agency. When they remake the rules, they are no longer mere manifestations of the system.

These changes have created a second important shift in the relations of production: they threaten to render the state all but irrelevant to the effective operation of capital by moving decision-making authority to corporate-dominated bodies such as the WTO and delegitimizing all forms of state intervention that do not serve corporate interests. (Suppressing unions and providing prison labour are approved state activities, which explains why China has been graced with high levels of foreign investment despite refusing until recently to liberalize investment regulations.) This situation goes beyond liberal-democratic state collaboration with capital because it restricts state autonomy to set the terms of and establish limits to that collaboration. State co-operation is now secured not only ideologically, but legally. While certainly consistent with the trajectory of liberal capitalism, the shift in political authority from collaborative nation-states to a World Trade Organization that will dictate deregulation and pre-empt new regulations is significant. Corporate hegemony and the loss of space for independent state authority present a historically unique moment in capitalist development, one that may present a significant shift in the relations of production.

Theorizing Agency

The conditions of possibility for and the possible forms of agency are central to post/structural debates in social theory. One thing that differentiates postmodern theories of structure from the critical school is postmodernism's obsession with defining the structure in such a way as to supply the material and space for freewheeling, undetermined agency. From this perspective naming the enemy fails to prioritize the structure's incompletion, which crucially provides the spaces for agency.

In order to evaluate this approach to agency, is important to understand and distinguish the effects of three faces of Foucault's legacy for theories of social struggle. First is his definitive caution about the subtlety of the operation of power, which recommends rigorous activist attention to the many sites and mechanisms of oppression. Second, Foucault's several studies drove home the frightening possibility that domination had in modern society begun to work in entirely new ways that we might enact on one another in the very act of attempting to dismantle the more obvious forms of oppression. Subsequent postmodern analyses have repeatedly documented the power of narratives, which structure even the most apparently liberatory gestures. Jane Flax challenges feminists to give up their 'dreams' of 'innocent knowledge' and take responsibility for 'locating our contingent selves as the producers of knowledge and truth claims' (1992: 447, 458).

Third, having carefully documented the incredible thoroughness with which modern domination constrains even knowledge and sexuality, at the end of his life Foucault was driven to make theoretical provision for agency by redefining power (1982). Since modern domination does its work through interiorized discipline, much of its operation becomes a 'relation' of power and thus most of its manifestations contain opportunities for agentic resistance. He argued that 'power relations' were only those relations of domination that included some possibility for escape. The resulting theory of agency has been grossly misinterpreted.

Subsequent postmodern theorists have emphasized holes and openings in the structure. They emphasize the importance of conceptualizations that can help to understand how it is that folks actually work amid the wires '"within the enemy's field of vision" and within the enemy's territory' (deCerteau 1984: 37, quoting von Bülow). This idea is actually neither new nor post-Marxist – anarchism has proposed for some time that structural changes can be accomplished by working 'in the interstices of the dominant power structure' (Ward 1982: 20). Nevertheless, postmoderns claim it as their own. Haraway (1983) theorizes Marcuse's white-collar workers as cyborgs, whose thrilling engagement with technology can invade employers' neat authority with infectious contradictions. Cyborgs are creoles, and the history of the African diaspora has shown the usefulness of adept appropriation of the techniques of domination. Supporting Haraway's theory, excavation of the rulers' cultures shows them to be already creolized (Nettleford 1994; Reagon 1994).

A version of this argument specific to the present concern with globalization challenges the conceptualization of globalization as existing. As mentioned earlier, the core of this critique is that such a conception overlooks globalization's 'partialness' (Chin and Mittelman 1997), where it fails, what doesn't interest it, and how it contradicts itself. Naming it capitulates to its totality in a way that is disempowering (Hirst and Thompson 1996). One of the more interesting arguments in this regard is Gibson-Graham's (1996/97) extension of women's resistance to the rape script. By disrupting the 'script' of total male power, women are able to believe in the possibility of resisting rape and to develop and teach one another techniques for escaping rape scenes (often incapacitating the rapist on the way out). Gibson-Graham worries that a story in which globalization is totalizing, as male power was seen to be, positions people as powerless.

Are these situations comparable? The disempowerments of gender are indeed (in part) physical, personal and intimate, and women are indeed capable (with some training) of matching men in hand-to-hand combat. The disempowerments of globalization arrive flanked by the police (or the military), with bulldozers for evictions, with trade rules to undermine local or national commodity markets. Individual skills are inadequate defence. Rape resistance training shows women how to attack men in their most vulnerable places. One question is whether globalization *has* balls? The insights of feminist struggle may not be applicable.

If totalized narratives about enemies are disempowering, why might third world scholars and activists find it useful to describe globalisation as 'recolonisation' (Raghavan 1990), as 'imperialist globalisation ... by multinational/trans-national corporations ... in haste to expand and tighten their rule in the world' (Declaration of Peoples' Conference Against Imperialist 'Globalisation', Quezon City, Philippines, 21–23 November 1996)? Perhaps clarity about the enemy and his intentions, while certainly terrifying, is *not* always disempowering. In the rape script every woman is isolated; in the corresponding script of colonial domination the victim is collective. Do terror, rage and empowerment operate somewhat differently for collectivities and for individuals who know they must face their enemies alone? Do history, culture and community play different roles in colonial struggles and in the highly immediate struggles of women for physical safety? Both material circumstances and meaning structures shape experience and even psyche; thus dis/empowerment may be quite different in different settings.

Since I am studying resistance to globalization, I shall retain the concern with the disempowering effects of a totalized vision of the enemy. Indeed, I shall trace this very issue inductively by examining how the social movements reviewed here understand their enemy. I shall also attempt to determine how the movements conceptualize their own agency/space of resistance.

The theoretical move to conceptualizing structure in such a way as to preserve holes for agency has been paralleled by the treatment of all forms of resistance as horizontally equivalent. The substance of the misreading, 'power is everywhere, so resistance is everywhere', is that the pervasive subtle activities of domination and the relationships that sustain them are somehow equally significant. This attention to a plethora of new sites of oppression wreaks havoc with the attempt to get organized about political economy. Does the fact that insidious forms of domination are *also* present in our sexuality and the way we categorize our knowledge mean that we should not this year prioritize the fight to prevent genetically modified foods coming on to the market?

Enthused by the empowering possibilities of new sorts of movements, researchers have proposed that almost anything could count as 'resistance'. Such proposals are sometimes imaginative attempts at respect for the constrained struggles of marginalized peoples and are sometimes downright silly, throwing aside what we know about ideological hegemony (and a long, complex discussion about consciousness) in favour of an entirely agentic cultural realm in which any sort of resistance is as promising as any other. Two of the most important axes of such resistance studies are identity and culture, which are briefly explored below as necessary to contextualize this study.

Iterations of identity   In 1980, Alberto Melucci coined the term 'new social movements' in recognition that the leading movements since the 1960s seemed to be mobilized around symbolic and informational issues rather than material ones, seemed less concerned about revolution than about the intrinsic benefits of participating in social movements, were integrating public political issues with private everyday life, and were expressing awareness of the global dimensions of social problems. Scholars and activists have for the most part agreed with Melucci that a shift has taken place, whether or not they agree with his diagnosis of it.

In response to various dimensions of the shift (which coincided with widespread Left disenchantment with the state socialist model), a number of important questions have been raised, such as: the make-up of the revolutionary class, the desirability and form of a 'revolution', the scope and unitariness of movement goals, their internal dynamics (particularly in terms of gender), pre- and post-revolutionary organizational structure (particularly the effects of bureaucratization), the usefulness or lack thereof of political parties and electoral projects, the role of the everyday and local, and the contributions of diversity and difference to determining strategy on all these things. The general strike as primary model of struggle is *gone*, as are hopes for unity and clarity among the oppressed and altruism among the privileged.

Melucci's term has been widely applied to a related but slightly different phenomenon, which is the organizing of movements around *identity* as not only an analytic frame for articulating experiences of oppression, but also as an increasingly absolute principle for mobilizing. For a while it seemed that movements might cease to be massified at all, as local identity-based groups pursued liberation in highly particularistic ways. It has indeed seemed that temporary, shifting particularistic alliances form the best framework for organizing when people feel misunderstood even by their allies and when individuals' desires for community are complex and changing. Since people find themselves on the receiving end of a series of different oppressions as they move through different sites, the goals of analytic clarity and unity have been abandoned. With identity as the gateway to politics, altruism has become impossible.

Identity has become a resource, a frame, and a political opportunity. It has reshaped notions of constituency, constrained solidarity, and created a new language of legitimacy. But most importantly, it has reached the status of a paradigm, shaping the way we conceptualize movements and the tools we use to build them. It has been naturalized as a way of understanding how individuals and groups make politics. Omar Kutty (1996) argues that it is the new reality of modern selfhood. Poststructuralists have offered their support to a broad array of liberatory movements with the belief that fragmented, partial, provisional movements are more accurate representations of peoples' experiences, interpretations and desires as they struggle against the regimes that micromanage their lives. Melucci is to be counted among these latter theorists when he argues in *Nomads of the Present* (1989) that attempts to capture state power are 'obsolete', that 'the self' has become a more important form of property than capital and land, and that the success of social movements is to be gauged by whether they contribute to the creation of new 'cultures'.

What is this identity? Foucault argued both that any independent interiority was a 'myth' and that new subjectivities were the crucial liberatory combustible. Drawing on this theory, Stuart Hall (1996) has argued that identity emerges as a 'suture', the sewing together of internalized discourses and the potentially agentic forms of subjectivity created by processes of oppression. While the mobilization of subjectivity allows for agency, it is hard ever to know which mobilizations are simply the structure 'speaking' through subjects and which are genuinely agentic. Postmodern theorists need not be concerned with the genuine if identity, the penultimate politics, is only ever constructed *through* structuring discourses (ibid.), so its every arousal is already infected. Weirdly, Hall's fellow traveller Simon Frith (1996) argues that subjectivity gives rise to choice, and 'we can choose to be anything' – a totally agentic claim with neither nod nor wink to how choices are structured. The critical school would remind us here of how capitalism constrains choices, and even the choosing, via less liberatory forms of identity: the privileges of white-collar culture are also constraints, which close off many choice practices.

Marxists have worked hard to rearticulate their theories in ways that respond to the needs of a working class which, they now acknowledge, is made up of diverse constituencies – women, people of colour and queers are the most often addressed of these. Laclau and Mouffe's new common denominator, democracy, is a reconceptualization of the basic terms and goals of Marxism, which can be articulated in defence of both identity and material interests (1985). Queer theory attempts to move to a 'post-identity' position by articulating a political formation of solidarity against homophobia, gender constraints and race and class oppression (Ertman 2000). This move is most powerfully driven by the inability of gay and lesbian politics to include their own constituencies, particularly bisexual and transgender people, and by the ways in which politicized gay and lesbian identities disserved those with diverse practices and presentations (Jagose 1996).

Identity politics poses problems: no single identity ever completely captures anyone's shifting and complex sense of self; every articulated identity already excludes; and experience-based politics may not be critical analyses of what we are up against. Identity-based movements have come to be seen as a threat to class-based organizing. In response, some scholars are arguing that identity is neither new nor anti-class (Calhoun 1982). Diasporic connections among Africans have been a political formation for over a century (Gilroy 1993) and, while partly organized by the vibrancy of cultural commonalities, are most strongly realized by the shared experience of dispossession among diverse people living in Europe, Latin America, the USA and the Caribbean. Anti-colonial movements have not had pre-existing ethnic homogeneity as a basis for unity, but have commonality imposed by the depredations of imperialism. It is useful to recall that Black Power, as originally articulated, was an analysis not of ethnicity, but of social and political economy. The most militant US new social movements, the Black Panthers and Young Lords Parties, were class-based.

Among women's movements, while much work has been done in the private sphere of the family, the body and interpersonal gender relations, there is a constant emphasis on the economic concerns of women – their double day and low pay. The multiracialization and internationalization of women's movements have made clear that there is neither common identity among women nor even common liberal values (their relationships to tradition, religion and formalized politics being among the more divisive issues) (Basu 1995). What holds their tenuous conversations together is the consistency with which women are exploited materially. Gay liberation movements, perhaps the quint-essential example of non-economism in their concerns with safety and self-expression, still prioritize organizing around material interests, such as issues of employment discrimination, marriage and adoption rights that could bring financial and legal security to gay families.

Hall and his colleagues believe that we must continue to pursue identity in political theory. Just as Flacks (1988) and others argue that we may not like the fact that people watch so much TV, but we must take it into account as we strategize our organizing, so must we take seriously that identity is the medium through which people experience their politicization and their politics. Nikolas Rose warns that post-modern people may in fact be experiencing themselves as fragmented, uncertain, and complex, which will certainly inform the boundary-making of identity politics (1996). Homi K. Bhabha argues that responsible multiculturalists must do more than simply show up with their identity and their sense of coherent unity, they must also do the work of exploring the boundarylands of identity and culture, must acknowledge the 'cultures between cultures', and turn antagonisms into hybridity (1996). If how women have thought feminism is partly shaped by interpellated sexism, then they are responsible for sup-porting the hybrid identities formed in its margins.

Since both globalization and this study of resistance to it strive for international thoroughness, it will be important to track how identity is conceptualized in new movements emerging globally.

(On the misuses of) culture

> resistance movements shape and are constitutive of cultural processes ... As political and economic power become more diffuse and less institutionalized, so too will forms of resistance. Undeclared forms ... everyday activities such as what one wears ... or buys and consumes may qualify as resistance. (Chin and Mittelman 1997: 26, 34)

According to Fredric Jameson's schematization of the relationship between culture and liberatory political change, Frankfurt School theorists including Adorno and Habermas envisioned modern art as 'negative, critical, and utopian' (1998: 25). Many current arguments debate the relative contributions of modernism and postmodernism as liberatory cultural material. Foucault, as already discussed, was hopeful that postmodern creativity would create alternative forms of consciousness and subjectivity. Manfredo Tafuri challenges this popular conception, 'positing the impossibility of any radical transformation of culture before a radical transformation of social relationships themselves' (ibid.: 28).

The currently hegemonic perspective on this debate, after which Jameson's book *The Cultural Turn* is titled, is a feverish embrace of the cultural as political. The disciplinary formation of 'cultural studies' is organized to document identity-based organizing, tactical 'appropriations' of popular culture and commodities, and the creation of Foucault's hoped-for new 'subjectivities'. Thus I initially planned this book to include a chapter on cultural instances of anti-corporatism. In the cultural realm, musicians, bands, zines, artists and internetsia talk about themselves and each other as 'anti-corporate' or as 'sold out' from previous anti-corporate positions. Bands that claim to be or were described as anti-corporate are found in a wide range of genres, including punk, rock, folk, Caribbean, techno and dance. Insiders and outsiders are aware of the existence of 'hardcore anti-corporate fans', 'anti-corporate users', 'anti-corporate clients', 'the list's anti-corporate contingent', 'the anti-corporate crowd', 'anti-corporate rock and roll ravings', the 'anti-corporate look', and even 'anti-corporate atmosphere'. A collectible trading-card game includes anti-corporatism as one of its 'playable themes' alongside 'green', 'liberal' and 'government'. A number of cultural celebrities have used their corporate stages to promote anti-corporate political causes.

While some anti-corporate musicians, such as Ani DiFranco, resolutely refuse to sign with major labels, other anti-corporate cultural figures sometimes claim that accepting corporate money is subversive. Henry Rollins explains signing with a major label as 'It's like taking money from an evil giant … It's like a total jack move – it's total chaos … an attempt to take over popular culture from less entertaining forms of music.' These are the sorts of contradictions celebrated by postmodern theory as subversive. My concern is not only, as Jameson points out, that 'commercial culture' has been 'incorporate[d]' into art 'to the point where many of our older critical and evaluative categories … no longer seem functional' for distinguishing between capitalism and critiques of it (ibid.: 31). I am also concerned about our ability to recognize agency when we see it. To the extent that creativity is sometimes itself a capitalist effect (dressing fashionably would be one instance of this), what sorts of gestures are indication of critical confrontational activity? The appearance of anti-corporate ideas in corporate PopCulture[26] makes agency rather hard to track. After a fruitless search of the literature for some useful operationalization of agency, I still felt the need to distinguish between fashion and a fight – which do seem to have important differences.

Social movement activists have long recognized the role of culture. A community's shared values and visions provide a cultural *lens for critical analysis*. Third world critics of Western development models, such as Paulo Freire (1969), Pramod Parajuli (1991), and Sulak Sivaraksa (1989) explain how traditional indigenous culture is the basis for critiques of oppression and for new visions and techniques. People have secured the survival and development of their communities by creating cultures of resistance, in which culture is the *medium of struggle*. Rex Nettleford and Bernice Johnson Reagon describe cultural 'creolization' as the intentional process through which a community ensures its survival (both 1994). This means that creole productions of self are survival responses to conditions of oppression, responses that testify to peoples' creativity, vibrancy and tenacity. Indigenous cultures are in no way inauthenticized by this agentic process.

Cultures of resistance not only inspire techniques of struggle but also serve as spiritual bulwarks against and oases of escape from dehumanizing forces (Scott 1990). It is important to be clear that while culture plays important roles, it was never the only medium of, for example, slave rebellions. Likewise, religious institutions are often community institutions that are used for organizing urgent responses to many kinds of problems; this does not make the response primarily a religious one. The struggles that are often cited as showcasing the power of culture did not rely upon that medium alone. Presumably, the postmodern creation of new 'subjectivities' (Foucault 1982) and 'cultures' (Melucci 1989) will bring new meanings, alternative spaces and media of struggle all at once.

Are postmodern uses of culture agentic? If humans and society are driven primarily by meaning-making (Lévi-Strauss 1963), if capitalist media and ideology systematically drain and resupply the cultural material available (Mills 1951; Marcuse 1964), and if ownership of the mass media is nearing monopoly levels, we can hardly call the resulting culture agentic despite the observation that consumed culture takes on a life of its own (Said 1978; Nandy 1983), no longer under the direct control of capitalist knowledge and image production. The high hopes of the bricoleurs (deCerteau 1984) depend on a Weberian desperation (1904–5) – the only way out is individual creativity and charisma (not persistent collective action based on community values). Butler (1990) proposes a diffuse, still highly individualized, strategy of appropriative 'subversive repetitions' of the enemy's mind-numbing chants.

While young people have 'appropriated' corporate fashion, Nike has become very effective at exploiting people of colour as employees and consumers. According to Zak Sinclair, Niketown stores combine high-tech surveillance of customers, individualistic brainwashing through 'motivational catchphrases', 'eroticized images of African American men in agony', slavery imagery, and phenomenal sales of the ultimate status symbol.[27] As Sivanandan argues, this culture does damage before it can be appropriated: 'You do not eat a hamburger ... watch television ... listen to pop music ... without losing your ability to hear other voices, your ability to reflect, weigh, meditate' (1989: 12). Neither side of the post/structural debate has taken to heart the admonishments of Althusser, Gramsci or Foucault regarding the insidious effects of power on seemingly independent social institutions like the internet. (For some of today's Marxists, the effort to avoid accusing anyone of false consciousness has led to analytic paralysis in this regard.) Somehow, despite their adulation of Foucault, poststructuralists have concluded that consuming television can be resistance. If everything at hand was designed to beguile us, to lure us into not paying attention to the real problems, can this material really be 'reappropriated'? Can it actually be used for any kind of 'radical break' (Benjamin 1940)? And what of the army behind the chanters?

The celebration of cultures of resistance has not managed to articulate very well *how* such culture can impact structure. Would it help to make a distinction between resistance and struggle? Conditions are resisted – and it's true that *anything* can be resisted. Many gestures, actions, thoughts, and interpretations are counter to hegemony and therefore resistive. We might want to understand struggle as another kind of thing – collective, strategic, waged against an identified enemy. The most impressive examples of cultural movements are feminism and gay politics, where cultural work has changed the quality of daily life by making alternatives livable and challenging oppressive social norms. Again, cultural change was only one component of these movements, which also worked for structural changes. And the cultural work is the subject of long-term communal dialogue; it is neither as momentary nor as individualistic as the theories it has inspired. Another way of exploring this is to ask whether particular PopCultural forms of resistance make explicit analytic links outside of cultural practices or merely exist as subversive reaction.

Because of my concerns with evaluating the significance of cultural gesture *as* social movement, I decided not to include purely cultural movements in the study. However, I do track the uses of culture by the movements.

Discourse 'Naming the enemy' is not only a structural proposition, it is also a discursive one. This study emerged from the conjoining of two discursive moments. The first was the recognition that communities all over the world, urban and rural, first and third world, face quite similar social, economic and environmental devastation at the hands of corporations (Starr and Rodgers 1995). The discursive aspect of this insight was that one discourse could be appropriate for such diverse peoples. The second moment was a meeting at the Los

Angeles Labor/Community Strategy Center, at which an organizer informed potential members they should clearly understand that the multi-racial Center was 'anti-corporate'. The fact that a social movement was actually using this structural analysis suggested an opportunity for the emergence of a coherent movement from many different social sectors. Thus 'naming the enemy', the formation and mobilization of anti-corporate discourse, is one of the primary concerns of the study.

How can we theorize the role of discourse in challenging globalization? The simplest proposal is that if invisibility is crucial both to the system's legitimacy and to its continued relatively unimpeded operations, then discourse can bring 'sunshine' to the workings of corporate hegemony (even if only briefly), can disrupt divide-and-conquer tactics, and can raise questions about social processes and who benefits from them. However, as they systematically destroy alternatives, corporations will need invisibility less. Stuart Hall, among others, acknowledges that insurgent discourses build new communities (and identities) around alternative ideas (see Gamson 1992).

A set of Marxists, from Gramsci to Laclau and Mouffe (1985), theorize ongoing discursive struggle for hegemony (from which position it would presumably be possible to make changes to the material structure and its mechanisms). Haraway (1983), as already mentioned, suggests that it may be possible to invade hegemony, to become it and then to change it. (We might note here that essentialist liberal feminism and other 'change from within' strategies have not succeeded in doing so.)

The notion of political 'opportunity structures' (Eisinger 1976) or 'world-systemic openings' (Foran 1992) could be extended to the issue of discourse by proposing that official ideologies are more permeable in some places than others or during crises of legitimacy. Thus in the USA the notion of 'product safety' made possible limited gains in corporate responsibility for a time, whereas limitations on the rights of private property have made little headway. The recent 'economic meltdowns' created a momentary crisis of legitimacy of deregulatory neoliberalism, a discursive pause during which Malaysia re-erected economic boundaries.

For Piven and Cloward (1977) truthful speech has no power of its own. Disruptive mobilizations can create possibilities for power, which would include discursive space. Flax (1992) agrees, but for different reasons. She argues that 'it is far from clear what contributions knowledge or truth can make to the development of ... discursive communities which foster ... an appreciation of and desire for difference [and] empathy'. Patricia Williams, Haunani-Kay Trask and other scholars argue that the tragedy of race is not, as my students tend to insist, a tragedy of ignorance or lack of information. Flax opposes discourse as an attempt to communicate the truth but supports it as a discussion about values.

Habermas agrees with Flax that dialogue is important, but sees it as a route to truth. In Richard Harvey Brown's words, for Habermas 'reason is transcendental creativity, an agency or activity that shapes or informs the world but stands above it' (1987: 64). This 'standing above' insists, first, that thinking is not hegemonized by structure and, second, that the activity of doing it, the practice (of 'rhetoric' for Brown, of 'communication' for Habermas) is what is liberatory (as opposed to material/political rearrangements). George Myerson points out that Habermas does not allow for the significance of 'refusing to respond on someone else's terms!' (1994: 87) – the radical refusal of negotiation and insistence upon self-determination. Nancy Fraser (1989) explains that such discursive negotiations do not take place on level ground in terms of resources, qualifications, authority and sanction (even if the insurgents can somehow gain access to unofficial ideas) – the game is rigged.

To summarize these positions crudely :

- Discourse carries precious bits of truth and helps to build the movement.
- Ideological hegemony matters and struggle for it is possible.
- Discourse is not where it's at.
- Dialogue is itself transcendent and transformative.

Anti-corporatism In one of the more celebrated efforts to establish common territory in the post/structural fracas, Ernesto Laclau and Chantal Mouffe's 1985 *Hegemony and Socialist Strategy* argues for a new unifying factor for social movements. In place of socialism, we should look for 'extensions of the democratic imaginary'. Such a framework makes space for 'infinite surfaces of emergence' – thus identity movements, political economic ones, and struggles with the terms of everyday domestic life can be equally valued in the struggle for liberation. On the heels of Laclau and Mouffe, Carl Boggs predicted that these many struggles all had the same enemy (I've italicized it):

> vital new phase in the historical struggle for democratization ... clash with the imperatives of *corporate hegemony* in extensive areas of social life ... generalized revolt against domination ... all forms of social hierarchy ... corporate and state spheres through which [patriarchy and racism] are reproduced and enforced ... [and the] technocratic infrastructure which ... rationalizes and legitimates the various types of domination. (1986: 50)

Stuart Hall was also paying attention to such possibilities and a few years earlier had proposed that Marx's *Grundrisse* (1857) 'demonstrates how it is possible to think of the "unity" of a social formation as constructed, not out of identity but out of *difference* ... as the "unity of many determinations"' (1980: 68). Allowing the revolution to emerge from multiple struggles need not be a capitulation to poststructural anti-economism. Hall points out that the contradictions of capitalism arise in different ways at different times and places. Laclau and Mouffe insist that not only the enemy but the inspiration for struggle (democracy) is widely shared.

In 1974, Barnet and Müller had proposed three possible future discourses of anti-globalization, based on existing critiques: anti-growth, anti-consumption, and anti-hierarchy. The most popular current approach was articulated by Richard Falk in 1993 as 'globalization from below' (the second mode analysed here). It is democratic, humanitarian internationalism. An edited volume by Brecher, Childs and Cutler (1993) presented a range of international activists' ideas about what this kind of internationalism might look like. Leftist scholars have embraced 'cross-border alliances' and labour internationalism as the model for dealing with globalization. Brecher and Costello (1994) propose a 'Lilliput' strategy. Once the Lilliputs have established their power, they will replace the 'corporate agenda' with a 'human agenda'. This will include democratizing global institutions, establishing basic human rights globally (including the right to self-organization), allowing plurality of economic systems, and rebuilding the public sector.

In 1994 Barnet and Cavanagh perceived that 'territorially based

forces of local survival seeking to preserve and to redefine community'
will be the basis for challenging the forces of globalization (the third
mode analysed here). Since the nation-state has been in disrepute
among leftists for some time now, scholars have not theorized how to
retake it as a tool of defence against globalization, despite the importance of the state to many of the social movements which are
actually mobilizing against globalization and specifically against their
nations' collaboration with multinational corporations (the first mode
analysed here).

This book takes a slightly different approach from that of examining
anti-globalization. I am interested in movements that are opposing
the agents of globalization, corporations. In the USA (inventor of
constitutional rights for corporations), anti-corporatism was part of
the populist tradition. It has other historical roots as well. Late 1970s
socialist commentators were divided over early US anti-corporate
movements. Some expressed concern that first world anti-corporate
activism would remain 'defensive and issue-oriented', would be expressed only as a consumer movement, or would be co-opted by non-
socialist organizations (Vogel 1974; Boyte 1977, Rotkin 1977). But
Harry Boyte also noted that the movement as it appeared in the 1970s
was 'incubating a longer range vision of decentralized, radical democracy'. John Judis (1976) warned that only short-sighted leftists would
ignore the 'proletarianism' and 'socialist possibilities' of anti-corporate
projects like Tom Hayden's 1976 Campaign for Economic Democracy.
In 1979 Paul Starr was encouraged by anti-corporate populism's connections with the working class, but concerned that it 'lacked concrete
economic strategies'. Sociologists (socialist or otherwise) have not
mentioned anti-corporatism since. They are also not discussing anti-
globalization movements systematically.

The first question this study traces is how the movements understand their enemy. Critical globalization scholars do not write about
the humble partialities of postmodernism. One of the analytic threads
to be pursued is whether the movements studied, individually and
collectively, envision their activities as partial (dealing with one of
many problems) or total (dealing with the systemic core of the
problems of their world). Is it possible to see and describe the enemy?
Do the movements critique growth? Dependence? Colonialism? Consumption? Capitalism? What mediating tools are used?

Collectively corporations have succeeded in defining the corporate good as the public good; the discursive delegitimation of their logics and actions challenges this dangerous equation. If cultural hegemony seems to threaten the possibility of knowing anything at all (note how effective corporate media have been in dismissing scientific consensus on global warming), then discourse on corporate 'legitimacy' (and 'delegitimation') are important processes. What is the significance of movements' discursive aspects? Helena Norberg-Hodge theorizes that a narrative of a totalized enemy could be empowering in that instead of feeling overwhelmed with a plethora of separate social problems, people could realize that those problems have a single source which is damaging social health in many ways (at IFG 1997). If structure *has* returned, we should expect a parallel shift in social movements.

And if things are pretty well structured, how can social movements be agentic in the face of corporate hegemony? Meditating on my computer's screen-saver, I wonder about all the ways we could 'fuck globalization'. Can we attack it? Can we undermine it? Can globalization be seduced and taken advantage of? Can we turn our backs on it, muttering to one another: 'Fuck that!'? Do the new movements draw on postmodern theories of struggle? Do they use identity? Pop-Culture? Do they create new cultures? What theory do they put forth of effective action? What are the sites? Is secular politics important? Disruption? Infiltration? Is the movement revolutionary, sweeping away and replacing existing systems, or does it attempt to use existing institutions for its own purposes? Do anti-corporate movements seem willing to link up with other movements across the boundaries of ideology, race, class, nation, first/third world divides? Are they linked up with each other? Which movements are less well connected?

Recently, scholars have begun to recognize the need for an 'alternative political economy' as part of the struggle against globalization (Amoore et al. 1997, Pieterse 1997; Robinson 1998/99), but they have not acknowledged the existence of any. Latham (1997) usefully suggests embracing Polanyi, arguing for movements that are 'self-consciously heterogeneous but take provisionism as the central and unifying task'. The second question this study traces is the movements' vision of how to rebuild the world. How do they define development? What scale of economy is imagined? Is 'progress' a goal? (How is it defined?)

What role does technology play? What is the source of information about organizing society? Is community important? What kind of political decision-making system is proposed? What role, if any, does the nation have? Is multiculturalism part of the vision and how are multiple oppressions addressed?

This chapter has explored theoretical issues at stake in the emergence of an international anti-corporate social movement. The following three chapters present reports on 15 ideologically distinct movements organized into three modes of struggle. The three modes are contestation and reform, 'globalization from below', and delinking/relocalization. The analysis of the movements appears in the concluding chapter, which returns to the theoretical issues raised here. It is unlikely that I will manage to answer all the questions above. Please join me in asking them of the data, asking them of your own knowledge and experience, and asking new ones as we work to respond to globalization.

Notes

1. Sulayman Nyang argues that 'the globalisation of morality is the product of imperialism and colonialism ... a new hegemonic order ... in examining the moral contents of the Declaration of Human Rights, one searches in vain for any reference to moral and religious concepts drawn from the Third World' (1998: 131–2; see also Trask 1993).

2. As articulated by Shiva at IFG 1997.

3. At IFG 1997.

4. Shiva at IFG 1999.

5. At IFG 1997.

6. Wallach at IFG 'Teach-In on Economic Globalization and the Role of the World Trade Organization', 26 and 27 November 1999, Seattle (USA). Hereafter 'IFG 1999'.

7. IFG 1997.

8. UNDP 1997.

9. Dorene Isenberg, 'The European Monetary Union: Greenspan's federal reserve writ large', *Dollars and Sense* 214, November/December 1997: 11–14, 39.

10. IDB Northern Ireland, www.INVEST-NorthernIreland.com. Advertisement in *Hemispheres*, the United Airlines Magazine, April 1999.

11. Tony Clarke, and IFG 1997.

12. David Bacon, 'Still Hungry' in *Z Magazine*, 10(1) (January 1997): 28–31.

13. Harry J. Gray, chairman and CEO of United Technologies Corporation, in Brecher and Costello 1994: 69.

14. Martin Khor, quoting a corporate spokesperson's statement at IFG 1997.

15. Lori Wallach, Richard Grossman, Congressman David Bonier, at IFG 1997.

16. Brian Burgoon, 'The job-eating villain: is it NAFTA or Mexico's currency crisis?', *Dollars and Sense* 206 (July/August 1996): 12–16, 42.

17. Wallach at IFG 1999.

18. At IFG 1999.

19. At IFG 1997.

20. IFG 1997.

21. Lori Wallach at IFG 1997.

22. Shiva at IFG 1997.

23. Obviously, all enterprises operating within a capitalist system are by necessity M-C-M'. But if we arrange economic forms on a continuum from C-C to M-M', then small businesses would be 'more' C-M-C than corporations.

24. Revealed in Disney's effort to bar a shareholder resolution. Hearing before the Securities and Exchange Commission.

25. International Trade Union Conference, 'Strengthen Pro-Worker Trade Unionism, Oppose Privatization', Kathmandu, 10–13 December 1994 (38 trade unions from 15 countries represented).

26. I'll spell it this way to differentiate it from more transhistorical forms of popular culture.

27. Zak Sinclair, 'Don't think. Just do it. Tripping in Niketown USA', *Third Force*, July/August 1997.

. . . .

CHAPTER 2

Contestation and Reform

Everyone must realize that McDonalds sucks, and you must do your part to put the fucking place out of commission. *'Screwing over your local McDonalds', www how-to guide*

§ THE first of the three modes of anti-corporatism is composed of movements that seek to impose regulatory limitations on corporations or force them to self-regulate. These movements contest the legitimacy of neoliberal reformulations of the role of the state and the necessity of subordinating social priorities to 'international competitiveness'.

The use of the word 'reform' to describe this mode does not mean that these movements take a liberal approach to capitalism. All three anti-corporate modes discussed here are quite thoroughly critical of capitalism (although they don't call it that) and none is ameliorative. Movements of this mode reject growth, prioritize non-economic concerns, and critique dependency and consumption – stances not permissible in liberal reformism. 'Reform', then, signifies a strategic approach commonly taken by this mode, mobilizing existing formal democratic channels of protest, seeking national legislation, mounting judicial challenges, mobilizing international agencies, boycotting and protesting.

In response to structural adjustment, people's movements are using a variety of tactics to challenge the destruction of the social contract and to strengthen the state's position relative to neoliberal licences for corporate hegemony. For the peace and human rights movements, corporations are increasingly appearing as the culprits. Land reform movements, first and third world alike, are putting limits on the market, removing land from its reach and demanding government accountability for basic protections. New explicitly anti-corporate movements, such as the movements to halt genetic engineering and biological patenting, are demanding re-regulation of corporations and even pressuring them directly. Cyberpunk, rather than working through government, attacks corporations directly, hoping they will stumble and become vulnerable to democratic processes. For all of these movements, 'Corporate rule' is wrong because it it undemocratic.[1]

Fighting Structural Adjustment

... because globalisation is all about paying no taxes, states are becoming bankrupt.[2]

Structural adjustment conditionalities require liberalizing investment policies, privatizing public industries and services, downsizing civil service employment, suppressing labour organizing, lifting costly regulation from business practices, devaluing currency, and cutting social spending and subsidies. All of these changes facilitate corporate entry into the economy and provide opportunities to capture markets. Like free trade agreements, structural adjustment packages undermine national sovereignty. Third world debt is a lever that enables first world institutions to retake governance of the third world, by shifting authority from national priorities to those of first world neoliberal advisers. In the first world, the necessity of 'international competitiveness' and European unification justifies these same practices – ironically in the name of the very social contract that they unravel (the promise of prosperity through exports) (Bello 1994).

By the mid-1980s, impoverishment and unrest in structurally adjusted third world countries led United Nations agencies to argue for 'adjustment with a human face'. From 1985 to 1992, 56 'IMF riots' or 'austerity protests', including demonstrations, strikes and riots, were waged in Latin America, the Caribbean, the Middle East, Africa and Eastern Europe (Walton and Seddon 1994). In the 1990s, protests defending social welfare policies erupted in Western Europe and Canada. In the United States, little mass mobilization has occurred around cuts in social programmes, but critiques of 'corporate welfare' have gained popularity.

Recent third world protest against structural adjustment has included Haitian resistance to secretive privatization plans, which forced the resignation of Haiti's neoliberal Prime Minister Michel in 1995. In South Africa, resistance to the IMF heated up in 1996 and involved riots, strikes and organizing among community groups, health workers and media. The Campaign Against Neoliberalism in South Africa called for the closure of the local World Bank office. In 1998, 10,000 Indonesian students led resistance to economic policy and lack of democracy. They occupied radio stations and regional parliament buildings. In spring, mobilizations estimated in the hundreds of thousands occurred in Yogyakarta and Jakarta. Despite the success in forcing General Suharto's resignation, students and the urban poor denounced President Habibie as well, for conforming with IMF-mandated abolition of food and fuel subsidies and for failing to implement democracy. Protesters neared one million.[3]

In the first five months of 1998, 400 farmers in Andhra Pradesh, India, committed suicide in response to structural adjustment-type policies in a context where the army has killed 600 peasant activists since 1992. In 1999, residents of Kanxoc in Yucatan, Mexico, ejected a representative of the government agency administering the privatization of collective lands; they declared that they would rather lose government agricultural subsidies than privatize.[4] In a January 1999 pastoral letter, the Venerable Society of Jesus (Latin American Council of Jesuits) denounced neoliberalism as 'a sin', a violation of justice according to religious principles, and insisted that alternative economic approaches are possible.[5]

Students at Mexico's largest university, Universidad Nacional Autónoma de México, went on strike in April 1999 in protest against policies including privatization, subsidy to 'the bankers and to the great industrialists' paid for by cutting 'resources to the education of the population'. The students announced that they were 'on strike, because we are not arranged to accept that the University closes its doors to the children of the workers' (Consejo General de Huelga, 2nd Manifesto, 23 April 1999). Over 100,000 students participated in democratic proceedings to decide the direction of the strike. The students expressed solidarity with many other social sectors, calling on people 'to fight shoulder to shoulder with the workers, the students, the farmers, to reveal themselves and resist the *privatizadora* (privatization) attack'. In February 2000, after the government and the students organized competing referenda, the strikers were attacked and many were arrested, and incredible support emerged from their parents and other civil society sectors.

Illustrating the limits of the much-heralded South Korean modernization-induced 'transition to democracy', the government has prosecuted leaders of the two-day May 1998 car-workers' strike, which demanded renegotiation of the 1997 IMF loan, which has led to the 'sacrifice' of workers. Nearly 100,000 unionized workers struck at 130 companies. In September 1998, Seoul hosted an international conference of 'People Against the IMF' accompanied by a massive demonstration of unemployed and fired workers, some now involved in illegal unions of the unemployed, organized by the Korean Confederation of Trade Unions. In October 1999, the Korean Federation of Bank and Financial Labor Unions became the first trade union to sue the IMF for damages caused by the imposition of structural adjustment policies.[6]

First world nations with popular movements against structural adjustment policies include Sweden, where in 1995 the General Synod of the Church of Sweden blamed economic globalization and 'increased confidence in the market as a forum for solving society's problems' for threatening the 'weakest members of society' as the government abandoned responsibility for the individual. In late 1995 France was host to general strikes in protest against cuts in the welfare system, health, civil service and education. An estimated five million – mostly public-sector and wildcatting private-sector workers – were involved. Citizens supported the action and one day a BBC journalist 'could not find a single traffic jam bound commuter opposed to the strike!'[7] An observer noted that workers appeared to be 'radicalized' by the situation; fearing government 'manipulation', they resisted reformist unions' effort to settle rapidly.[8] In late 1996, the French unemployed held their first strike (the official unemployment rate at the time was 12.7 per cent). For a month, 'the organizations of the unemployed demonstrated, petitioned, and occupied public buildings'. The movement continued to grow.

> From October 1998, every month, throughout France, demonstrations or occupations have taken place with the slogan 'Nothing Has Changed!' This has helped to mobilise all those who find themselves even worse off than they were last year, and added to the determination that a total reform is neccessary. Key dates have been 3 December and 21 December. The huge mobilisation for a 'Christmas Bonus' of 3000 francs started in Marseille with 20,000 demonstrators in the streets, and this led to actions in 50 towns and cities.[9]

In addition to ongoing protests directed at national governments, these movements have been internationalized in important new ways. Jubilee 2000, started in the early 1990s, active in 60 countries and drawing extensive religious support, demands cancellation of 'the unpayable debts of the world's poorest countries by the end of 2000'. The organization has assembled a series of human chains demanding debt relief, including 70,000 people surrounding the G8 Summit in Birmingham in May 1998; 35,000 surrounding the G8 Summit in Cologne in June 1999, accompanied by 50,000 in London, 10,000 in Edinburgh and 15,000 in Stuttgart; and 30,000 in November 1999 at the Seattle WTO Ministerial. Jubilee 2000 also calls for the 'restructuring of international trade and investment to benefit ordinary people'.[10] It is supported by labour, women's organizations, environmentalists and students. The Afrika Coalition is comparing debt forgiveness with the historic struggles to abolish slavery, describing the enemy as 'debt bondage'.

Another international network, 50 Years is Enough, has 170 member non-governmental organizations worldwide from 50 countries. Debt reduction is only part of its goal. It aims to reform World Bank, IMF and other international financial institution activities to be open, accountable and supportive of 'more equitable development based on the perspectives, analysis, and development priorities of women and men affected by those policies'. Its alternative vision is 'small-scale community-determined solutions that promote economic self-reliance, as well as economic and social justice'. Regional organizations critical of international financial institutions have also been formed in Latin America, Eastern Europe and Asia. The European Bank for Reconstruction and Development (EBRD) is the target of protest about the imposition on Central and Eastern Europe of Western economic models and developments (such as nuclear power) that benefit multinational corporations. Central and Eastern European Bankwatch Network is a network of NGOs that monitors the activities of international financial institutions, including the European Investment Bank, which, they explain, 'lends more money every year than the World Bank, while having only one environmental expert on staff [while] the World Bank has hundreds of experts on environment and sustainable development'.

In November 1999, Jubilee 2000 South Africa hosted a 'South–South

Summit'. According to Njoki Njoroge Njehû of the 50 Years is Enough
Network, the conference agreed on several analytic positions organized
around the concept 'Don't Owe–Won't Pay!' First, they reject the
IMF/World Bank pretence at debt relief via the HIPC (heavily indebted poor country) classification, which is merely another form of
imposing structural adjustment. Second, they 'repudiate' Southern
nation debts 'on the grounds of illegitimacy and the tremendous
ecological and historical debt owed *to* the South by the North for
centuries of exploitation, slavery, and colonialism'. Third, they demand
restitution (prosecution of those responsible for debt) and reparations
for the damage done by debt and other exploitation. These movements
are insisting that civil society organizations in each country receiving
debt relief be granted authority over the use of national resources
freed from debt service.[11]

The World Bank and IMF created the HIPC category in response
to these movements, but they require these countries to implement
more structural adjustment in order to qualify for debt relief.[12] The
June 1999 meeting of the G8 was heralded by Jubilee 2000 as indication of a 'paradigm shift' as the G8 repudiated the IMF and spurred
its own commitment to debt relief for poor countries.[13] In March,
September and December 1999, Canada, the USA and the UK respec-
tively announced intentions to write off bilateral debt as countries
come through the HIPC process. (They will only forgive after HIPC
in order to avoid that money being used to pay other creditors.)
Canada has also gone ahead and forgiven Bangladesh's debt to it,
which is significant because Bangladesh is not on the HIPC list.[14] Like
the HIPC process, the bilateral relief proposals may include continued
structural adjustment conditionalities, which are unacceptable to
Jubilee 2000 and 50 Years is Enough campaigners.

The Center for Alternative Structural Adjustment/Bretton Woods
Reform Organization was founded in 1991 by Davison Budhoo, former
senior economist of the IMF. Budhoo explains that his goal is to
'destroy the World Bank/IMF as technical institutions by doing what
they say they're doing – only we need to do it better'. The alternative
programme 'is based on the principle that a healthy economy does
not rely on exports for income and on imports for daily needs ...
provides for the needs of the people in a sustainable and egalitarian
way that fosters self-reliance'. This includes rural and non-rural

agriculture devoted to food security, priority on small-scale labour-intensive, high value-added enterprise, affordable energy and technology for rural areas, elimination of primary resource, mineral and grain export, and micro-credit at low or no interest rates along the Grameen Bank model.

Alternatives to structural adjustment are even beginning to be co-opted, as World Bank President James Wolfensohn participated in the July 1997 launching of the Structural Adjustment Participatory Review Initiative, supported by many civil society organizations, labour unions (accounting for one-quarter of members), and by World Bank employees 'who have known for some time about the negative impact of structural adjustment programs, but have been afraid to speak out'. The Initiative is a massive, supposedly participatory investigative process, 'designed to yield recommendations'. The results of official participation in the generation of 'alternatives' are yet to be seen. The World Bank's interest in Grameen Bank-type micro-credit organizations is of some concern, given that this could be a mechanism to indebt third world people individually as well as collectively. I'd been saying this for a while and finally John Samuel confirmed my fears, stating that 'development itself is increasingly being treated as a business', arguing that a mythology has developed around the Grameen Bank that 'sells a neoliberal market-oriented ideology of development', and informing us that Citicorm, Chase Manhattan and American Express co-sponsored the World Bank's Microcredit Summit.[15]

Struggles against structural adjustment are implicitly anti-corporate. They oppose and seek to reverse government collusion with corporate priorities, they refuse the legitimacy and necessity of adjustment policies, and they insist upon national sovereignty in the face of the neoliberal onslaught. All over the world, people's movements are forcing national governments to examine the effects of domestic neoliberal policies. These hurt both domestic economic elites and the poor, as multinational corporations externalize more costs while receiving priority access to low-cost inputs. People are pushing their governments to acknowledge that facilitating corporate projects does not alleviate poverty; this is a challenge to modernization theory.

In response to neoliberal policy in the USA, an unusual multi-ideological coalition came together in 1997 under the name of the Stop Corporate Welfare Coalition. The coalition created a list of targets for reducing federal handouts for corporations. The targets included the Market Promotion Program (which subsidizes foreign advertising of Pillsbury, Dole, McDonalds and Jim Beam, among other US corporations), timber roads into national forests, plutonium pyro-processing, the Overseas Private Investment Corporation, the Export–Import Bank and the International Monetary Fund.

Another multi-ideological coalition of socialists, free-marketers and environmentalists is working to expose the secrecy and, in Indonesia's case, illegality, of Congressional appropriations for IMF bail-outs. Free-marketers are arguing that public funding of sports stadiums – the shibboleths of local economic development – is unconstitutional subsidy of private corporations.

While the conservative economic institutes are concerned that corporate welfare 'distorts the market economy' and leads to 'inefficient' production, liberals learn that the conservative premises of 'free enterprise' and 'reducing federal spending' can be the basis for budgetary critiques that address concerns of environmental and social equity movements. They agree on criteria for corporate welfare, many of which reveal how corporate subsidies contradict useful legislation. This promising movement is playing an important role in the public discourse on corporations. The next step for this movement is to expose why corporate welfare exists by analysing corporate power and the ideological role of corporate growth and its promises.

Campaign finance reform, like corporate welfare reform, is a multi-ideological populist issue on which left and right politicians and social movement organizations are cooperating, exposing corporate influence in campaign finance and calling such influence 'anti-democratic'. This movement directly challenges corporations' 'free speech' rights, accorded by the 1886 Supreme Court decision giving them the rights of citizens. Building a critique of such rights and delegitimizing them could be important to dismantling corporate hegemony internationally. As Kevin Danaher of Global Exchange suggests, 'even if it didn't pass, a constitutional amendment stating "a corporation is not a person" would force corporations to clarify why they want such rights'.

The anti-corporatisms of corporate welfare reform and campaign finance reform differ slightly: campaign finance reform clearly theorizes corporations as intentionally villainous, while corporate welfare reform could be interpreted as positioning corporations as cheerful freeloaders, taking advantage (as anyone would) of bungling government pro-grammes. A complete critique must link the two, showing that corporations purchase politicians in order to protect not only direct subsidies (corporate welfare) but also indirect subsidies (regulatory and deregulatory benefits) and also how corporate priorities have been embedded into federal and local government definitions of 'the public good'. Campaign finance reform has been easily co-opted, hopelessly confusing the issue; this has not been so easy with corporate welfare reform.

Peace and Human Rights

Peace and human rights movements are analysed together here because they are interwoven ideologically and share personnel. Both are well established and diverse movements that have both institution-alized and informal structures and employ a range of tactics. Moreover, both have become discourses that go beyond their organizations; their interrelated discourses can be articulated within other struggles. Thus it is significant that these movements have begun to include cor-porations among the enemies of peace and human rights.

The peace movement is a first world moral phenomenon, which opposes first world military imperialism and excessive militarization of first world societies. (Third world opposition to first world military colonization and nuclearization takes the form of struggles for political sovereignty; it is not an attempt to 'reform' national governments. Thus it will be considered in the section on sovereignty.) Since much of the peace movement is targeted at state practices and the dis-semination of non-violent conflict-resolution techniques, it often does not appear to be anti-corporate.

The peace movement's international humanitarian work in pro-viding emergency assistance to war refugees has brought peace organizations such as the American Friends Service Committee to critical perspectives on development and the role of corporations in war and exploitation. Similarly, the Asia Pacific Center for Justice and Peace includes in its list of areas of work 'long-term ecological sustain-ability and local and national self-reliance, in order to reverse the devastating environmental, social and cultural impact of exclusively market-driven development schemes'. Even august organizations like the Carter Peace Center are critiquing mainstream development, concluding that 'the most appropriate development policies and strategies come from within a country, not from outside'.

Disarmament campaigns do recognize government–industry collusion in using the military–industrial complex as a form of economic development. Although corporations are only part of the problem, as profiteers they have become warmongers. The disarmament movement regularly takes direct action against nuclear weapons, testing and production. The use of direct action has enabled the international disarmament movement to be powerful despite its relatively small numbers. A UK religious group, The Prince of Peace Ploughshares, in advertising their attempt to disarm an Aegis destroyer, explains: 'We see these ships as blasphemy against God; as byproducts of national weakness, fear and hatred; as robbery from the poor, as technology bent toward pride and lawlessness. In the judgment of God's Word, they should not exist.' The Ploughshares' analysis lists 'corporate global domination' among the 'madnesses' of the world. Their critique shows the ideological advancement of the peace movement, which discovered that military aggressiveness is often connected with the interests of corporations, and has subsequently focused more attention on their state's military support for corporate projects in the third world. They connect militarism to poverty, corporate global domination and international racism. Peace activists contribute important direct action knowledge gained in tax resistance, human blockades and breaches of military facilities.

Few versions of the peace movement put forth general critiques of capitalism, and I did not find any putting forth generalized critiques of corporations. The peace movement's idea of converting weapons factories to peaceful goods production is a particularly problematic vision, echoing the corporate promise that industrial production is the road to peace. This is a problem with clear historical precedents: following the Second World War, war technology was converted to a 'peaceful' industry – agriculture – resulting in the promotion of petroleum fuel, herbicidal chemicals and re-equipped tanks. This conversion commodified formerly free farm-based inputs, raising the stakes for small farmers and eventually resulting in massive loss of topsoil, toxification of food, mutated pests and industrialization of the land. Tragically, this 'swords into ploughshares' project shifted the entire cosmology of farming from collaboration and husbandry to a war against nature. The Spring 1997 issue of *AdBusters* magazine documents how military imagery is still used in advertisements for agro-industrial products.

In its anti-corporatism, the peace movement focuses on public–private collusion in the pursuit of war for profit. It uses multiple strategies, including institutional democratic processes and direct actions against corporations and military sites. The peace movement laid an important foundation, but now needs a more thorough vision of how imperialism is crucial to capitalism and militarism is utilized by corporate 'development'. It would be unfair, however, to say that such visions are absent. Many participants in the peace movements are also participants in various movements for economic democracy (such as sustainable development and labour movements), and more recently they have joined the anti-structural adjustment and anti-FTA movements.

Organizations like the Women's International League for Peace and Freedom, whose work has for decades been focused on military issues, have now turned to anti-corporate political economic campaigns. A Bangor, Maine (USA) peace organization called Peace through Interamerican Community Action has built a Clean Clothes anti-sweatshop campaign, which has resulted in city resolutions on selective purchasing, partnerships with retailers, and a consumer pressure network. The same shift is occurring in human rights organizations. The object of the 2000 Session of the Permanent People's Tribunal will be violations of human rights perpetrated by multinational corporations. Although most of their tribunals investigate political repression, they have recently had two tribunals on the IMF and World Bank (1988, 1994), two on Industrial Hazards and Human Rights (1992, 1994), and one on Workers' and Consumers' Rights in the Garment Industry (1998).

Human rights, though enshrined in the 1948 International Declaration of Human Rights, must still be pursued by multiple means, including legal cases, direct action and boycott. International human rights work has frequently recognized the role corporations play in supporting abusive governments. Human rights organizations mount campaigns to bring political attention to acts of specific corporations. Both the Non-Aligned Movement and indigenous peoples' human rights groups acknowledge that globalization, liberalization and trans-national corporations are threats to peace, self-determination, human rights and cultural integrity.

Human Rights Watch claims that the critical focus on corporations became stronger in 1996 with publicity about famous brands' third world sweatshops. The organization now has a special initiative on corporations. In the anti-apartheid movement of the 1980s corporations were used as leverage against the South African regime. Boycotts and divestiture movements sought to strip university, union and other large investment portfolios of holdings in companies doing business in South Africa, using corporations as a means to undermine the government. Shareholder resolutions are a new tactic through which first world citizens can attempt to constrain corporate behaviour. (Shareholder resolutions can easily be defeated when the majority of stock is owned by the corporation.) In Germany an organiztion called Critical Shareholders organizes small shareholders' votes at meetings of 30 major German corporations. 'The "Critical Shareholders" are not the ones who first ask how high their dividends are, but where they come from.'

In November 1995, human rights groups publicized the role of Shell Oil in the executions of Nigerian activist Ken Saro-Wiwa and eight other Ogoni activists. In his testimony at the military trial, Saro-Wiwa stated that Shell Oil had been waging 'ecological war' against the Ogoni people and the Niger Delta region. Sanctions and boycotts were called for against the Nigerian government *and* specifically against Shell. Shell has admitted to paying the military[16] – so not only can corporations wage war, they can also have their enemies put to death by the state. Shell was actually represented by counsel at Saro-Wiwa's trial. Chevron has admitted to 'authorizing the call for the military to come in' and transporting Nigerian soldiers to an oil platform in company helicopters, where the soldiers shot and killed two protesters and wounded several others.[17] In January 1999, the government also killed (possibly with the use of oil company heli-copters) a number of Ijaw people who had given the companies an ultimatum to leave the region. Disruption of oil production has caused Shell to close an export terminal. The Free Nigeria Movement is an international solidarity movement that blames transnational corpora-tions for enabling the ruling military regime to stay in power. They are boycotting and calling for disinvestment from three of these companies: Coca-Cola, Motorola and Royal Dutch/Shell.

While recognizing specific corporations' role in human rights abuses is certainly an improvement, human rights campaigns' model of abuses as deviances, rather than as systemic, ignores the engine of human rights abuse. Externalizing costs is what corporations do. A regulation here and there will not change the engine that constantly produces the need for absurd regulations like 'Thou shalt not befoul the air and water and kill the fish'.[18] Like the peace movement, human rights has no generalized critique of corporations. It presumes they can be reformed, or forced or shamed into conforming with human rights principles. Moreover, the dependence on existing political organizations fails to deal with *why* governments (even democratic ones) refuse to enforce such agreements. Plans for enforcement are delimited by the requirements of the state imperative to keep corporations happy. Corporations (and the US Export–Import Bank) use the logic of 'constructive engagement' to argue for continued operations in league with states known for human rights abuses. But the record on this kind of engagement has been murderous; constructive engagement legitimizes corporate operations in the places where it is most convenient and repressive regimes make it more convenient.[19]

Another approach to social justice pursued by human rights activists, along with some environmentalists, is 'fair trade'. The idea is that direct links with first world consumers can enable small-scale third world producers to retain more profits and more control over the production process. This facilitates better working conditions and more environmentally and culturally sustainable practices alongside increased financial security. The effectiveness as a first world marketing device has in some cases greatly enriched corporations, such as the Body Shop, while providing relatively little benefit to third world producers. In addition, these new relationships do nothing to reduce third world producers' dependency. Lastly, the idea that first world consumption can contribute to enhancing human rights contradicts the larger truth in which first world consumption is in fact the cause of many human rights abuses via corporate production techniques, military support for corporate interests, extraction of resources, and pressure on third world national policy. Fair trade not only offers up justice for consumption, it simultaneously disguises a refusal of justice.

In all the most important ways, fair trade changes nothing about first world/third world relations. This can easily be demonstrated by how critical third world scholars theorize their catastrophe: dependence, colonial relations, invasion of markets, commodification and *export*.

Peace and human rights campaigns and activists continue to develop their theories about enemies and alternatives. Contact with other movements plays an increasingly important role as activists search for more powerful explanations of the problems they struggle against. These movements have fostered extensive first world/third world/ fourth world contact, which has facilitated new organizing against genetic engineering and free trade. These new projects are increasingly anti-corporate. Through new alliances and connections, both movements are also gaining exposure to political economic critiques and alternative economic visions.

> We want an end to poverty, exploitation, imperialism, militarism, racism, sexism, heterosexism, environmental destruction, television, and large ugly buildings, and we want it fucking now. (Raze the Walls! A US-based prisoners' rights group)

Land Reform

Land reform movements are first and third world, rural and urban, informal and legal. All appeal to existing national governments to provide more just use of land within the existing economic order. Thus they are indeed reformist. At the same time, by challenging the commodification of land and market distribution of it, they challenge enclosure.

In Latin America, massive popular movements are organizing for rural land reform. They reject industrialization of agriculture and export agriculture, arguing that 'agribusiness violates the human right to healthy food – in order to maximize profits'. They see neoliberalism, structural adjustment and globalization as enemies, because 'sovereignty of communities who are highly dependent on the markets or subsidies for their food supply is endangered'.[20] Goals include healthy food, secure local food production without corporate inputs, quality of livelihood, and rural self-determination. Indigenous people and urban workers are among the diverse participants. These movements use legal channels, both international and national, as well as land occupations to demand land rights in what scholars are describing as 'the new agrarian reform'.

In Brazil, the Landless Workers Movement, Sem Terra, organizes displaced smallholders, urban workers and farmworkers and has managed to settle over 200,000 families. The movement demands legal titles for these settlers and confiscates property for land reform. Apparently, 83 per cent of Brazilians support land reform and 40 per cent see land invasion and occupation as an appropriate political strategy.[21] The movement uses diverse ideology, sometimes articulating itself as a union, sometimes as a mass organization. It aims to be decentralized, but has a national voice to facilitate dialogue with government, media and other groups. The structure is highly democratic, including about half of the leadership from the settlement camps.[22] The settlement camps also are run in a highly participatory democratic way. Their slogan was originally 'Without land reform we don't have a democracy' and is now 'Agrarian Reform – The Struggle for All.' They challenge 'multinationals possessing large portions of land, sometimes bigger than many countries in Europe'.

In Ecuador, 3,500 indigenous communities blocked roads and highways to halt commerce and successfully won land reform in 1994 against the government's attempt to privatize agricultural land. Subsequently, the revised laws included acknowledgement of indigenous communities' agricultural practices, and prioritized production for internal consumption. The privatization of water was halted. Kilusang Magbubukid ng Pilipinas (The Peasant Movement of the Philippines) is an armed, militant 'peasant federation'. It struggles for revolutionary agrarian reform and economic nationalism and freedom from foreign industrialization so as to achieve food security through sustainable agriculture and local production. The Adivasi (indigenous peoples) movement of India initiated a Land Entitlement Satyagraha[23] with a 3,000-km foot-march from December 1999 to June 2000 to 'launch a massive movement of non-violent direct action and civil disobedience on land issues', promoting 'occupation of governmental land' and resistance to 'capitalist globalization' which is 'depriving people of their rights and means of livelihood'.

Food First Information and Action Network, with national sections in three continents, defines itself as an 'international human rights organization for the right to feed oneself'. Via Campesina, an organization including peasant organizations from 37 countries of Asia, Europe, North and South America and Africa, claims that neoliberalism is the 'cause' of impoverishment and environmental degradation. It recognizes women's contributions in food production and the role of racism in third world problems. It demands participation in international organizations, including the World Bank, United Nations and WTO. It seeks 'food sovereignty' and explicitly blames transnational corporations, which 'deny peasants and farmers the possibility of controlling their own destinies' (Tlaxcala Declaration of the Via Campesina 1996). Confédération Paysanne is an organization of French origin that articulates land reform issues as crucial to the survival of both first and third world farmers. It sees 'food sovereignty' as dependent on the 'implementation of sustainable development and solidarity of peasants all over the world'.[24] First world farmers must realize the effects of commercial competition and subsidies on farmers of the South, and change their farming practices to support all farmers. The Confédération is a member of Coordination Paysanne Européenne and of Via Campesina. It opposes WTO, Codex Alimentaris, genetic engineering and multinational corporations' dictates, which leave farmers with no choices and no democratic processes. Its motto is 'Food Sovereignty'.

Third world urban squatters' anti-corporatism is implicit. Shantytowns account for a third to half of the populations of third world cities of Asia, Africa and Latin America.[25] Out of need and incredulity, squatters refuse to surrender the commons (and the social cosmology of commons) to urban regimes. Their settlement solutions (built with locally available and discarded materials) have won the admiration of a few first world urban planners. In cases such as the Orangi Projects in Pakistan, minor technical assistance implemented by squatters' own organizations have improved the quality of the building and sanitation systems still using only squatters' own resources (Ekins 1992: 188–92). Worldwide, squatters' confrontation of the privatization of the city is both massive and fragile. The impressive institutionalization of squat communities is matched by the solidity of the bulldozers that are sent at whim to destroy entire neighbourhoods.

In Chile, the political movements of shantytown dwellers use both confrontational tactics and party politics. They are affiliated with both communist parties and conservative ones. Some shantytowns have won official rights and delivery of public services. In others, a plethora of self-help groups have developed to support women, religious minorities and youth, to provide credit, to pursue permanent vertical housing, to install sanitation, and to achieve democratic participation in existing government.

European urban squatter movements seem to be youth movements, are associated with hardcore and punk music, art, anarchism and 'antifa' (antifascism), and show familiarity with anarchism and Marxism. European movements make explicit connections between squatting, anti-fascism and anti-capitalism. Members of the Rivermen squat community (founded 1989) include members of a band which, in 1993, made a tour called 'Youth Accuses Imperialism ... probably the first rock attempt to reject the westernization of Russia which started after perestroika'. The band 'stayed the right wing attack' while preaching 'antifa manifests to the fascist crowd'. Apparently these Eastern European youths see connections between the Western development model and fascism.

A web page of links for 'Anti-Fascism and Squatting' advertises its links as 'important Anti-Fascist and Autonomist groups in Europe'. It goes on to say that German, Danish and Italian squats 'are by far the most militant and well organized in the world'. German antifa movements emphasize that the roots of fascism are in capitalism, and also work regularly on issues of patriarchy. They engage in demonstrations against 'fascist training centres' and direct actions such as bombing deportation prisons and other means of government repression of Kurds.[26]

Efforts to displace Amsterdam squats have led to street battles and public support for squatters, followed by government negotiations and provision of alternative sites.[27] The movement embraces *pro deo* (self-defence in court) and accuses speculators and government of 'disturbing the peace ... manslaughter ... violation of human rights, sexism ... ' among other things. The following description of squatting illustrates the somewhat postmodern epistemology of this quite structural movement:

> Out of the anonymity of the city ... the decision is made. We're going to squat ... Then the heroes appear. They're already part of the other

reality, to which we are still en route ... The space was to be found literally in and outside the 'dominant system'. The city is ours ... The violence against the door was the transgression of the law which gives life its fixed form ... The first thing done after the squat was to repair the door. ('Squatting Beyond the Media', Amsterdam)

In introductory materials, the European Squat!Net answers the question 'What do we *really* want?!' with 'We don't really want an internet magazine – We want squatted houses and freespaces everywhere.' One of their mottos is 'Squat the World'.

Homes Not Jails, San Francisco (USA), physically takes control of vacant and abandoned housing in order to house homeless people. It bases weekly actions on the claim that 'human rights (specifically the right to housing) far outweigh property rights. No building should be left abandoned or vacant for real estate profiteering when people need housing.' It also engages in civil disobedience as an educational project to show how use of vacant buildings can solve homelessness problems. It has done sweat equity projects, and has taken legislative actions. It is legally challenging San Francisco's double standard in enforcing laws against squatters while not enforcing laws against landlords who have flagrantly violated rent control and eviction laws for the purposes of increasing profit.

Squatting works to delegitimize profit-based systems for distributing needed goods. Unlike other movements of very low-income people, these movements have few scholarly allies, and their critique is organic. Correspondents for homeless newspapers base their analyses on their own experience, the political, social and cultural contradictions they observe on downtown streets. They also observe and learn from the contradictions of private property: homeless people have no legal means of confiscating vacant housing, but the police legally confiscate homeless persons' personal property at whim.

Not all first world attempts to de-commodify land are waged by the landless. In Britain, an organization called The Land is Ours demands 'reclamation of commons spaces', 'low impact, high employment uses of the land', and protection of lands for Gypsies and travellers. The group makes celebratory occupations of unused land to bring attention to the misuse of land for superstores and luxury housing. The movement draws on the tradition of the Diggers, who in the mid-seventeenth century declared the land 'a common treasury for all'. Continuing to insist that enclosure of land for private use is 'tantamount to the impoverishment and enslavement' of neighbours, current Diggers organize celebratory land occupations of various lengths as well as 'permanent Digger colonies that assert the right of access to rent-free land'.

All of these movements participate in direct action and aim, eventually, to build legal structures to protect the de-commodified arrangements they have carved out. Sometimes this takes the form of enforcing constitutional rights. Other times it means the creation of new legal institutions. One formalized version of land de-commodi-fication is the community land trust. Communities purchase land and then lease space to homeowners, businesses and apartment complexes. Community ownership insulates the land from market forces and ensures that individuals will not sell their land for personal profit. The US version of this concept was developed by Robert Swann of the Schumacher Society.

Urban growth boundaries are another political technology being implemented by environmentalists and small farm interests. Specu-lation at the metropolitan edge drives farmers out of business, and sprawl destroys green space. Growth boundaries enable urban areas to stabilize farmers' tenure just outside the growth boundary. But the US Greenbelt Alliance also has a decentralist and self-reliant vision. They ask people to 'Imagine your metropolitan area if you had to get all your food and take all of your vacations within a fifty mile radius.' This vision encourages urban areas to maintain quality of life rather than assuming (in a colonial/imperial tradition) that they can get food and pretty views from other places.

In the USA, a variety of anti-growth initiatives have been politically successful as urban populations have moved to protect the quality of urban space, to limit sprawl, to create 'greenbelts' or urban growth boundaries, and to place moratoriums on non-residential growth. Far from being a leftist issue, in 1998, control over growth emerged as a major political issue in state electoral campaigns, bringing victories to Republicans as well as Democrats.[28] Affluent communities find that zoning, height limits and historic preservation designations have been useful legal mechanisms to block growth in attempts to maintain architectural charm and open space and to block increased traffic.

Although mostly used in service of aesthetics, historical preservation has also been used to defend buildings and spaces used by low-income people. Corporate invaders and speculating developers have learned to pursue their goals despite these mechanisms, however, by putting more trees in the parking lot or adding a layer of architectural detail to their box stores. Without creating an analysis of 'charm' and culture that is fully political economic, localities will have difficulty keeping control over land.

Low-income urban communities have articulated political economic critiques of 'gentrification', through which real estate is made more desirable for high-profit corporate uses while poor people are permanently displaced, community networks are destroyed, and the jobs created are either temporary or low-wage. Opposing growth as a goal of the city (Logan and Molotch 1987) challenges corporate priorities (and government collusion).

Taken (artificially) as a whole, movements that challenge commodification and development make an exciting multi-class movement. Including anti-fascist punk youth, wearily determined (and oft-arrested) homeless activists, wealthy historical preservationists, organizers and housing advocates in low-income urban communities, and third world landless workers, these anti-profit movements have important contributions to make to anti-corporateness: they indicate the broad social diversity of support and demonstrate the power of the epistemological project of delegitimizing corporate logics of growth, profit and enclosure. These movements spend most of their time and energy defending non-market goods, spaces and values.

Both third world and first world land reform movements are attentive to issues of sustainable development. They see their enemy as the failed national attempt at modernization and seek to recover healthy rural lives that reduce inequality. Beyond achieving land reform, however, the movements aim for self-determination and decentralized governance. According to a 1998 report by James Petras, rural land reform movements are inspiring expanded politics, allying with unions and urban movements with the agenda of 'reversal of all the major free market counter-reforms; the re-nationalization of basic industries ... the socialization of ... banking, foreign trade ... and ... agrarian reform, which limits cheap exports'. Long struggles for territorial and institutional autonomy coupled with the intense effects of globalization put these movements in an excellent position to lead popular movements that aim for structural change. Their political economic agenda focuses on the nation-state as a vehicle for protecting the economy. At the same time, they are wary of electoral politics and liberal democracy: 'The closer to parliament, the further from the people.'

The Explicit Anti-Corporate Movements

The error is in naming the enemy – which is neither trade nor global-ization. The real target is corporate rule. The fact that the Seattle protest was neither left nor right, reform nor revolution, only shows the breadth and depth of the rebellion against corporatization. (James MacKinnon for AdBusters[29])

There are a number of mobilizations that are explicitly organized around limiting corporate power. The most vibrant of these is the movement to oppose genetically engineered agricultural inputs. Genet-ically engineered seed, unlike traditional hybridization, centralizes control over genetic decision-making in corporate laboratories and reorganizes the genetic resources of the crop around the corporate priorities of commodification of agricultural inputs. Through the use of 'traitor' technologies, biotech companies can programme crops to turn on or off stages of the growth cycle only with the application of company sprays. Release of genetically modified (GM) organisms into the environment threatens to damage other cultivars as well as wild plants. Corporations are also moving to patent biological resources that are the scientific heritage of third and fourth world peoples. Resistance to genetically engineered crops and biopiracy has been strong in many social sectors and geographic regions.

Farmers are resisting pressure to use the new seeds and are up-rooting and burning crops in field trials. Such direct action has occurred in many countries including India, the UK, France, Korea and Ireland. US activists have finally joined together and have undertaken 20 such direct actions in the last six months of 1999. Small farmers insist that their methods are both sustainable and sufficiently productive, and offer a viable alternative to transgenic crop design. In 1998, Andean farmers forced a US patent on quinoa to be dropped. The movement describes transnational corporations as seeking to colonize the third world via seed patents; they are also described as 'criminals'. In Brazil, the Landless Workers' Movement has committed to 'destroy any genetically engineered crops planted in Rio Grande do Sul state' and a Brazilian federal court has halted commercial release of Monsanto's soy despite Brazil's dependence on soy exports.[30]

European consumers have led the charge against genetically modified foods and are demanding protections. There are also strong movements in Japan, New Zealand, Bangladesh and Mexico, and a small movement in the USA. In response to consumer outrage, McDonalds, Burger King, Nestlé, Unilever and Kentucky Fried Chicken have announced the removal of genetically engineered soya and corn from their menus in UK outlets.[31] Most Japanese food manufacturers have abandoned GM ingredients.[32] France's largest supermarket chain, Carrefour, has removed all GM foods from its shelves. In 1999 UK supermarket chains announced that they would be phasing out genetically engineered products. In addition, leading chefs and restaurateurs announced that they would post and adhere to Greenpeace's Anti-Genetic Engineering statement in their restaurants. The Guild of Food Writers, the Academy of Culinary Arts, Eurotoques, and Slowfood have endorsed the campaign.

In response to farmer and consumer protests, many national governments have begun to act against GM organisms either in imported foods or as agricultural inputs. The EU has banned GM foodstuffs from domestic production and entry.[33] Parts of Australia are banning GM foods from schools. The French Conseil d'Etat has banned Novartis GM maize from planting. Thailand has banned GM seed and in the interests of protecting native corn varieties from GMO contamination, the Mexican government banned import of seed from the USA.[34] The Africa Group, the Like-Minded Group of Developing Countries and NGO alliances have firmly opposed patents on life and demanded regulation of genetically modified organisms. The 1993 Convention on Biodiversity has been weakened by the WTO Trade Related Aspects of Intellectual Property Rights (biopiracy) treaty and the 2000 Biosafety Protocol (to protect from harmful effects of GMOs) may also be challengable under the WTO, which does not allow for use of precautionary principles.

Direct action protests typify anti-corporate mobilizations. Act Up, an international AIDS activist organization, confronts the profiteering behaviour of the pharmaceutical companies, challenging their role in international AIDS conferences. According to Tom Swindell, who protested at a recent conference, 'This entire AIDS conference was bought and paid for by the pharmaceutical industry as a way to hype their deadly drugs.'[35] A web page called McSpotlight posts weekly actions against McDonalds from all over the world. Such protests include educational street theatre, postering, and lowering corporate flags to half mast. But McDonalds is targeted as 'just one example' of the problem. 'Any of the other big corporations' can also be critiqued for the 'take-over of the world's economy and the transformation of people's everyday lives', resulting in 'wage slavery, hunger, break up of the independence and self-sufficiency of local communities, abuse of resources ... and the suppression of people's genuine needs and desires' all 'backed by governmental institutions'.

> It gobbles whole mountains and forests, drinks rivers dry, spews toxic waste, and enslaves whole populations. It has all the rights of a citizen, but few of the limitations. It can cross national borders as if they were cobwebs. It is immortal, and can therefore amass wealth and power beyond the capabilities of mere mortals. It has powers that dwarf and control governments. It controls the newspapers, radio, and television, and so it controls the 'truth' ... We are talking about the CORPORA-TION. (Earth First! 'End Corporate Dominance International Day of Action' October 1996)

Critical Mass, an international bicycle activist group, uses direct action to expand bicycle rights and inconvenience automobiles in order to halt the corporate project of automobile use. Policy emphasis on truck-based transport empowers (and subsidizes) corporations to constantly relocate production to rural areas with cheaper labour. Meanwhile the paving industry pushes hard for government road-building contracts.[36] Anti-roads opposition (most active in England and Germany), always explicitly anti-corporate, mounts celebratory direct actions by occupying proposed highway lands, moving into treehouses in threatened trees or tunnel dwellings in the path of proposed roads, blocking roadways, torching road-building equipment, and hosting street parties. The US organizations Alliance for a Paving Moratorium and Earth First! have produced the *Road Fighters' Direct*

Action Manual, which shares 'the latest tactics and technology' for 'defending the Earth' with 'serious road fighting'. The *Auto-Free Times*, a US magazine, promotes struggles for bicyclists' rights, closure of existing roads, new utility and house-bike designs, and bike-based businesses (delivery and gardening services), while critiquing the relationship between transport-technology speed and quality of life, the political role of oil companies, and globalization issues.

The European organization Reclaim the Streets was founded in London in 1991, initially with the slogan 'FOR walking cycling and cheap, or free, public transport, and AGAINST cars, roads and the system that pushes them'. Early actions included the spontaneous painting in of bike lines, 'subvertising' by modifying billboard advertisements, and site invasions to block road building. In 1995, the tactic of street parties was initiated as part of motorway blockages, of which the 1996 block of the M41 highway involved 8,000 people and lasted nine hours. The focus of campaigning has remained anti-car, 'but this has been increasingly symbolic, not specific'. The organization critiques government road-building as 'good for the economy' because it indicates 'economic growth' when really it is anti-ecological and anti-social. 'Our streets are as full of capitalism as of cars and the pollution of capitalism is much more insidious.' Thus it proclaims solidarity with workers, opposes privatisation and challenges the government's neoliberalism. A 1997 party in Trafalgar Square had the title 'Never Mind the Ballots ... Reclaim the Streets!' Its other main goal is encouraging direct action, and they do this by embracing the history of the liberatory carnivals and revolutionary festivals. By 1997, autonomous Reclaim the Streets 'disorganizations' had been formed across Europe.[37]

Another tactic used by anti-corporate groups is to organize boycotts. Boycotts are grounded in the corporate responsibility campaigns of the late 1970s and the 'standard-setting' movement. One of the most famous of these was the 1977–86 INFACT campaign against Nestlé's deceptive and dangerous marketing of infant milk formula in Africa. INFACT's next campaign was a boycott of General Electric from 1984 to 1993 (when GE gave up nuclear defence contracts) to punish the company for its role in military production. In 1997, INFACT published an exposé on the human costs of corporate influence, this time focused on effects on the USA. Rainforest Action Network led a successful boycott against Burger King's use of beef raised on former rainforest land and is now focusing on Home Depot's sale of old growth wood.

A boycott called 'The Great Boycott' has been called against 'the eight biggest pesticide companies on earth'. The goal of the boycott is to develop 'a long-term publicity campaign to isolate the major criminal poisoners of the planet, so that no one wants to do business with them'. The Great Boycott is seeking university and investor disinvestment from these corporations and a consumer boycott of all their products and those of their subsidiaries. Campaigns in specific industries are very popular. Baby Milk Action (UK) and the International Baby Food Action Network (Switzerland) work on abuses by infant formula sellers. The Clean Clothes Campaign (Europe) provides solidarity to workers' organizations. United Students Against Sweatshops (US) pressures universities to ensure that insignia merchandise is not made in sweatshops. Coordination gegen BAYER-Gefahren (Germany) investigates the Bayer chemical company.

In 1982 Ralph Nader, a longtime advocate for product safety and consumer rights (bases of the anti-corporate movement), established Essential Information (USA), an organization dedicated to supporting people in dealing with local issues in their communities. Essential Information includes the Multinationals and Development Clearinghouse, which works with Southern hemisphere activists and organizations fighting corporations. The Clearinghouse provides information about specific multinationals and about how to oppose development projects, including World Bank projects.

Another group of organizations compile information on corporations and share strategies for fighting corporate power. These include the Polaris Institute (Canada), Project Underground (USA), which focuses on the mining and oil industries, Corporate Environmental Data Clearinghouse (New York), the Transnational Information Exchange (Amsterdam), the Transnational Resource and Action Center (USA), which runs the CorporateWatch web page, Corporate Watch (UK), a separate organization, Stichting Onderzock Multinationale Ondernemingen (Centre for Research on Multinational Corporations), Amsterdam, which documents and critically researches the role multinational corporations play in the international economic relations between industrialized and less-industrialized countries, the Asia Regional Exchange for New Alternatives (Hong Kong), the IBON

Philippines Databank and Research Center (Manila), and People's Action Network to Monitor Japanese Transnationals (Tokyo).

Alongside these research organizations are journals and newsletters that focus on corporations, such as *Third World Resurgence*, based in Penang, Malaysia, *Oil Watch*, based in Quito Ecuador, Essential Information's *Multinational Monitor*, which publishes an annual 'ten worst corporations' issue, Fairness and Accuracy in Reporting's *Extra!* and Counterspin radio show, which 'focuses public awareness on the narrow corporate ownership of the press' resulting in 'allegiance to official agendas'. Corporate Watch (UK) has a magazine of the same name.

Recently, new national grassroots membership organizations in Canada, Europe and the United States have emerged specifically around the issue of corporations. They express standard left values of social justice, peace and human rights, but emphasize the corporate invasion of government and economies as the explanation of social justice problems. The Canadian explicit anti-corporate group, the Council of Canadians, explains that 'a corporate agenda has force-fed us an unhealthy diet of policies benefiting a few powerful transnational corporations, but eroding the incomes and quality of life for most Canadians'.

The Corporate Europe Observatory, with headquarters in Amsterdam, is working to oppose the United Nations' 'Global Compact', which endorses corporate self-regulation. The Observatory participated in an October 1999 conference in Cordoba, Spain, which resulted in a declaration of 'Challenging Corporate Power'. The declaration includes 'rejecting the current agenda-setting role of business and anti-democratic alliances between corporations and states', rejecting self-regulation and insisting upon enforceable standards rather than failed self-serving 'codes of conduct', and 'limiting economic concentration and dependency on mega-corporations is a necessary part of any attempt to roll back corporate political power, and allows the social and environmental agenda to reclaim political space'. A French organization called ATTAC (Association for Taxation of Financial Transactions in Order to Aid Citizens) was founded in 1998 after an article by Ignacio Ramonet in *Le Monde Diplomatique* received a tremendous response. It is now one of the first world organizations actively making international connections against globalization, neoliberalism and structural adjustment. One of their projects is the Tobin Tax, which would put a small international tax (.05 per cent) on speculative capital, the proceeds of which would be used to alleviate poverty.[38] ATTAC is allied with the World Forum for Alternatives (Sénégal), the National Federation of Peasant Organizations (Burkina Faso), the Policy and Information Center for International Solidarity (South Korea), and the Karnataka State Farmers' Association (India).

Alliance for Democracy (formerly Citizens' Alliance) in the USA echoes standard left visions of economic democracy, environmental justice, family welfare, anti-militarism, anti-racism, women's rights, etc., but claims that 'the heart of the Alliance' is 'ending corporate rule'. One of the main projects of the Alliance is undermining corporations' legal legitimacy by challenging their charters and state corporation law. This approach has been developed by Richard Grossman of the Program on Corporations, Law and Democracy. Some anti-tobacco campaigns are now urging revocation of Philip Morris' corporate charter. In 1995, the Community Environmental Defense League petitioned the attorneys general of Delaware and West Virginia, asking them to revoke the charters of WMX Technologies (a toxic waste corporation that has been fined repeatedly for illegal acts) and CSX (a shipping company also involved in the toxic waste industry).

In November 1997, the first International Symposium on Corporate Rule was held in Port Elgin, Ontario, Canada. Delegates included 85 people from Asia, Africa, Europe, Latin America and North America. The closing statement read: 'We came together to consolidate our efforts to expose and confront corporate rule in all its forms.' The group emphasized the interconnections between 'how corporations have subverted true democracy in some countries and reinforced brutal autocratic regimes in others; how they have exploited workers, pillaged resources, ravaged the environment, weakened labour laws, and widened the gap between rich and poor with particularly devastating effects on women and children; how they have enshrined the goal of maximizing profits over all human, cultural, social and ecological needs; and how they have seized control over the reins of public policy making in all our countries'.

A US anti-corporate tactic is the enactment of a constitutional amendment called 'The Seventh Generation Amendment'. The amendment draws on a Native American principle of living and making decisions (particularly about resource use), always keeping in mind the health and welfare of the people seven generations in the future. The Amendment was initially drafted for state legislatures by the International Law Center for Human, Economic, and Environmental Defense. Another legal strategy is 'three strikes and you're out' for corporations (mimicking the punitive criminal justice crackdown and cleverly extending corporations' legal claims to the rights of persons). Any corporation that racks up three strikes of serious health, safety, environmental or labour regulations would have its charter of incorporation revoked. Selective purchasing/contracting is another way to cut corporations off from the public till in punishment for violating standards. The US state of Minnesota no longer allows corporations to engage in farming.

The explicit anti-corporate movements attract activists from peace, human rights, sustainable development, social justice and indigenous movements, whose analyses seem so far to be fairly compatible. These movements' focus on corporations as enemy provides a powerful explanation of the changes happening in the world. While mostly working on national issues, these movements are committed to linking up with third and fourth world peoples. Political action is organized in a range of campaigns and actions ranging from analytic research to playful street theatre, but always clear about the anti-corporate critique. A majority of participants are also sustainable development advocates and practitioners, which provides the vision for much of the movement.

Youths' views on these issues show up a little more informally. While youth may not be invited into the scholarly section of the movement, their analysis is consonant. A youth zine article laid out a 'strategy for the destruction of the PROFIT SYSTEM', which urged readers to 'choose not to consume ... boycott the mall and all of its products', 'choose not to produce ... the work you do for any company benefits them far more than it benefits you', and unite with other people to share survival resources and skills.

Cyberpunk

> In this case the medium is not the message, the message is the mes-
> sage, and the message is: Wake Up!! Turn off your television sets and
> read a book, or get to know your neighbours. Take a walk, enjoy the
> polluted air. Get angry and do something about it. Don't let the people
> at the top distract you from what is really going on. Don't let them
> tell you what the problems are ... We've allowed big business to con-
> vince us that money is more important than people for too long. We've
> convinced ourselves that our goal to maximize profits will help all of
> us in the long run, instead of widening the gap between rich and
> poor. We believe that we can continue to abuse the planet and it will
> continue to be able to sustain us indefinitely.
> **Join the Cyberpunk Revolution!**
> For all those who refuse to bow down to the system, who realise
> that you cannot change the system from within ... willing to do more
> than put a band-aid on a gaping wound. The only way the Cyberpunk
> Revolution can work is if we all work together.

Cyberpunk is a philosophy and identity that developed out of several
early 1980s novels about the 'near future' in which rapid technological
development, corporate totalitarianism and decline of political coherence and the nation-state result in culturally bleak, highly regulated
life in 'the sprawl' (metropolitan/suburban area). Surveillance and
repression are constant, but hardy and clever marginalized/alienated
individuals survive, undermining the system and playing with it. Cyberpunk is a very self-conscious movement, which publishes histories,
bibliographies (including extensive attention to postmodern texts),
philosophic tracts (referencing Jacques Derrida), literary debate (on
science fiction and cyberpunk fiction) and political analysis of itself as
a movement (and as a part of 'Generation X'). Cyberpunks are
attempting to create a community, are interested in and committed to
debating its values and practices, and are puzzling through pluralism.
There is a great deal of discussion of both individuality and community.

William Gibson, author of *Neuromancer* (1984), is considered the
'theorist' of the cyberpunk genre and his visions about the future are
taken seriously. In this future, 'very shortly people will be identified

more often with consumer products than any other form of ethnic or cultural identification' and 'corporations will "modify" their employees in various ways so as to improve their efficiency'. Despite this bleak vision, cyberpunk is also described as 'optimistic', in that it imagines that the struggle for freedom will survive. The people who maintain this struggle are those who are marginal to the system in some way. The exercise of tech skills buys them *survival* without being incorporated into the system and *pleasure* from the play and adventure of slipping in and around the fingers of power. Their skills are not a function of formal education, but sort of a technological street training.

Cyberpunks critique technology, even while joyfully using it. They acknowledge its power and repressive capacities. Not all cyberpunks agree that technology is neutral. They analyse the issues of ownership, control and democracy in the consequences of technology. Fortunately, technology is also *vulnerable*, and, also fortunately, a fun form of self-expression. The general struggle against the system (power and its tech) echoes Jean Baudrillard's theory of new social movements: the enemy becomes generalized. Power (centralization) is the enemy; the task of social movements is the 'annihilation of the legitimacy of the state' and of *all* 'parties of order' (Aronowitz 1992: 261). The liberatory vision of the future is unclear.

One of the common threads of the diverse cyberpunk movement is the emphasis on the relationship between individuals and technology. As always, it's important to be very careful about understanding the role of individualism. Individuals are theorized as having agency within the system as a function of their skills. But cyberpunk is also celebrated for its 'communal atmosphere' in which 'we who walk on the fringes of culture need to hold each other's hand'. Cyberpunks are very interested in saying what they are, but always with lots of respect for others who may disagree with their definition.

As an active social movement, cyberpunk has several subgroups: *Hackers*, 'people with a deep understanding of how their computers work', break into computer systems. *Crackers*, 'the real-world analogues of the "console cowboys" of cyberpunk fiction, break into all sorts of technology ... for illicit gain or simply for the pleasure of exercising their skill'. *Phreakers* break into phone systems.[39] *Cyphers* crack codes. *Cyberchic* cyberpunks are interested in raves, fashion and music. The explicitly *political* cyberpunk movement is about freedom and access. All except the cyberchics are actually involved in confronting and attempting to undermine corporate power.

According to Steven Levy, the original 1980s hackers 'aimed to promote decentralization, open access to computers, and easily modifiable technology and computer code, fighting the corporate mentality'. Steve Mizrach (aka Seeker1) explains that 1990s hackers subscribe to a Hacker Ethic, 'declaring that they will not "hack" personal privacy or the personal computer user, instead declaring that their 'targets' will be large, unresponsive corporations or bureaucratic government organizations'. One reason given for the *apparent* aggressiveness of 1990s hackers is that 'control over computers is an act of self-defense'. It also is a form of political expression. 'Phreaks, in "hacking" the phone system, are simply acting in the centuries-old tradition of American radicals who have always challenged the ways in which corporate and government structures prevent people from free association with their peers ... challenging the notion that "to reach out and touch someone" should be a costly privilege rather than a right.'

Mizrach asks what it is that cyberpunk is countercultural against. The answer: 'the culture of the multinational corporation, which viewed information as proprietary; the culture of the new information and service economy, which offered rebellious underachievers only McJobs or McData Processing positions; and the culture of the Compute Establishment, which made lots of dumb rules about where one could and could not go in cyberspace'. The author goes on to say that the rebelliousness of the slogan 'information wants to be free' was not 'evident at first glance'. Cyberpunks see widespread illegal software piracy as an 'insurrection'. Cypherpunks' provision of public-key cryptography is a 'rebellious act'. Cypherpunks (or 'cryptoanarchists') believe that people should use non-state encryption to protect themselves from the state's attempt to monopolize data encryption theory and technology. Some even believe that independent encryption 'can ultimately destroy the State' by camouflaging monetary transactions and thereby making taxation impossible.

Hacking that is accused of destructiveness, virus/logic bomb/trojan writing, is the 'vanguard' or the 'Weather Underground' of the movement, practising 'political terrorism' by shutting down entire computer systems. 'Imagine what would have happened if someone was able during the Persian Gulf War to infect the military C3I system with a virus and paralyze the US' force coordination ability. That would have stopped the war a lot sooner than any "give peace a chance" sit in.' Hacking can be heroic. The movement has a strategy to undermine corporations that looks something like a swarm of bees, pestering in many places, distracting, and throwing their enemy off balance.

A review of the zine *Cybertek* defines cyberpunk as 'making use of available or appropriated technology to obtain, analyze, and disseminate real information through legal or illegal channels'. It prioritizes information 'relating to survival or personal freedom'. Examination of a list of cyberpunk zines documents cyberpunk's consistent criticism of centralization of control over technology, privatization, and profiteering. The list shows the development of institutions to support challenges and insurgent alternatives and documents a deep and diverse interest in science and technology. The zines are animated by a distrust of corporate projects and trust in the abilities of creative individual 'explorers' as well as a grim sense of humour. They include: *Journal of Pills* critiquing medicalization, providing 'recipes'; *2600: The Hacker Quarterly*, 'the ultimate guide ... including 'a *very* detailed guide to AT&T's new switch, the 5ESS'; *Intertek* with articles on 'the history of ownership' and 'the incompatibility of capitalism and information'; *MediaMatic* including 'speculation about just how soon cyberspace will become reality in the sense of an individual's more or less being able to live there'; *Extropy* journal of transhumanist issues ... such as the mechanics of space travel and uploading human consciousness to computers; *Taper's Quarterly*, 'a zine about taping live music concerts that specifically discourages the exchange of money for recording'; a cryonics news magazine recommending deanimation schedules, investment advice and resurrectionist poetry; *Dropout*, with info on mainstream media's biases and new developments in underground media; and *S.E.T. Free: the Newsletter Against Television* – 'obviously they are small and terribly underfunded'.

Cyberpunk legends William Gibson and Bruce Sterling have become actively anti-corporate. In a May 1993 speech to the National Academy of Sciences' Convocation on Technology and Education, Sterling worried that schools will soon be 'auctioning [children] off to the highest bidder'. He encouraged teachers to adopt cyberpunk philosophy by resisting the seduction of technology (and rationalization of its corporatization), prioritize 'values ... the only things that last', and 'hack the rest'. He gave as an example the history of the internet as 'a post-apocalypse command grid' for the military. Its transformation into a site for free speech was accomplished by citizens who 'had the courage to use the network to support their own values, to bend the technology to their own purposes. To serve their own liberty.'

Perhaps the most sophisticated political interpretation of cyberpunk came from Pam Rosenthal, a business computer programmer ('I move money around'), who proposes that cyberpunk literature reveals 'a hunger' for 'worlds articulated by present and future science and technology in terms of ideological and narrative structures that are resolutely pre-capitalist, pre-democratic, even pre-industrial'. Marxism worked to bring the 'magic space' of imagined equity into the real space of workers' daily lives. Postmodern life presents 'increasing immiseration of real space' and 'growing enrichment of fake space'. Rosenthal suggests that there is a political connection between these two, one which cyberpunks can expose. People 'who are favorably situated within the flow of data' must try to 'live history' by interrogating the relationship between the cybernetic spaces of production and the spaces where people live[40] – and, presumably, build a new Marxist relationship between them.

Cyberpunk is clearly populist. Its narrative is the American yeoman, free because he has worked hard to wrest sovereignty over his space. Heroic forefathers struggled to establish a civic space that must be protected through creative individual effort and collective concern. Independence is crucial to 'liberty'. Technology (including capitalism, racialization) can be managed through populist democratic processes, through dialogue. The totalizing forces will not quite totalize. Cyberpunk trusts the people as long as power is equitable. Thus they oppose corporate power and control. Technology-based analysis serves as a mediating tool for apprehending corporations' power to structure society.

Recently, cyberpunk techniques have been adopted by political hactivists, who have developed two approaches to activism in cyberspace. Political hacking can take the form of adding different messages to official websites, such as a hack of China's human rights agency's new website in October 1998 which read: 'China's people have no

rights at all, never mind human rights.'[41] This is a worldwide phenomenon, practised by Portuguese, Mexican, Serbian, British, Dutch,
Canadian and Pakistani hackers. The other form is cyber civil disobedience, which takes the form of 'flooding' or other means of
blocking traffic to a given website. One of the organizations facilitating
this is Electronic Disturbance Theater, which provides the software
needed for cyber civil disobedience. Their Intercontinental Cyberspace
Liberation Army issued a press release that stated that 'bands of
netwarriors around the world ... are converging in cyberspace to
instigate information warfare, netwar, against the PRI controlled
Mexican government'.[42] The UK Electro Hippies organized a 'virtual
sit-in' as part of the global protests against the WTO 1999 Seattle
Ministerial. They had over 105,000 participants on November 30 and
over 137,000 on 1 December (see Wray 1998).

Discussion

Movements in this mode sometimes fail to challenge fully the
consequences of the corporation, opposing only specific behaviours
or state collaboration with corporate priorities. Historian William
Appleman Williams tracks the ideological and political events that
enabled corporations to dominate the US political economy. This
history, and the conception of the corporation that was wrought,
have shaped the logics of corporate rights institutionalized today in
free trade agreements. Perhaps more importantly, these early definitions also came to shape the logics by which citizens attempted to
limit corporate power.

During the 1880s, corporate and political leaders, concerned by the
immanent possibility of class upheaval, sought to establish a more
organized economy than was possible in the earlier *laissez faire* mode.
After a period of debate between *laissez faire* restorationists, socialists,
labour syndicalists and anarchists, the group that gained hegemony
was a coalition of humane 'Progressives', mostly former gentry and
corporate leaders. Progressive corporation syndicalism and Christian
Capitalism recognized organized labour as a junior partner in the
development of a smooth-running national economy. While some
members of the Progressive movement had humanitarian motivations,
few were willing to question the centrality of private property or the

role of imperialism as the base for American prosperity. Indeed 'overseas economic expansion provided the *sine qua non* of domestic prosperity and social peace' (Williams 1988: 355).

Today, many United States leftists still see themselves as Progressive, perhaps betraying the precise limits of their humanitarian commitments – their willingness to make peace with a corporate political economy. The movements discussed in this chapter are likewise limited. They attempt to organize national governments to regulate corporate activities more effectively, or they mobilize people to demand standards or concessions from corporations themselves. Movements demanding 'corporate responsibility', 'voluntary codes of conduct' or 'standard setting' have, as David Vogel predicted in 1974, convinced corporations that they should make an appearance of 'cleaning up their act'. Progressive movements do slowly gain moral ground, but they offer corporations methods of relegitimizing themselves. The framing of corporations as *enemy* by the movements in this chapter expands the Progressive movement in new directions.

The major challenge for first world movements in this mode is to commit themselves to the material consequences of their humanitarian sympathies. Some of the explicit anti-corporate movements seem to fantasize that first worlders can maintain their current living standards, consumption and technology while relieving third world debt, destroying the military–industrial complex, and rescuing third world workers from inhumane working conditions on the global assembly line. If first worlders are to support third world land reform they will have to change their eating practices considerably.

What is the material relationship between first world social justice and third world social justice? Calls for a renewal of the social contract to provide first world justice can be achieved only on the back of third world resources and markets, suggesting that third world survival depends on a new approach to justice in the first world.

Some of the movements discussed in this chapter are single-issue or interest-based movements that are expanding to general anti-corporate perspectives in the face of relatively recent advances in corporate hegemony. The strengths of the movements discussed are their emerging clarity about the enemy and their growing willingness to challenge the assumptions that empower corporate hegemony. The emergence of a set of movements that call themselves 'anti-corporate' and mobilize against specific corporations as 'just one example' has expanded the politics of boycotters and peace and human rights activists. Even (or especially) cyberpunks, the least institutionalized of these movements, are self-conscious and articulate about naming the enemy.

Collectively, these movements can be seen experimenting with ways to bar the corporations' paths and turn them back. Their techniques range from legal challenges to cybertech infiltration to direct action to decommodify land and food. They mobilize in churches, corporate retail outlets, plantations, busy streets and payphones. They involve 1960s peaceniks, seasoned politicians, NGO leaders and development workers, landless poor and alienated youth. None of these movements is organized as an identity movement. Class, as well as the defence of private property, could keep squatter movements, cyberpunks and anti-roads movements divided from more scholarly and legalistic participants. In the third world critical development scholars who oppose structural adjustment are allied with peasants and indigenous people, but in the first world scholars/activists may not see cyberpunks, homeless squatters and other insurgent street scholars as allies. This division may hinge on privilege. For educated first worlders, opposition to road-building and development seems absurd, while in the third world it is modernization that is absurd.

For the most part, the movements discussed in this chapter do not go so far as to articulate an alternate vision. The exceptions would be the anti-roads and pro-bicycle movements, the alternative structural adjustment programmes, and third world land reform movements, which have sustainable subsistence visions. We now turn to another set of movements, which seek to surpass the *realpolitik* of comprador states through new kinds of political systems.

Notes

1. Alliance for Democracy, USA.

2. David Ransom, 'Globalisation – an alternative view', *New Internationalist*, 296, November 1997: 7–10.

3. Mike Head, 'Indonesian students demand Habibie's resignation', *World Socialist Web Site*, 9 September 1998; Chris Latham, *Green Left Weekly* 352, 19 March 1999.

4. *Diario Yucatan*, 3 May 1999.

5. 'The short run', *Dollars & Sense*, 223, May/June 1999: 5.

6. Soren Ambrose, 'South Korean union sues the IMF', 50 Years is Enough Network, *Economic Justice News*, December 1999/January 2000: 8, 13.

7. Kevin Brandstatter, Swindon, UK.

8. All unattributed quotes are from primary data collection.

9. Yvonne Rocomaure, 'French unemployed actions: demand for total reforms' Paris, 22 December 1998, posted to LabourNet.

10. Jubilee 2000 Afrika Coalition.

11. Njoki Njoroge Njehû, 'Jubilee South and the Johannesburg Summit', in 50 Years is Enough Network, *Economic Justice News*, December 1999/January 2000: 10–12.

12. David Holtzman, 'Ring out the debt, ring in prosperity?', *Dollars & Sense*, 223, May/June 1999: 9.

13. Ann Pettifor, director, Jubilee 2000 Coalition UK, 'What does the Köln Agreement mean for the Jubilee 2000 campaign worldwide?' 24 June 1999, http://www.jubilee2000uk.org

14. Jubilee 2000/USA, 'Drop the debt!: news and action from the Jubilee 2000/USA campaign', January/February 2000, Washington DC.

15. John Samuel, 'The holy cow of microcredit', *Third World Resurgence*, 112/113: 6–8.

16. Essential Action, 'The Skinny on Shell', 1998 at www.essential.org

17. Democracy NOW!, Pacifica Radio, 28 May 1998.

18. Paraphrase of Winona LaDuke, speaking at University of California, Santa Barbara, 13 November 1997.

19. Arvind Ganesan, 'Corporation crackdowns: business backs brutality', *Dollars & Sense*, 223, May/June 1999: 10–13, 23.

20. Rolf Künnemann, 'Agrarian reform: a human right', Food First Information and Action Network.

21. Bill Hinchberger, 'Land of no return? Not Brazil', *The Nation*, 2 March 1998.

22. *Do or Die: Voices from Earth First!*, 7, Brighton, East Sussex, UK.

23. 'Satyagraha' is a Gandhian term that means 'struggle for truth'.

24. Jean Cabaret, Confédération Paysanne.

25. *Economic Review*, Sri Lanka, April 1987.

26. *Radikal*, April 1995, trans. Arm the Spirit (an autonomous, anti-imperialist information collective), Toronto, Canada.

27. From Freedom Press, London.

28. Neal R. Peirce, 'Sprawl control: a political issue comes of age', *Washington Post* Writers Group 1998.

29. 'First we take Seattle', *Adbusters*, Spring 2000.

30. Peter Rosset, 'The parable of the golden snail: third world farmers see in biotech crops a first world disaster in the making', *The Nation*, 27 December 1999: 22.

31. *Daily Mail*, 23 February 1999.

32. David Bartruff, 'Japan to bring in mandatory tests for GM foods', *Nature*, 23 December 1999, vol. 402: 846.

33. 'Thailand to ban altered seeds', *Associated Press*, Monday 18 October 1999.

34. Peter Rosset, 'The parable of the golden snail'.

35. 'Well being', posted by the San Francisco Medical Research Foundation, August 1996.

36. Elisa Peter on NAFTA and EU agreements and trucking, *Auto-Free Times*, Arcata, CA, Spring 1997.

37. 'The evolution of reclaim the streets', *Do Or Die* #6, Summer 1997.

38. Sputnik Kilambi, 'Mass attac', *New Internationalist*, 320, January/February 2000: 21.

39. A friend living in Brazil intermittently called me from a liberated payphone that was temporarily providing free long-distance calls. This is the only piece of data I have suggesting the worldwide spread of cyberphreaking.

40. Pam Rosenthal, 'Surfing history, Hacking metaphor: two or three ways to know yourself in cyberspace', UC Berkeley, 25 March 1994. The essay references Dungeons and Dragons, Derrida, Manuel Castells, William Gibson and an essay by Erik Davis entitled 'Techgnosis, magic, memory'.

41. Amy Harmon, '"Hacktivists" of all persuasions take their struggle to the web', *New York Times*, 31 October 1998.

42. Bob Paquin, 'E-Guerrillas in the mist', *Ottawa Citizen*, 26 October 1998.

CHAPTER 3

'Globalization from Below'

> an array of transnational social forces animated by en-
> vironmental concerns, human rights, hostility to patriarchy,
> and a vision of human community based on the unity of
> diverse cultures seeking an end to poverty, oppression,
> humiliation, and collective violence. *Richard Falk*[1]

§ THE basic idea of 'people's globalism' or 'globalization from below'
is that people all over the world are commonly threatened by environmental degradation, abuse of human rights and unenforcement of
labour standards, and that powerful global alliances can be formed to
make corporations and governments accountable to people instead of
elites. Barnet and Cavanagh call this a 'global civil society' that will
'develop a democratic global consciousness rooted in authentic local
communities' (1994: 430). Instead of wielding the nation-state as a
defence against globalization, these movements perceive the need to
globalize resistance to match the globalized structure of neoliberal
exploitation.

This approach to anti-globalization is consonant with Marxist and
international humanitarian hopes: Workers of the world – that is, all
those dispossessed by the ravages of corporate hegemony – unite and
rebuild the world! It is a hopeful vision that assumes the possibility of
international, democratic, non-violent revolution to be achieved by
the rising up of peoples' movements everywhere. Corporations are
wrong because they generate manifold injustice. The movements of
this mode are devotedly democratic, holding Western democratic
ideals both as fundamental goals for their movements and as the anvil
on which to shatter corporate rule.

Mark Ritchie (1996) documents that cross-border movements have
purposefully worked across national borders, particularly in the

agricultural sectors and among indigenous people. They have used self-interest as the basis for solidarity. Relationships have been built between local organizations, not just national ones. The movements have been long-term – as long as 20 years. And personal relationships formed in these long movements have enabled committed solidarity in response to new issues.

The necessity of global politics is old hat to environmental and socialist movements. The labour movement, rapidly globalizing its capacities, is often positioned as the natural leader of 'globalization from below'. This chapter also includes two new social movements, the incredibly effective international movement against free trade agreements and Zapatismo, which may be the most sophisticated practice of 'globalization from below'.

Environmentalism

One of the major accomplishments of the environmental movement is overcoming national boundaries and embracing both a global definition of the problem and an internationalist solution. This internationalism has taken several forms: assembly of international expertise to publicize the global environmental crisis, political campaigns to require the United Nations and other governance organizations to officialize attention to the problem, international solidarity in support of particular local struggles to protect the environment, and sharing of principles, visions and techniques. In addition, environmentalist ideology has changed from being primarily focused on regulatory schemes within existing governance structures to challenging the industrial mode of production and the corporate interests that refuse to change to less harmful practices and products.

The European green parties provide an excellent example of these developments. While struggling for electoral posts and legislative changes within nations, they are also organized in an all-Europe Federation, echoed by a youth federation. They have agreed to 'guiding principles' (Masala, Finland, 1993), which seek to re-embed economic functions within ecological limits. They acknowledge European responsibility for pioneering destructive and exploitative industrialization all over the world and they express the intention to cancel the debts of the poor countries. They criticize regional monetary consolidation as a financial arrangement designed to meet corporate needs, not those of everyday people. Corporations would be completely controlled by new democratic processes that would prioritize ecological security and social justice. They acknowledge the need for multiculturalism, indigenous peoples' rights and gender equity. Their political projects include citizenship rights for immigrants, industrial conversion, peace-keeping and guarantees for democratic rights. Typical of the 'global-ization from below' perspective, economic conversion would involve rational planning organized around the replacement of 'dangerous and wasteful' sectors and the reorientation of trade policy to support social justice goals. While some manufacturing would remain large-scale (in highly regulated corporate operations), the Greens also acknowledge the desirability of local ownership and small-scale production, including informal-sector enterprises.[2]

The pan-European youth federation challenges progress and in-dustrial society because they 'require mobility that brings about anonymous solitude' and cause 'depersonalized and disintegrated pro-duction activities, thereby depriving work of its meaningfulness', while destroying 'cultural heritage'. Some of the national parties also have more radical perspectives, such as 'all land belongs to the community occupying it, never to individuals' (UK). The Scottish party explicitly challenges multinational corporations' inappropriate power and ad-vocates 'self-sufficient, regionally based economies ... reducing the exploitation' of the third world by 'scaling down ... economic policy to community level'. The Irish party, Comhaontas Glas, advocates that 'All political, social, and economic decisions should be taken at the lowest effective level.' Sadly, the first 100 days of Red–Green government in Germany (February 1999) indicate that facilitating 'corporate com-petitiveness' is driving policy.

Greenpeace provides another model of 'globalization from below' by actively intervening in corporate environmental destruction in many parts of the world and building arguments that require global response, such as the 'carbon logic' analysis of the greenhouse gas crisis. It is campaigning against national subsidies to fossil fuel industries, arguing that existing supplies are already at four times the total amount that can safely be released into the atmosphere for the next 100 years. Tax breaks and licences for further exploration and development of more sites are suicidally unnecessary and limit the possibility of energy transition. While participating in national and local campaigns, Greenpeace has also built an international presence and constituency, and appears as an international voice for ecological concerns.

Greenpeace's direct action campaigns have been copied by other movements, such as ECODEFENSE!, founded in 1990 in Kaliningrad, Russia, which has successfully worked to close five chemical and nuclear plants, halt a construction project that was 'exploding the mountains', and stop an oil terminal from being constructed, as well as reducing logging and the hunting of wolves and participating in international solidarity.

The most vibrant and anti-corporate parts of the international environmental movement are the local struggles against logging, mining (including of gold), oil extraction, shrimp farms and dams. These struggles are almost always waged against specific corporations and there are often several attempting to exploit a particular area. They frequently affect indigenous peoples, who blockade roads, occupy sites and refuse to relocate from valleys scheduled for submersion. 'This is not development, but theft' of 'our land, our rights, our culture, and our future', says an indigenous leader.[3] National governments, which have often given licences and leases to the corporations, refuse to recognize indigenous rights and respond to protests by making them illegal, harassing, arresting, beating and killing people.

First world organizations, including Greenpeace, Amnesty International and Cultural Survival, have assisted in building international outrage at both the corporations and the comprador behaviours of third world governments. Clearly emerging from these campaigns is a logic that conjoins environmental, indigenous and human rights abuses, showing how corporate exploitation of natural resources endangers self-determination, democracy and the very survival of indigenous peoples such as the Akawaio and Arecuna of Guyana, the Penan, Kayan, Iban and Kelabit of Sarawak, Malaysia, many Amazonian peoples, and the Saramacca Maroons of Suriname. Environmentalists are acknowledging indigenous claims that biodiversity can best be protected by protecting human diversity. The Sarawak campaign successfully targeted investors, showing them the 'internal contradictions' of the Bakun Dam, but the Malaysian government kept on. The Mitsubishi corporation alone threatens communities in the Philippines, Malaysia, Papua New Guinea, Bolivia, Indonesia, Brazil, Chile, Canada, Siberia and the USA.

A similar kind of campaign is the growing anti-golf course movement. Golf courses threaten indigenous lands and cause environmental damage through pesticides, excessive water use and elimination of biodiversity – all for a luxury land use providing high-risk profit to transnational corporations. Indigenous resistance to use of water and sacred land for golf in Tepoztlán, Mexico has brought violence, political imprisonment, and death to those who protested against the project. First world environmental organizations have acted in solidarity. The most important first world response is the Global Network for Anti-Golf Course Action, founded by a Japanese market gardener, which has stopped 300 proposed courses in Japan and has also provided solidarity pressure to stop courses elsewhere. Thailand and Malaysia have resistance organizations, working with activists from Hawai'i, Hong Kong, India, Indonesia and the Philippines.

The United States environmental justice movement challenges the toxification of communities of colour. In the 1993 letter sent by environmental justice activists to President Clinton in which they asked him to issue an Executive Order, corporations were named as the cause of environmental injustice. The February 1994 Executive Order on Environmental Justice promises to 'ensure that hazardous substances are controlled in such a way that all communities receive environmental protection regardless of race or economic circumstance'. But the implementation of this order has positioned corporations as 'partners' and 'stakeholders' in addressing environmental justice. In contrast to officialized environmental justice, which accommodates corporate interests, materials from grassroots organizations consistently focus on specific corporations and corporations in general. Unlike the government, corporations are in no doubt that they are the enemy of environmental justice. They fight back, filing Strategic Lawsuit Against Political Participation (SLAPP) suits against environmental justice organizations. The distinction between grassroots and official definitions of environmental justice suggests that the grassroots ideology is significant. It is not the articulation of the environmental injustice *problem* that poses a threat, but the naming of corporations as the enemy.

Environmental campaigns have become increasingly explicit about naming corporations as the enemy. For example, Rainforest Action Network (RAN) has participated actively in the Mitsubishi boycott, struggles to save particular forests in North and South America and Africa, in debates over alternative forestry strategies, and in defence of the rights of indigenous peoples. RAN included a member survey in a 1997 Action Alert, asking members to select the 'biggest problem facing the rainforests' from the following list: 'transnational corporations, government inaction, or over-population'. This example suggests that the shift to an anti-corporate movement may be increasingly explicit among organizations not initially founded with such a perspective. The Sierra Club has become more similar to Greenpeace (whose anti-nuclear and anti-whaling work led it to an anti-corporate stance long ago) in 'directly targeting corporations', which is seen as a 'new front for the Club' so as not to 'have all our eggs in the basket of public policy'.[4]

Labour

> 'Globalization' means the gradual dismantling of norms of work, collective bargaining, and independent organizations of the working class ... And this is done always in the name of 'modernization', 'competition', the 'market'. More and more, the poor and workers are becoming mere beasts of burden, numbers for the bean counters of the multinational corporations and the governments in their service ... Doesn't the exchange of a few crumbs – the so called 'social clauses'[5] ... represent the destruction of everything we have built? (Brazil Workers' Conference)[6]

As assembly lines have stretched across the globe and production processes sufficiently flexible to make it easy to exchange one workforce for another nearly anywhere, unions have recognized the need to build global organizing capacity. This takes the forms of company-specific unions, which pursue their jobs from country to country organizing new workers; industry-wide or sectoral unions; and international inter-industry solidarity campaigns. Labour's new awareness has overcome the divide that formerly positioned first world workers' standard of living as dependent on third world workers' cheap labour.

A union organizer explains that 'the power of transnational companies' is a 'common ground' for workers. It has enabled workers to challenge the logic of 'international competitiveness', recognizing that such a logic will drive all wages down. 'The turmoil in Europe tends to put the lie to the "global competition" myth, i.e., German workers must sacrifice to compete with the French … When your boss talks about "global competition", he's referring to the contest among the trans-national corporations to see who can beat-up workers best.'[7]

Unions are widely recognizing the need to bring the standards of all workers up in order to make all workers safe. In May 1999 the 22,000-member Service Employees' International Union, Local 1877 (USA), partnered with Mexico's Telephone Workers' Union. Both represent janitors and other service employees.[8] Unions' participation in the anti-free trade agreement movements has radicalized unions, in that they are now challenging 'neoliberalism', 'privatization', and 'comprador' governments. According to Kommunal, the Swedish Municipal Workers' Union, privatization makes it necessary for former public-service workers to direct their organizing to the transnational companies winning contracts for privatized services. In January 1999, a South African metalworkers' union demonstrated in protest about the arrest of South Korean unionists and accused the ruling regime of being 'in cahoots with the multinational companies'. Meanwhile the Korean unions are aware of the need to 'fight the unfair labour practices caused by Korean enterprises abroad'.[9] Nepalese unions challenge hegemonism, bureaucracy, feudalism, imperialism and com-pradorship.[10] An international trade union conference in Kathmandu recognized that parts of the union movement embrace neoliberalism, 'equat[ing] the "free market" with democracy'. It blamed this on 'the 40-year multi-billion dollar "cold war" lead by the United States against any nation, government, people, or class that stood up for its right to independence, self-determination, or non-capitalist economic develop-ment'.[11]

The 'comprehensive campaign' strategy has been developed in the last ten years as unions have struggled for power in an aggressively anti-union economy. This strategy uses media, informational picketing, presence at shareholder meetings, attention to interlocking director-ships, and attempts to embarrass owners and presidents of corpora-tions. The comprehensive campaign targets an entire corporation, including its shareholders, subsidiaries and public relations messages. The effectiveness of this campaign is best attested to by the 1995 effort by US corporations to get Congress to declare comprehensive campaigns an 'unfair labor practice'. Consumer organizations such as the European Banana Action Network have pressured corporations to improve conditions. That group has also defended European governments' right to preferential trade with former Caribbean colonies (where corporations do not own the farms).

In 1995, the National Labor Committee (USA) was able to document wages as low as 12 cents an hour in Haitian factories producing for Disney. Six thousand grammar schoolchildren were organized to write Disney about its labour practices. By 1997, Disney had reviewed its corporate code of conduct and agreed to minimal inspection of contractors' factories. The Committee announced that this was 'totally inadequate, but it shows that companies do respond to pressure'. Does this kind of 'response' portend the possibility of reversing the power relationship between multinational corporations and people? Founded in 1998, United Students Against Sweatshops (USA and Canada) now has chapters on over 125 college campuses. It continues to protest about universities that have joined the Fair Labor Association, which essentially permits manufacturers to monitor themselves, and demands that their campuses join the Worker Rights Consortium, which is an independent non-profit organization that verifies compliance with a code of conduct written by student activists. The December 1999 Holiday Season of Conscience Day of Action resulted in anti-sweatshop actions in 40 cities across the USA. Nike campaigns resulted in a 25 per cent wage increase in Indonesia in October 1998 and another in March 1999, some improvements in working conditions (such as the shape of the chairs), and disclosure of 41 factory locations in October 1999.[12]

While such campaigns offer the possibility for people of colour to unify around diaspora exploitation, even when successful they do nothing to reduce third world workers' dependence on meagre manufacturing wages and the resulting dependence on multinationals. Such campaigns did not acknowledge the economic instability of these production facilities in a capitalist system, or the ecological unsustainability of the rate of consumption that justifies them, or the dependency of the entire Haitian economy on imported jobs and imported basic goods (both controlled by multinational corporations). In mid-1997, Disney's contractor, H.H. Cutler, was moving Haitian production to China and the National Labor Committee was changing its campaign to 'We want to work with [Disney and Cutler][13] ... With an enormous international effort, we may again be able to keep Disney in Haiti.'[14]

In anti-sweatshop campaigns workers have had to push beyond traditional definitions of workplace and employer. Most garment workers are employed by small contract firms who sew for 'manufacturers' (the names on the labels). Since contractors are themselves marginally profitable local entrepreneurs who must bid for every job, they do not have the financial margin to upgrade sweatshop conditions. (The large profit margin is at the manufacturer and retailer part of the chain.) Because non-payment of wages by contractors (and contractor failure) is common, pressuring the contractors is futile for the unions. Manufacturers have no legal responsibility for the working conditions or payment of wages because the contractor is the legal employer. Garment workers have devised innovative strategies to pressure the high-profit manufacturers to take responsibility for conditions in the factories. Instead of accepting manufacturers' legal irresponsibility, workers in California have repeatedly introduced legislation requiring joint liability for working conditions and wages between manufacturers, retailers and contract shops. Anti-sweatshop organizing has resulted in the dissolution of this legal boundary. Even the weakest, most unenforceable corporate 'codes of conduct' accept some responsibility. This is a good example of how the law is neither an absolute boundary for social movements nor an absolute defence for corporations when there is sufficient popular pressure.

As unions face declining membership due to layoffs and unemployment, some turn to organize new sectors of the workforce, such as teachers and service workers. In Latin America, where layoffs have decimated union memberships, teachers are in the forefront of labour struggles.[15] Justice for Janitors is another new approach to the union movement in the USA. It is disruptively organizing janitors in entire industries, buildings or downtown areas, rather than organizing by employers.

These movements are 'new' labour movements in so far as new constituencies are taking the lead, purposely evading the straitjackets of labour law and compromised labour organizations, and even challenging legal issues of contractual lines of responsibility. In the USA, as in the environmental justice movement, the non-responsiveness of mainstream established organizations to the special conditions faced by communities of colour resulted in the development of parallel organizations.

For the most part, even the most international new labour movements rarely think beyond the corporate form. They do not aim to reorganize work, but to re-establish the social contract. International solidarity will make it possible for social priorities to be imposed on corporations. Workplaces will be increasingly democratized. Social welfare will be extended and women and minorities will be treated better. International democratic organizations will finally enforce labour standards, so that corporations will have nowhere to escape them.

Unions acknowledge the need 'to gain insight into the global activities of transnational employers'[16] and then explain that 'these companies must exercise the level of responsibility and accountability that accompany their position within the global economy'.[17] There are a few signs of broader anti-corporatism. The 'comprehensive campaign' has an anti-corporate sensibility shown by the development and distribution of information about corporate activities generally, not just in a particular workplace. A rare example of the potential emergence of anti-corporatism is an article in the newsletter of the 'rank-and-file' of the Australian State Transit Authority Workers Union, entitled 'Anti-corporate plan unveiled!' Also, the largest Canadian trade union issued 'corporation trading cards' to popularize a generalized critique of corporations.[18] However, the goals and the kinds of solutions sought by these campaigns are not ultimately anti-corporate goals. Corporations are sites for delivery of social justice; there is nothing inherently wrong with them as institutions. Unions make no critique of industrialization, centralization, standardization, consumption, ecological limits or growth. At the protests of the 1999 Seattle WTO Ministerial, where 'sea turtles and teamsters' got 'together at last!', union folk tried out a new language of environmentalism. But it is not fair to say that this alliance has gone beyond the political. I say this not because, as many commentators wrote, environmentalism ultimately threatens jobs and that will bring about the end of labour support for it (indeed, labour history is replete with examples of unions taking material risks in solidarity), but because the entire system to which labour articulates itself is ecologically senseless.

Seeking improved wages and working conditions refutes the moral and social legitimacy of infinite corporate profits but does not reach beyond the corporate form – or the corporate job, the 'modernization' paradigm of growth as the basis for social welfare, or excessive consumption as the foundation of the economy. In February 1997, labour leaders gathered in conjunction with the Davos World Economic Forum Annual Meeting endorsed growth and positioned it as necessary for dealing with unemployment, addressing inequality, and for achieving democracy. In 1998 a major annual conference of European unions critiqued the European Monetary Union, but only on the basis that it 'will not guarantee employment and growth'.[19] Unions' vision of economic life is totally dependent on corporations. Unions are not putting resources into developing alternatives to 'jobs' as a source of economic security.

A few unusual moments in union discourse did propose an alternative political economy: The Korean Confederation of Trade Unions announced its interest in policy measures 'to protect and promote small and medium enterprises and agriculture'. A US union opposing Wal-Mart did so in order to protect 'local retailers who otherwise get driven out'.[20] A leader of the Liverpool dockers strike says: 'Where you can't guarantee employment, maybe you have to stop talking about unemployment and start talking about people having their own skills ... services ... generated within the community on a cooperative basis. ... a swap or some other system.'[21]

Socialism

Socialism is certainly *not* dead. Beleaguered socialist parties continue to educate and to expand their politics through solidarity with people's organizations. Many socialist parties continue to struggle for hegemony. These struggles emphasize democracy and social equity. They express international solidarity with other people's struggles, but their discourse is primarily national. They support trade union struggles (which do not always support the socialist parties in return), and they participate in electoral politics. They sharply critique the comprador state, which invites in and facilitates the operations of corporations. Many criticize other aspects of the state, such as imperialism, militarism and criminalization.

Some socialist parties are truly global. The Socialist International, which has 130 member parties, explains that the challenge of globalization is 'nothing less than the beginning of a new, democratic world society' that will prevent 'blocs, nations, and private corporations' from controlling 'the political structure of the planet as a mere by-product of their own interest'.[22] Its vision includes democratization of international financial institutions and, on a more local scale, a mixed economy including self-managed cooperatives, public enterprises, some decentralized production, and strong unions in companies that remain private. The World Socialist Party (New Zealand) also sees that socialism must be global. It claims that socialism in the sense of communal ownership has not been tried; the existing so-called socialist nations are actually state-owned capitalism. In the future they seek, there will be 'no more transnational corporations or small businesses and therefore nobody will own the world'. Democracy will take place in communities, regions and on a global scale, which the party says is possible based on existing technology. The Socialist Party (Ireland) advocates regional socialism in Europe.

In critiquing 'big business' socialism seems anti-corporate, but its critique is not actually of the *bigness* of big business. In other words, it does not focus on the distinctive problems of bigness, such as centralization, standardization, cultural homogenization and colonialism. Often socialist parties do not distinguish between large and small businesses (or, as in the quote above, see them as equally problematic). Their anti-corporatism is only a reflection of historical specificity. Two exceptions to this are the Democratic Socialists of America (USA) and the Democratic Socialists of Australia, both of which are explicitly anti-corporate, focusing specifically on the role of corporations in dominating political processes. The Australian party critiques the Greens for not 'taking a clear stand against the right of big businesses to own and control the economy'. None of the socialist parties articulated a critique of growth. The absence of a critique of bigness means that socialist parties have little hesitation in relying on state systems for delivery of social goods.

Cuba's recent transformation of its agricultural system to organic methods, made necessary by the lack of access to petroleum and chemical inputs formerly supplied by the USSR, provides several important lessons for socialist thinking that are relevant to its anti-corporatism. First, the experience has demonstrated the efficacy of self-sufficiency in basic needs. Second, the success of the transition has been facilitated by the diversification of forms of production and distribution, including smaller-scale farms and the (re)development of micro-scale urban agriculture, as well as a profusion of daily farmers' markets. Third, the crisis enabled Cuba to rediscover indigenous medicines and the value of traditional farming techniques, such as the use of oxen. Fourth, a critical analysis of the food system enabled dietary changes appropriate to the ecology. At the same time, Cuba's success in this massive transition demonstrates that some involvement of central planning can be supportive of sustainable practices (Rosset and Benjamin 1994).

Cooperatives practise socialist principles on a daily basis. Cooperatives include producers' associations (farming, crafts, fishing, transportation and manufacturing) and consumers' associations (replacing private retail), and associations that make the producer and consumer one, such as housing associations and credit unions. The first workers' cooperative was founded by weavers in Rochdale, England in 1844. The principles laid down, which are still adhered to by most cooperatives, included participatory democracy, cooperative education for all stakeholders, equal distribution of surplus, voluntary association, limited interest on share capital, and cooperation with other cooperatives.[23] Such alternative economic institutions have taken on a life of their own, perhaps independent of formal socialist doctrine. They now often embrace (or even emerge out of) environmental and social values, such as employment of disabled persons or access to safe food.

Italy has the largest sector of cooperatively owned production industries in the world, outstripping even the Basque Mondragón system.[24] The Seikatsu Club consumers' cooperative in Japan practises panchayat-style democracy, with many layers of elected representatives and high rates of participation by women. The Seikatsu Club 'is calling on the public to create a self-managed lifestyle in order to change the present wasteful lifestyle, which is a fallout of the present capitalism-controlled society ... One of our directions is to create local based economies' (1988 in Ekins 1992: 132). The club has become concerned with food safety and the ecological aspects of products, opening its own organic dairies to secure safe milk and manufacturing its own soap from recycled cooking oil. It employs members in production collectives and forms independent political networks to achieve its ecological campaign goals, electing many women to local posts. It is also spreading its organizing to South Korean women. 'We refuse to handle products if they are detrimental to the health of our members or the environment ... even if members make demands for them ... And through our purchases and consumption, we are attempting to change the way that Japanese Agriculture and Fisheries are operated' (Seikatsu Club 1988 in Ekins 1992: 131–2).

The Union of Czech and Moravian Production Cooperatives assists members in finding domestic and foreign producer and trade contacts. The Uruguayan Confederation of Cooperative Entities' 600,000 members account for 3 per cent of the GNP and 10 per cent of agricultural production, but 90 per cent of milk production, 70 per cent of the sugar, and most of the honey. The Confederation organizes itself to 'meet people's needs', particularly by developing inter-cooperative relationships. North America has 50,000 cooperative organizations of various kinds, including agricultural, retail, worker-owned cooperatives, and credit unions, involving twelve million people. There are 500 institutionalized food cooperatives in the USA among other buying associations.[25] Some of these organizations (like food coops) are loosely linked through national associations, overlapping board memberships, and cross-honouring of memberships. The Self Employed Women's Association in India (founded in 1972) has over two hundred thousand members and seeks both communal self-reliance through Gandhian development and individual self-reliance for women (which means 'control and autonomy' over their own lives). The organization facilitates the development of cooperatives (84 employ over eleven thousand women in dairy, artisanal, trading and vending, service, and land-based enterprises) as well as waging legal battles to defend the rights of self-employed workers, and providing services such as healthcare and water harvesting.

What facilitates the emergence of cooperatives? In India, a 1946 milk strike enabled the cooperative form (led by the Amul cooperative) to take over the national milk production system, eliminating 'rapacious milk contractors'. Clearly, the exploitative role of middlemen played a role in politicizing farmers. Perhaps more important, however, was that the farmers owned the means of production and could thereby stage the strike, which gave them the power to hegemonize an entire sector of the economy. Where means of production remain in the hands of small producers, it could be possible to socialize the economy sector-by-sector. It would seem that the availability of socialist public discourse could facilitate a high level of cooperative organization, as in France, where nine out of ten farmers and 9 per cent of the crafts sector are members of a cooperative, 12,300 stores are retail cooperatives, 700 transport businesses are cooperativized, and 12.5 million citizens use cooperative banks. But the emergence of the Seikatsu Club in Japan suggests that socialist discourse is not necessary. Other legitimizing discourses, such as food safety and environmental sustainability, can lead to the desire to develop producer/consumer control over the production process. Where communal ownership of land is facilitated by land reform processes, such as through the *ejido* system in Mexico (now facing neoliberal dismantlement), cooperative organization has been a common form of economic association particularly effective at pursuing social justice at the local level (Cornelius and Myhre 1998).

Socialist economic institutions are anti-corporate, but more implicitly so than parties. Party socialism relies on statist implementation of social welfare. Alternative institutions propose that socialist principles can be enacted on a local, everyday scale. While not explicitly anarchist, the operation of some cooperatives within capitalist nations follows a more anarchist model than a centralized socialist one. (Anarchism will be discussed in the next chapter.) The development of alternative organizations is seen as a way to initiate community transformation, through the transformation of basic institutions of social reproduction. They are an effort to politicize daily life and to construct viable alternatives to the existing economic structure. This valuable experimentation could facilitate socialist transition, by providing models of dealing with issues of democracy, bureaucracy, diversity and coordination.

Anti-FTA

Our resistance will be as transnational as capital![26]

A striking new social movement burst upon the world stage in the 1990s. It is striking for its internationalism, its ideological unity, its diversity, its size and its effectiveness. Thousands of people's organizations, including trade unions, environmental organizations, farmers' and fishworkers' associations, youth groups, women's organizations, indigenous peoples' organizations, anti-roads activists, peace and human rights groups, and many more are engaging in highly co-ordinated, articulate and celebratory mass protests against free trade agreements. Corporations are constantly criticized, democracy is always embraced and internationalism is actually achieved.

The May 1998 Summit of the World Trade Organization in Geneva was accompanied by worldwide protests, many of which took the form of Reclaim the Streets street parties, which were educational non-violent protests, performances and dances, with up to twenty disc jockeys and lounges with couches and carpets. Ten thousand people surrounded the WTO meeting in Geneva itself (many more attempted to get there but were turned back at Swiss borders) while simultaneous protest parties were held in cities and towns all over the world. Three thousand people partied in Prague, the Czech Republic, two thousand each in Turku, Finland and Sydney, Australia, one thousand at an unannounced party in East Berlin. Hundreds of thousands of farmers, workers and tribal people demanded that India withdraw from the WTO. Fifty thousand marchers from 'four cardinal points of the country' converged on Brasilia. Along the way, they camped in front of supermarkets to protest against the unaffordability of food.[27] Many smaller events were held, including several ritual burnings of the WTO agreement (one fire initiated with use of 'a fair traded candle made in Soweto by the cooperative Ukukanhya [Light in Darkness]'). Anti-MAI events were held in 20 cities in the Netherlands in April 1998 and a 'wild dance party ... blockaded a six lane highway' in Utrecht. Many actions occurred in Spain, including the posting of a massive banner announcing 'Iberdrola, BBV, Telefonica and the other multinationals are destroying the world' and including a drawing of 'a bleeding South America being squeezed by a hand that wears ... the symbol of the Euro and the logos of several TNCs'. In Ottawa, Canada, banners announced 'World Trade Organization – Global Government for the Rich' and expressed solidarity with Chiapas.

Other sites of protest include the meetings of the World Economic Forum at Davos, which was protested about by 192 organizations from 54 countries, claiming an aggregate membership of twenty million people, in 1998. In 2000, the city denied protest permits but 1,000 people managed to protest anyway. A thousand protesters blockaded the 1999 Conférence de Montréal, which gathers government leaders to celebrate globalized economies. The movement uses celebration as a form of protest, creating moments in which people control public space and contrasting such fun with the day's automobile proceedings. There are constant efforts to educate fellow global citizens through fliers, symbolic challenges to corporate franchises, performances and dialogue. An Inter-Continental Caravan originated in India and toured Europe during May and June 1999 to protest against agricultural multinationals and free trade.

In late November 1999, the awakening movements of the USA came together seventy thousand strong in the most extraordinary mobilization in recent memory. Hard-won coalitions between labour, environment, human rights, farmers and youth groups bore fruit as a variety of complementary direct actions (including Reclaim the Streets-style dance parties) shut down the WTO Ministerial meetings in Seattle for an entire day. Simultaneous protests were held in Geneva, where a march of 2,000 farmers and 3,000 city people (a new alliance) converged on WTO headquarters. Seventy-five thousand French participated in actions in 80 different cities, including 5,000 farmers, who met in Paris along with their farm animals for a protest feast. Other protests were held all over, including Milan, Berlin, Amsterdam, Buenos Aires, Israel and Colombo (Sri Lanka), with small protests in major US and UK cities. In Manila 8,000 people rallied at the US embassy and at the presidential palace to protest against Philippine participation in the WTO. They returned to the embassy a couple of days later to protest against police treatment of Seattle protesters. Many protests were held in India, including ten districts of the Punjab New Delhi (protest at Gandhi's burial site), Bangalore and the Narmada valley. In addition to opposing the WTO, Indian protests emphasized the 'Monsanto Quit India' campaign, a new land rights movement, and opposition to dams and other World Bank projects.

These protests are among the largest in recent history and their momentum is growing steadily. They involve significant scholarship and educational components, particularly in the case of the Multi-lateral Agreement on Investments, whose implementation they have significantly disrupted. A Joint Non-Governmental Organization Statement on the MAI to the Organization for Economic Cooperation and Development has been endorsed by 560 organizations in 67 countries. It demands that negotiations be suspended until a social, environmental and development assessment is completed; binding, enforceable agreements on environment, labour, health, safety and human rights standards; democratic dispute resolution mechanisms that enable civil society to 'hold investors to account'; limiting the 'expropriation provision so that investors are not granted an absolute right to compensation for expropriation' as it undermines national sovereignty; and that the negotiation process be changed into one that is participatory, transparent and permits withdrawal from the agreement.

In addition to street protests and scholarly interventions, the movements are organizing their own fora to build consensus on alternative policies. In April 1998, a People's Summit with representatives from the whole continent of South America was held to respond to the Presidential Summit of the Americas in Santiago, Chile, which is trying to negotiate a Free Trade Area of the Americas. Malaysian NGOs hosted a series of conferences in parallel with the November 1998 APEC (Asian FTA) summit in Kuala Lumpur. These included the Third International Women's Conference with the theme 'Women, Resist Globalization! Assert Women's Rights!', a Peasant Forum entitled 'Throwing Off the Yoke of Imperialist Globalization', and the People's Assembly on APEC. Convenors included the Peasant Movement of the Philippines (KMP), the Anti-Imperialist World Peasant Summit and the Asian Peasant Women's Network. The movements involve primary leadership from third world countries and the protests there tend to be larger. The collaboration between the first, third and fourth world activists seems to be effective. In addition, the ideas put forth and the practices of the protests defend all social sectors, including squatters, youth, women, political prisoners and queers.

Coordinating organizations of the movement include the People's

Campaign Against Imperialist Globalization, representing 34 countries, which met in 1996 Quezon City (Philippines) and in 1997 in Vancouver, and held a conference against mining transnationals in Manila in 1998, accompanied by a protest against mining and APEC. Founded in 1997, the People's Global Action Against 'Free' Trade and the WTO includes 300 delegates from 71 countries. The Geneva founding conference was 'largely housed in squatted halls and houses', building strong connections with youth and homeless movements and establishing low-cost operational resources. Its manifesto states that its activist strategy is 'to actively disobey and disrespect all the treaties and institutions at the root of misery' and also a commitment 'to building a new world ... deeply rooted in diversity'.[28] People's Global Action challenges Western science, education, gender relations, dependence on consumerist consumption, and the internalization of 'understandings of human dignity' distorted by the promotion of 'beneficial effects of global competition' that actually 'constitute direct violations of basic human rights'. Their four priorities are: rejection of the multilateral trade system, destroying (not reforming) the WTO, direct actions (not lobbying), and being a 'basically democratic' organization.

The Joint Action Forum of Indian People against the WTO and Anti-People Policies (also founded in 1998) is composed of 50 people's movements. It describes the WTO as 'our brutal enemy', which is 'converting us into objects of Transnational Corporations' economy of consumerism', and resolves to 'build a pro-people egalitarian social order through a genuinely democratic process'. The World Forum of Fish Harvesters and Fishworkers has formed in 25 countries. The International Forum on Globalization (IFG), founded in 1994, is an alliance of 60 leading activist economists representing 19 countries. A 1995 position statement 'views international trade and investment agreements ... combined with the structural adjustment policies ... to be direct stimulants to the processes that ... create a world order in the control of transnational corporations'. The most important US organization is Public Citizen, which did a great deal of the organizing against NAFTA, fast-track authorizations, the MAI and the WTO. It even loaned a staff member to help the Direct Action Network organize protests at the WTO 1999 Seattle Ministerial.

High-profile participants in the international anti-FTA movement have included the late Sir James Goldsmith, reputed to be the richest man in Europe, George Soros, one of the most influential players in international currency markets,[29] and Bernard Lietaer, one of the architects of the European common currency. Even more remarkable than their participation is the extent to which a wide variety of affected movements, such as peace, human rights, consumer associations, farmers and environmentalists, have become active campaigners.

Some property crime violence has occasionally accompanied the protests, but the convenors of the May 1998 protest of the WTO announced that they 'regretted the damage ... but that this violence was nothing compared to the violence organized in the WTO building'. In other Geneva actions, non-violence was announced and people even marched on their knees to emphasize it, but the police 'responded with incredible violence, kicking and bludgeoning under the TV cameras for more than an hour'. Arrestees were beaten in custody.[30] In Seattle, where European observers noted the extraordinary non-violent discipline of protesters, police violence stole the show in what my group could only conclude was an effort to use any means necessary to distract attention from the success of the non-violent direct action. Formal and brutal informal suspensions of the constitutionally guaranteed rights to free speech and assembly have subsequently been regularized to frighten people from participating in non-violenct direct action.

The visions put forth by this movement include an embrace of Rousseau, whose statue was the destination of a Geneva march by 1,000 silent (gagged) protesters to bring attention to their non-inclusion in the destruction of the social contract. The National Alliance of People's Movements, India, while protesting the WTO and 'anti-sovereign agreements', asserts 'the right to have the land, water, forest, mineral, and aquatic wealth localized in each village community, to have a local eco-socio-economically decentralized planning for equity and sustainability' including indigenous technology, local markets and non-consumerist living. The fisherfolk movement Pambansang Lakas ng Kilusang Mamamalakaya ng Pilipinas, along with demanding the government to withdraw from the WTO and regional free trade agreements, envisions 'reorient[ation of] our food production and market to feed the Filipino people and not aristocrats abroad'. People's Global Action's vision is to 'reconstruct sustainable livelihoods' by 'transform[ing] our daily lives, freeing ourselves from market laws and the pursuit of private profit', 'develop[ing] a diversity of forms of organization at different levels', and forming a 'decentralized economy and polity based on communities' rights to natural resources and to plan their own development, with equality and self-reliance as the basic values'. The International Forum on Globalization also envisions 'more diversified, locally controlled, community-based economics', to be supported by better international agreements focused on 'the needs of people'.

Zapatismo

> Our blood and our word have lit a small fire in the mountain and we walk a path against the house of money and the powerful. Brothers and sisters of other races and languages, of other colors, but with the same heart now protect our light and in it they drink of the same fire.
> (Fourth Declaration of the Lacandon Jungle, 1 January 1996)

Zapatismo is a sovereignty movement, insisting on self-determination rights for the indigenous peoples and peasants of the Lacandon forest region of Chiapas. But it is different from most indigenous sovereignty movements (discussed in the next chapter) because at the same time, it is a movement of 'intuition'[31] that calls out to all Mexicans and all people of the world to express Zapatismo in resistance to oppression and as expression of self-determination and dignity. The Zapatista National Liberation Army institutionalized the internationalization of this struggle by hosting the First Intercontinental Encounter against Neo-Liberalism and for Humanity in Chiapas in April 1996, attended by 3,000 international delegates from 43 countries. A European conference of the same title was held in May in Berlin; the 1997 Encounter was held in Spain.

Zapatismo embodies the theory of 'globalization from below' quite thoroughly. First, its analyses insist on the prioritization of political economic concerns. While 'indigenous heart' gives birth to the political force that 'descends from the mountains' in the form of the Zapatista army (4th Declaration), the enemies are economic elites who 'pillage the wealth of our country', who have 'sold half our country to the foreign invader', who 'don't care that we have nothing, absolutely nothing' (1st Declaration, 1 January 1994), 'the omnipotent power of the cattle ranchers and businessman and penetration of drug traffic' (2nd Declaration, June 1994), and the anti-democratic political system that supports these elites.

Zapatistas know that to their enemy, 'known internationally by the word "neoliberalism"', indigenous people and peasants 'did not count, we did not produce, we did not buy, we did not sell. We were a useless figure in the accounts of big capital.'[32] The movement's naming of neoliberalism as the enemy critiques the dominant governmental mode of organizing the economy to benefit corporate activities and priorities. In March 1995, Subcomandante Insurgente Marcos wrote that 'the tanks and the helicopters and thousands of soldiers came saying they were defending national sovereignty and we say that that was being violated in the financial arrangements, not in Chiapas'. The true enemy was recognized because: 'When we rose up against a national government, we found that it did not exist. In reality we were up against great financial capital, against speculation and invest-ment, which makes all decisions in Mexico, as well as in Europe, Asia, Africa, Oceania, the Americas – everywhere.'[33] The Third Declaration spells out the collaboration between Mexican and first world elites:

> At the end of 1994 the economic farce with which Salinas had deceived the Nation and the international economy exploded. The nation of money called the grand gentlemen of power and arrogance to dinner, and they did not hesitate in betraying the soil and sky in which they prospered with Mexican blood. The economic crisis awoke Mexicans from the sweet and stupefying dream of entry into the first world. (3rd Declaration, January 1995)

The enemy is confronted with the cry 'Enough!' The Zapatistas say 'we are the possibility that it can be made to disappear ... tell it you have alternatives to its world'.[34]

In aiming an international movement against neo-liberalism, Zapat-ismo rejects export-based economies, international lending agreements, free trade, privatization and other forms of economic liberalization that are devastating first and third world countries alike for the benefit of corporations. 'In the first world it is less clear, but it is the same.'[35] The Zapatistas continue and extend Mexican struggles for land reform as the core of economic change: those who work the land should own it, large estates will be turned into non-taxed collective farms, the purpose of production will be for peasants to feed their families. 'And all debts owed by poor peasants to either the government, foreigners, or the wealth elite will be abolished.'[36]

The second way Zapatismo manifests globalization from below is in thoroughly and constantly addressing multiple oppressions: race, gender and sexual orientation. One-third of the military troops are women and one-half of the members of the civilian organization are women. Both the take-over of San Cristóbal and an important unit in the December 1994 rupture of the military blockade were commanded by a woman, Mayor Insurgente Ana Maria.[37] Marcos notes that the government and media have carefully concealed the role of women as leaders in combat. In March 1995, he wrote about how the women have come into their own power: 'When we governed, alcoholism dropped to zero and it's because the women were ferocious and said that booze just made men beat the women and children and commit other barbarities and so they gave the order no booze.' In addition, the movement has expressed support for queers, first world people of colour, indigenous peoples and ecological perspectives. At one point, expressing the spirit of Zapatismo, Marcos wrote 'in San Francisco, Marcos is gay … Marcos is all of the minorities who are untolerated, oppressed, resisting, exploding, saying "Enough"' (in Johnston 1997).

> In the world of the powerful there is no space for anyone but them-selves and their servants. In the world we want everyone fits … The Nation which we construct is one where all communities and lan-guages fit, where all steps may walk, where all may have laughter, where all may live the dawn. (4th Declaration, 1996)

They insist that the only way to provide justice and dignity for indigenous people is to change the entire racialized system of the nation. During an indigenous peoples' march on Mexico City, Zapat-istas refused the mayor's greeting and overturned ballot boxes to show disdain for false inclusions.[38] Zapatista supporters even try to speak to the government soldiers as allies: 'You're behaving like animals. Aren't you also sons of peasants?' (Landau 1996). 'You don't understand why you are here. You are indigenous. Analyze it.'[39]

Zapatismo is one of the more sophisticated attempts at 'new globalization from below' forms of democracy. The Zapatistas insist that power 'be collective and communal', a lesson they claim to have learned at the insistence of the indigenous communities. The political practice of this principle has shown in the initiation of a national dialogue the Zapatistas call the first between 'peaceful civil society' and 'a clandestine and armed group' (4th Declaration), resulting in a 1995 plebiscite of over 1.3 million Mexican citizens who ratified the Zapatista demands and a 1999 'consultation', in which 2.5 million Mexicans expressed support for indigenous people, demilitarization and the Zapatista principle of 'govern by obeying'. These civil society ventures were undertaken in response to an earlier dialogue with Mexican civil society from which the Zapatistas heard the desire for a peaceful solution. The resulting 'consultation' included 15,000 electoral-style polling places and also, according to the option of the community, decisions taken according to traditional customs. The Zapatistas' civilian strategy is to create non-electoral approaches to changing Mexican politics. The hyper-democratic 'govern by obeying' principle is being extended by Zapatistas into other struggles, such as the prison movement, Voice of Cerro Hueco. It involves a leadership council that is held tightly accountable to regular general assemblies.[40]

The principle also shows in ultra-democratic internal policies. In response to the Mexican government's proposal for peace agreements, the Zapatistas 'in an unprecedented democratic exercise within an armed organization, consulted its entire membership on whether or not to sign'. The predominantly indigenous membership refused, 'seeing that the central questions of Democracy, Liberty and Justice had not been resolved' (2nd Declaration). In the process an example was documented of the use of indigenous culture as a tool of political analysis:

> They advised us to be prudent and to sign the peace (agreement) … They asked us to prudently surrender and live … All afternoon we talked in the Committee. We tried to find the word 'surrender' in some language but we couldn't. It doesn't translate into Tzotzil nor into Tzeltal and no one remembers that word in Tojolabal or in Chol. We spend hours trying to find an equivalent … Someone arrives with rain pouring off the cap and the rifle, 'Coffee's ready', they tell us. The Committee, as is customary in these parts, takes a vote to see if they'll have coffee or continue trying to find the equivalent of 'SUR-RENDER' in the language of truth. Coffee wins unanimously. NO ONE SURRENDERS. Will we be alone?[41]

This democratic sensibility also appears in the practice of political speaking. The films *The Sixth Sun* (Landau 1996) and *Zapatista* (Big Noise 1998) include many images of villagers confronting the soldiers, each one speaking to a soldier, each person making their own argument, embracing the soldiers sent to oppose them in a cacophony of dignity, dialogue and democracy.

In articulating democracy, multiculturalism and perfect clarity about the enemy, Zapatismo is a model of 'globalization from below'. The plan for rebuilding the world is a little unclear. One aspect of it will be 'One no, many yeses',[42] meaning that it is necessary to clearly name an enemy, but there may be many different kinds of strategies for how to rebuild the world, and those strategies can coexist.

Discussion

The movements of this mode are organizing very significant new forms of internationalism. In response to NAFTA, collaborations have emerged between Mexican and US labour organizations, farmers' organizations and people of colour. These organizations are working to educate themselves about the similarities of their situations across the first world–third world border. The Zapatistas' courageous stance catalyses international commitments from first world social justice allies and fourth world indigenous peoples' groups, some of whom commit their own bodies. Harry Cleaver argues that the rapidly mobilized support for the Zapatistas was made possible by the cross-border anti-NAFTA movement infrastructure. This support included physical actions as well as lobbying. 'There can be no doubt that their actions – and the subsequent rapid circulation of their findings and declarations ... (along with all the other forms of protest in Mexico and without) ... contributed to blunting the states' military counter-offensive and [forced it to] undertake negotiations with an armed enemy it quite clearly would have preferred to squash (if it could, which is by no means obvious)' (Cleaver 1994). Support for the Zapatistas came from indigenous people from the entire South American continent.

Not the least important of this new internationalism is the development of alliances among indigenous people. The anti-FTA movements show the strong base of international solidarity that has been built by development scholars and activists through years of challenging World Bank and IMF policies. Critical frameworks and knowledge developed in North–South collaboration enable the rapid development of analyses and international campaigns that focus on the concerns of the poorest of the poor.

While enthused about people's globalization, each of the movements also does powerful work locally. Environmental movements take great risks to defend particular forest stands and fisheries, and unions risk everything to draw the line on exploitation one workplace at a time. These movements are in total opposition to the necessity of injustice and destruction. The Zapatistas are transforming the conditions of life in the villages they work with, particularly for women, while holding their own in a war against the Mexican government. Among other projects, the Zapatistas are proving that it is possible to build a sustainable, humanitarian and democratic autonomous regional community.

While the solidification of labour internationalism, particularly across first world–third world borders, and new strategies are hopeful and exciting, this movement seems to be the least anti-corporate of the movements studied here. The rest of the movements in this mode agree on a total critique of their enemy – environmentalists, anti-FTA activists, Zapatistas and socialists all agree that the whole damn system has got to go. Nevertheless, socialist parties stay separate from these other movements as a result of lack of interest – might socialists be right that the other movements have an inadequate analysis of the system? Critical political economy firmly positioned outside socialist politics makes the anti-FTA movement an important and new political framework. The leading organizations are both scholarly and activist and have gained both great legitimacy and mass international support quite rapidly. The anti-FTA movement firmly insists that economic globalization 'is not inevitable' and the Zapatistas breathe hope by challenging it in seemingly impossible ways.

The liberatory vision of 'globalization from below' is still being worked out. There are many unanswered questions about how it will be organized, what forms of unity are possible, how it will avoid bureaucracy, and how it will manage diversity. Perhaps the most important question is the vision of the future. Will unions look beyond the *good* corporate job towards transformative visions of the economy? The scholarly anti-FTA movement is working out alternatives, as are the

Zapatistas. Indigenous perspectives and alternative epistemology play an important role in framing possible alternative democracies and economies. The movements in the next chapter are devoted to this project. They have articulated sophisticated non-corporate paradigms for rebuilding the world.

Notes

1. In Brecher et al. 1993: ix.

2. Dr Caroline Lucas, Green Party Spring Conference in London.

3. All unattributed quotes are from primary data collection.

4. John Byrne Barry, 'Making corporations accountable', *The Planet*, 5(6), July/August 1998. Last quote from Mike McCloskey, chairman and former executive director of the Sierra Club.

5. These are the toothless labour and environment side-agreements added on to FTAs to quell protest.

6. Preparatory to the Western Hemisphere Workers' Conference against NAFTA and Privatizations, Porto Alegre, Brazil, 26–27 July 1994.

7. Len Wilson, 'Fighting the world economic order', *Industrial Worker Online*, January 1996.

8. Diane E. Lewis, 'Unions flex new muscle as overseas ties grow', *Boston Globe*, 23 January 2000.

9. Korean Confederation of Trade Unions, 'KCTU international policy'.

10. General Federation of Nepalese Trade Unions, Kathmandu, Nepal, 'Objectives, principles, and basic demands'.

11. International Trade Union Conference, 'Strengthen Pro-Worker Trade Unionism, Oppose Privatization', Kathmandu, 10–13 December 1994; 38 trade unions from 15 countries represented.

12. Global Exchange, press release, 16 October 1998; *National Public Radio Morning Edition*, 'Nike announces raises for workers in Indonesian factories; critics say it's not enough', 24 March 1999; Steven Greenhouse, 'Nike identifies plants abroad making goods for universities', *New York Times*, 8 October 1999.

13. National Labor Committee, 'Jobs threatened: urgent action alert in solidarity with Haitian and US Workers', 28 July 1997.

14. National Labor Committee, 'Are human rights campaigns necessary?', 28 July 1997.

15. InterPress Third World News Agency, 'Labor challenges Mercosur', *Industrial Worker*, January 1999.

16. International Union of Food, Agricultural, Hotel, Restaurant, Catering, Tobacco and Allied Workers' Associations (IUF), international federation, 'What It Is'.

17. International Federation of Commercial, Clerical, Professional and Technical Employees (French acronym FIET), 'Introducing FIET'.

18. Tony Clarke at IFG 1997.

19. 'Visions for a new Europe – Euro-FIET sets the scene for the 21st Century', 8th Euro-FIET Conference, Cardiff, 29–31 March 1998. from *FietNet News Issue*, 4, 24 April 1998.

20. This is the UFCW.

21. Mike Carden, in David Bacon, 'Liverpool dockers', *Z Magazine*, 12 (2), February 1999: 9–13.

22. Socialist International, 'Declaration of Principles', 97.

23. Rebecca Em Campbell, 'Rural worker-owned cooperatives', *Permaculture Activist*, 38, February 1998: 8–10.

24. Tim Huet, 'Can coops go global?: Mondragón is trying', *Dollars & Sense*, 214, November/December 1997: 16–19, 41–2.

25. Ibid.

26. This phrase became popular in the J18 (18 June 1999) anti-FTA protests. I was not able to establish its origins.

27. This protest was simultaneously against structural adjustment and against free trade.

28. People's Global Action Manifesto, March 1997.

29. 'Capitalism is more totalitarian than communism' (according to Khor at IFG 1997).

30. People's Global Action Bulletin, 2, July 1998.

31. Marcos in Big Noise 1998.

32. The Indigenous Clandestine Revolutionary Committee-General Command of the Zapatista National Liberation Army, Planet Earth, July 1996, in Richard Greenleaf Rowley, 'The Zapatistas and the modern state', *Prevailing Winds Magazine*, 4: 16–19.

33. Big Noise 1998.

34. Ibid.

35. Ibid.

36. Jason Wehling, 'Zapatismo: what the EZLN is fighting for', *University Sentinel*, 10 January 1995.

37. Subcomandante Insurgente Marcos (National Commission for Democracy), March 1996.

38. Saul Landau, speaking at UCSB, 4 June 1998.

39. Big Noise 1998.

40. SIPAZ International, *SIPAZ Report*, 4 (2), May 1999.

41. Wehling 1995.

42. Michael Lane, 'Diary of the second Zapatista *Encuentro*', *Dollars & Sense*, 214, November/December: 8–9.

. . . .

CHAPTER 4

Delinking, Relocalization, Sovereignty

> If you do not concede our demand, we will no longer be
> your petitioners. You can govern us only so long as we
> remain the governed; we shall no longer have any dealings
> with you. *Mahatma Gandhi*, Hind Swaraj 1908

§ AS Helena Norberg-Hodge explains, even if 'globalization from
below' were to succeed in writing a different set of multilateral treaties,
'such international steps would not in themselves restore health to
economies and communities'. The movements of relocalization would
also be necessary. 'Long-term solutions to today's social and environmental problems require a range of small, local initiatives that are as
diverse as the cultures and environments in which they take place'
(1996: 394).

The third mode of anti-corporatism articulates the pleasures, pro-
ductivities and rights of localities. Corporations appear as threats to
locality whose powers can be evaded only by 'delinking' the local
economy from the corporate-controlled national and international
economies. Interlopers must not be allowed in. While Samir Amin
(1985) coined the word 'delinking', the concept was not new. The
movements in this chapter are long-term movements with well-dev-
eloped philosophies. Like movements in the other modes, they are
democratic, but they articulate a different form of democracy – the
practice of local sovereignty and the refusal of distant authority.

While scholars have complained about the need for an 'alternative
political economy', little attention has been paid to the many ongoing
practices of what I call 'relocalization'. Exceptions include Paul Ekins'
1992 *A New World Order*, in which he collected grassroots projects from
all over the world in the areas of housing, development, environment,
and health; the Jerry Mander and Edward Goldsmith edited volume,

The Case Against the Global Economy (1996); Richard Douthwaite's *Short Circuit* (1996); Michael Shuman's 1998 *Going Local,* which gives examples of community-based development in the context of the USA and Canada; and Maria Mies and Veronika Bennholdt-Thomsen's *The Subsistence Perspective* (1999), which both defends subsistence as a reasonable political economic theory and provides examples of how it works.

There are three distinct concerns that contribute to relocalization. The first is the need for economies in dialogue with their ecological bases and limits. The second concern is the need for community economic health. Anarchists, a family of socialists, have long insisted on local-scale economies. But they share with sovereignty movements and religious nationalists the third concern, political autonomy and the assertion of people's right to govern their own lives. The three concerns are mutually reinforcing, leading anti-globalization scholars to draw on Jeffersonian/Iroquois democracy, Swiss *gemeinde* (commune, the sub-canton unit), and Gandhian *swadeshi* in articulating a theory of local political authority founded on economic independence and local mutuality (Mander and Goldsmith 1996: 507–9).

Anarchism

Anarchism today is alive, youthful and international. Anarchism as a youth movement is involved with animal rights, feminism, anti-racism, concerns with police and prison abuse, music, homeless issues and free speech. As an international movement it is historically aware, intellectual and prolific. Anarchism is particularly strong in Sweden, Spain and Eastern Europe, and has many organizations worldwide.

The other myth is that anarchism is chaos. It is claimed by politicians, bosses and their hacks in the media that if there was no government there would be chaos. But did you ever wonder about society today and come to the conclusion that perhaps we are already living in chaos? At the moment thousands of builders are on the dole yet homeless people need housing to live in. The price of butter is scandalously dear yet every year the EC has to deal with a butter mountain. Thousands of people are dying of starvation around the world yet millions of pounds are spent every day on nuclear arms which have the potential for wiping us and the world out. (Pamphlet, 'Anarchism and , Ireland', Workers' Solidarity Movement, Dublin)

Anarchist organizing may look little different from socialist organizing. It proposes use of workers' unions, the general strike and other measures to strengthen people's power in relation to state and corporate power. Where anarchism differs from socialism is in the post-revolutionary vision – local autonomy of worker-collectives and no state. Why? 'The state is essentially a creation of class society. In a society where one group of people owned more than another then you needed a state to maintain this situation.'[1] Localized ownership of the means of production in a stateless society will enable local economic autonomy and will prohibit elite power. While vigorously internationalist, the future vision of the movement is about re-localization.

Anarchism includes a rich dialogue about its own history, its relationship to Marxism and its relationship to individualism. Some of the history that anarchists draw on is the role of anarchism in Korean anti-imperialism, the Spanish anarchist collectivist movement and anarchist feminism. In Spain in the 1930s anarchists developed non-state socialism in which enterprises were collectivized and smallholders were allowed to hold land and enterprises privately and trade with collectives, as long as they didn't employ anyone. In Turkey and elsewhere, anarchism is extending and deepening Marxist critique in the face of the failure of Western development and of the socialist states. Anarchist feminism includes both critique of the state as deliverer of women's rights and of traditional marriage as another site of authority and inherent inequality. Web pages have links with the free speech online campaign, concern with depleted uranium ammunition used in the Gulf War, temporary workers organizing, *Covert Action Quarterly*, the Great Boycott, police brutality, anti-prison work, feminist newspapers, homeless activism, gang truces, and the Black Panthers. A British organization called Class War explains that 'At present the capitalists invade all areas of our lives – in turn we will have to retrieve every part of them.'

One of the major issues for anarchists is the need to distinguish their movement from vulgar stereotypes, such as that anarchists promote chaos and violence. In the USA *The Anarchist Cookbook*, which some believe was produced by government counter-intelligence agencies and is mysteriously kept in print and commonly stocked in bookshops, contributes to this misperception. A critic writes: 'I would like to ask, if you are interested in blowing stuff up, that you not bother with Anarchism. Anarchists have to be concerned with building structures which can effect positive social change, and which have real grassroots control without any hierarchical structure.' He recommends that the real *Anarchist Cookbook* is the *Food Not Bombs* handbook, which has guidelines for 'food recovery' programmes, recipes for feeding lots of people, and information on how to deal with police harassment. *Food Not Bombs* does homeless activism that challenges commodification by feeding people for free in public places.

The online free speech campaign, known as the Black Ribbon Campaign, is one of the more visible current anarchist projects. Anarchist campaigners recognize that while both government and corporate control are autocratic and authoritarian, corporations are worse because people don't even have the 'potential' to have a democratic voice. They call this privatization 'the enclosure of the internet', making it into a 'commodity' controlled by 'corporate/government fiefdoms'. The purpose of the campaign 'is to illustrate that what people value most about the Internet comes from its anarchistic character: the free exchange of information and ideas among people around the world, without the intervention of a governing body'.

While anarchism is not a vibrant, rapidly growing movement, and while it languishes under discrediting stereotypes, its survival is significant for several reasons. Anarchist history, analysis and experiments provide a resource for other delinking movements that are moving to anarchism under different names. It provides a political space for a youth constituency and nurtures radicalism. Youth movements' sustained enthusiasm for anarchist thought, statistically insignificant though it may be, is important in delegitimizing liberalism and homogenizing consumerism; it is one of the few alternatives for youth. It also provides a theoretical opening for strict socialists to make the transition to supporting relocalization.

European anarchists have been very active in the anti-FTA and anti-structural adjustment movements. They have built links with third world peoples and were very supportive of People's Global Action's Intercontinental Caravans. In Europe, they form part of the backbone of these major movements. A last-minute addition to the landscape of anarchism as this book goes to press is the huge and significant role anarchists played in the protests of the 1999 Seattle WTO Ministerial in the USA. The anarchists who engaged in property crime got a lot of media attention, which detracted from the success of the protest.[2] In that context, no one wanted to draw attention to the fact that the entire event was organized according to anarchist principles. This was so explicit and so obvious that my entire group (which at no point has identified itself as an anarchist group) felt that we should also use anarchist principles in organizing ourselves during the week of protest. Many anarchist principles were in obvious use. There was no attempt at centralization, control, official messages, or forms of the protest as a whole. The only attempts at coordination were engaged in dialogically and person-to-person (in the spirit of the Critical Mass xerocracy) in forms such as T-shirts reading 'this is a non-violent protest' and invitations to direct action trainings. (This 'non-violence' was a completely successful campaign. The only reported assaults were perpetrated by WTO delegates and police.)

Community systems were the basis of organizing. Individuals were encouraged to form 'affinity groups', which, it was recommended, should have some sort of organization and designation of one or two people to do low-risk activities to support those doing activities with higher risk of arrest. Each group organized themselves for whatever activities (marching, locking down, hanging banners, street theatre, human chains) they saw as most strategic. Each different group had high-priority messages and actions they wanted to participate in. They collaborated with other groups for particular actions. Each group had their own decision-making structure. I observed the Red Noses having a quick meeting in which they made sure they had people filling several (apparently rotating) positions, including a spokesperson for the action they were about to undertake.

At the anarchist Convergence Center, all activists were welcome to build puppets and other props, have meetings, plan actions, recruit participants to their actions, and rest. The Center provided some basic services: housing assistance, meals, medical care and direct action training regarding how to prepare for arrest (these included special trainings for minors). People communicated about a whole variety of issues via big pieces of paper hung on the walls. There were a number of tactical teams, equipped with communications equipment. Also in an anarchist fashion, some groups decided to provide medical and legal services. Some people became medics in the midst of the tear-gas and nerve-gas. It is particularly important for non-anarchist participants and supporters to acknowledge that groups with different messages, tactics and skills coexisted without attempting centralized organizing. That coexistence was the material of the blockade's success. Everyone who participated has now experienced the anarchist alternative to bureaucratic top-down systems. We saw self-organization at work and it worked.

Sustainable Development

World historically, sustainable development is omnipresent, but unnamed. Fairly recently it has become a social movement, with ideology, activists and practices. In the third world, the movement often takes the form of ongoing critique of modernization, particularly in agriculture. Gandhian development is an example of the politicization of this dialogue, emphasizing '"the *khadi* mentality", meaning the decentralization of the production and distribution of the necessities of life' (Chowdhry 1989: 146).

One of the earliest first world articulations of sustainable development as a transformative practice was Bill Mollison's 'permaculture', founded in the early 1970s. Examining forests, Mollison hypothesized that it must be possible to design agricultural systems modelled on the dense functional interdependency of ecosystems. The resulting permanent, low-maintenance 'food forests' might then produce the level of abundance visible in nature. In developing what he calls the only 'design system' for sustainable development, Mollison draws on practices used by indigenous people all over the world. A sustainable system is one that in its lifetime will produce the energy required for its construction and maintenance. Water collection, sewage disposal, food, fuel and fodder are produced and managed on-site or communally. Mollison refers to permaculture practitioners worldwide as 'our own nation', indicating his vision of separation from, rather than collaboration with, existing political economic systems.

E. F. Schumacher was another early theorist of the movement. His 1973 classic, *Small is Beautiful*, proposed small-scale ecological economics that would provide meaningful livelihoods, peace and equity. In 1975, the Dag Hammarskjold Foundation published *What Now? Another Development*, which emphasized several important aspects of sustainable development. It must be needs-based, endogenous (based on cultural sovereignty), self-reliant and ecological. To accomplish such development, structural transformation in economic activities, power and social relations would be necessary (Ekins 1992: 99–100). Duane Elgin's popular (1981) book, *Voluntary Simplicity*, pursued environmental morality and first world visions of the good life simultaneously by proposing that great pleasures were to be had through gardening, bicycling and relationships with nature. Bioregionalism (named by Peter Berg, along with 'rehabitation') was popularized by Kirkpatrick Sale's 1985 *Dwellers in the Land*. Bioregionalism suggests that there are ecological bases for human geographies. Bioregions provide good guidelines for appropriate territorial delineations of self-sufficient economies.

Echoing Schumacher, development scholar (and permaculturalist) F. E. Trainer sees a shift to appropriate development for the rich countries as quite easy and realistic because of 'the magnitude of the present avoidable waste [and] the many alternative resource-cheap ways that are available' (1989: 504). He recommends:

> reduction or elimination of many unnecessary products, designing goods to last and to be repaired ... decentralizing ... moving food production closer to [consumption] ... increasing self-sufficiency of households ... edible urban landscapes ... [deprofessionalizing] tasks presently performed by bureaucrats and professionals ... increasing time spent 'working' in ... backyards ... local businesses, and community groups close to home. The central principle is the building of thriving, small-scale economics which are highly self-sufficient and integrated ... secur[e] from external economic fluctuations. (ibid.: 504)

Trainer's vision of sustainable ecosystems is based on an economy without import/export dependencies or transportation costs, which facilitates priority being placed on community, creativity and growing things. Such development focuses productive resources on meeting local human needs because necessary goods will no longer be imported and productive resources will no longer be used up in producing goods for export.

Indigenous people, through their own political groups, articulate a vision of sustainability, including the requirement of sufficient land to live with sustainable use of natural resources under autonomous collective forms of management. The Centre for Indigenous Peoples and Communities of Eastern Bolivia defines the necessary amount of land as 200 hectares per family (IWGIA 1989: 166–7). Sri Lankan and Indian alternative development organizations pursue culturally appropriate development on a village level, through religious and non-religious non-governmental organizations. Care must be taken as first world people recognize the value of third world knowledge resources. Without working to ensure self-determination for third and fourth world peoples, harvesting their knowledge is just more colonial theft (Vellinga 1971).

To achieve international equity, first world sustainable development movements focus on making the first world sustainable so as to reduce the extraction of third world resources. Sustainable development internationally means the first world taking responsibility for having underdeveloped the third world, and figuring out how to make the first world sustainable – Weinberg calls this 'scaling back of over-development' (1991: 159). By 1987, first world environmentalists had begun to recognize that 'to be more effective at saving tropical Rain Forests ... what we need is to get our foot off the throat of the Rain Forests ... Our tax dollars and our capital are financing a lot of destructive projects. Our corporations are cutting down the forests, and the overconsumption and the waste of our society and ourselves as consumers are all part of that problem.'[3] Internationally, a large number of governmental and non-governmental organizations promote sustainable development. In addition, there are many successful experiments with totally sustainable communities, many of which have communal governance systems. Such communities often have an educational component, offering courses and open access to their communities as working models.

Urban sustainability movements insist that cities can use resources responsibly and maintain a high quality of life. A host of enthusiastic inventors create designs for energy production and conservation, waste treatment, household heating, transportation and water management that make possible sustainable residences and communities. Consumption reduction movements try to get individuals to take responsibility for the externalized costs of their consumption. The Enough! Campaign, founded in 1992, headquartered in Manchester, England, introduces its anti-consumption message by saying that:

> any proposed solutions to the problems of world poverty, environ- mental destruction and social alienation will fail, unless they also address the role that the consumerist lifestyle plays in creating these problems ... in a world of limited resources, a system that advocates an ever-increasing level of consumption, and equates such consumption with personal well-being, economic progress and social fulfilment, is a recipe for ecological disaster ... if we in the wealthy nations want to see a just, stable and sustainable world, we are going to have to con- front the issue of how unfairly its resources are distributed in favour of a wealthy minority ... it is a myth to insist that rejecting con- sumerism also means rejecting our basic needs, our technology, our stylishness, or our quality of life.

Enough! distributes statistical data on inequality, the drawbacks of unsustainable consumption, the pleasures of neighbourhood-based economies, the impacts of anti-consumption on jobs, and critique of mainstream organizations. 'International Buy Nothing Day' was moved in 1996 to Black Friday, the largest shopping day of the year (the day after the US Thanksgiving) to intensify the anti-consumption message.[4]

Internationally, sustainable development advocates are increasingly critiquing agribusiness. The term 'inappropriate technology' is being used to refer to crops that are not indigenous to the climate, requiring excessive chemical or water inputs when traditional crops can be grown more easily. This usually happens when multinational firms promote the production of standardized (such as McDonalds' favourite Russet Burbank [Shiva 1991: 208]) or luxury export crops over traditional sustenance crops. Experts are recognizing that secondary infestations are increasing as a result of pesticide use; there are major economic consequences of out-of-control pest infestations that can be traced to the excessive marketing of pesticides by chemical companies. In response to the agro-industrial invasion, militant farmers' unions and farmers' cooperatives are cropping up all over. They seek social equity and express ecological concerns. They substitute social organization for advanced technology. For example, instead of advocating dams, they rebuild social water management organizations. Farmers in Southern Europe have returned to using irrigation cooperatives. The National Farmers' Union of Canada articulates sustainable farmers' focus on corporations as the enemy of sustainable development activists.

> Governments have let it happen that the control over the most basic needs of the people has been surrendered to an increasing degree to transnational companies. The undemocratising of this essential control is the central element of rural depopulation, urban slums and food related problems ... Sustainable agriculture must be based on a mutual understanding with our society: farmers have an obligation to society as providers of safe and nutritious food products and as the stewards of soil, water, air and natural landscapes; society in return will have to accept the role of enabling farmers to fulfil their obligations by providing safeguards against the loss of incomes below an acceptable level and the eviction from their farms and homes.

Farmers all over the world are rediscovering indigenous farming practices, including dense intercropping (mixed crops in one field), which produces a greater mass of food per acre, provides a complete nutritional mix, self-fertilizes in the form of mulch from the plants and is pest-resistant (Meyer and Moosang 1992). Fields are self-fertilizing because the mulch from all the different plants provides rich nutrients for the soil, trees provide nitrogen-fixing and decrease erosion, and natural pest predators – such as crickets, ladybirds, and grasshoppers – control pests (Lampkin 1990; Cleveland 1991; Goering et al. 1993). Indigenous farming technologies can be successful with minimal irrigation; Hopi Indians farm with less than ten inches of rain per year and no irrigation.

While extensive knowledge about organic agriculture exists in the world, agro-industry has invaded the systems of many farmers and entire regions; the remaining knowledge is scattered and threatened. Heirloom nurseries, seed museums and libraries, organic seed companies and demonstration gardens are playing an important role in the preservation and redistribution of this knowledge. Universities and research centres have been created to collect sustainable knowledge and train practitioners. Wageningen Agricultural University in Holland has a programme to 'develop and disseminate the scientific knowledge needed to sustainably supply society's demands for sufficient, healthy food and a good environment for humans, plants and animals'. The American Institute of Urban and Regional Affairs in Maryland offers a PhD in sustainable development. The University of Bonn has an Institute of Organic Agriculture.

In 1990 the largest-scale conversion ever undertaken from conventional to organic agriculture began. Cuba's organic agriculture revolution is but one aspect of a significant world-historical experiment with delinking. With the loss of socialist trading partners, Cuba suffered a 57 per cent decline in access to food, over a 90 per cent decline in access to chemical inputs, and over a 50 per cent decline in access to petroleum needed to run agricultural equipment. Suddenly in 1990 it was necessary to 'essentially double food production while more than halving inputs – and at the same time maintaining export crop production so as not to further erode the country's desperate foreign exchange position' (Rosset with Cunningham 1994). Fortunately, a group of Cuban scientists had been actively researching alternative agriculture since 1982. Predator pests are being introduced in place of pesticides. Traditional vegetables are being grown in greater quantities, and urban gardens are promoted.

Other sustainable development activities include urban composting programmes (in Vancouver, BC, the city provides bins and support) and even composting *services* (in San Francisco, USA, a small company sends cyclists to make weekly collections of compostables, returning compost for plants and gardens). Local environmental organizations provide educational materials on indoor composting techniques for apartment-dwellers. The Rainbow Plan in Nagai, Japan, is organized around processing urban compostables for local farmland and selling more local produce in town. Muto Ichiyo says of the plan:

> Processing urban organic garbage into compost is not a new idea; it's being tried by quite a few cities. The Rainbow Plan was new in the sense that it was guided by a clear vision of reconstituting the whole community of Nagai into a self-reliant and ecologically sound community worthy of being passed on to future generations. (Ichiyo 1998: 12)

Nagai's plan is an example of a model that analyses the 'foodshed' (Getz 1991; Hendrickson 1993) and strengthens the local 'marketscape'

(Green 1995) for local producers. Building new 'foodlinks' (Auld et al. 1999) between farmers, consumers and food-serving institutions provides security for farmers and eaters alike. New political economic formations are being conceptualized and built by the movement.

In 1965, a new approach to small-scale farming was begun outside Tokyo. Called in Japanese 'farming with a face on it', the basic idea is that urban families buy annual shares in a farm's produce and receive a weekly basket of the harvest. The system provides security for small farmers and healthy organic produce for families, and greatly reduces agricultural waste by reducing transportation (from an average of 1,300 miles to a maximum of 200 miles), storage, spoilage (25 per cent of agribusiness produce is thrown away), and chemical use (by avoiding monocropping). The first European 'Community Supported Agriculture' (CSA) was founded in West Germany in 1968. By 1978 a Zurich CSA was supplying vegetables to 400 families and milk to 600. The first US CSA was founded in South Egremont, MA in 1985. The original Tokyo CSA now feeds 400 Tokyo families. By 1994, 400 US CSAs were feeding some 80,000 people (and most CSAs have waiting lists). There are 80 projects in the UK, called 'Linking Farmers with Consumers'. CSAs encourage families and children to reconnect with farmers, farming and land by hosting harvest celebrations at the farm and also by encouraging members to pay part of their share in labour on the farm. People who purchase organic produce through a CSA pay slightly less than they would for commercially marketed organics. The system also plays a role in educating consumers to eat produce that is in season locally (Imhoff 1996).

Farmers' markets play an important role in rebuilding local food systems. In 1977 California small farmers won an important change in agribusiness law with the repeal of a Department of Food and Agriculture restriction that prevented family farmers from selling directly to the public except from their own property. The state started a farmers' market programme. California alone now hosts 300 weekly farmers' markets, up from only four in the late 1970s.[5] Certified farmers' markets require that all vendors actually grow the food they sell. In California, as elsewhere, the movement has been very successful in restoring non-corporate food options and a non-corporate economic arena. The US Department of Agriculture documents 2,500 markets, but admits it does not know about them all. In 1995 alone it learned about 750 new ones around the country.[6] Some farmers' markets accept food stamps and even the national government has provided special farmers' market vouchers through a social welfare programme. Recently, in response to demand, Paris has added two organic farmers' markets to its existing 70 open-air fresh food markets.[7] Farmers' markets improve nutrition and support local small-scale farmers. They also re-personalize and bring community into the economy.

US sustainable development has recently made a very important turn. The Community Food Security movement has focused on food issues in low-income urban communities. It works to link small farmers and the organic agriculture movement with low-income urban residents who often have little access to affordable food due to super-market redlining. As Cook and Rodgers (1996) note, 'supermarket chains have become a meeting point for agriculture conglomerates and middle class consumers – leaving small farmers and rural and urban low-income groups hungry'. The Community Food Security movement provides the tools to build 'a more democratic food system' by reconceptualizing the food economy around 'community need'.[8] The Community Food Security Coalition has developed new linkages between food banks, family farm networks, anti-poverty organizations, community development organizations, farmers' markets and the sustainable agriculture movement, seeking to organize them around 'the notion that all people should have access to a nutritious diet from ecologically sound, local, non-emergency sources'. Challenging corporate agriculture by de-concentrating market and production are seen as necessary elements of the movement. Low-income urban community organic agriculture programmes have been very successful as economic development, nutrition and youth programmes. New alliances include hunger activists, welfare advocates, economic justice activists, government food and health agencies, small farmers and other local food producers, and church and other charitable feeding programmes.

Toronto's food security programme (run by a 'food policy council') includes special CSA boxes with pre-cut vegetables for senior citizens and a Caribbean box including both local and imported vegetables for Caribbean cooks. In 1994, 43 boxes were sold per week; in 1997, 4,600 a week were sold, 50 per cent to low-income people. For the Toronto

Food Policy Council, food boxes are just the beginning. They assist organizations to get community kitchens and gardens started, they have an incubator kitchen for start-up businesses in the food industry, run a catering company and hold classes on making baby food at home.

Another way to provide food security to urban residents is by developing urban farms. Open urban land can be used for raising mixed crops for the sustenance of as much of the community as possible. In this way, community labour will be going to meet community needs, food can be de-commodified on a small scale, and good nutrition will be possible at low cost. Farmer Michael Abelman points out that even in Manhattan, 2,000 acres are available that could be used to provide food and jobs in neighbourhoods.[9] Jar Smit, President of the Urban Agriculture Network, encourages us to imagine an 'edible urban landscape'. Already 14 per cent of the food produced in the world is produced in cities. Where urban and suburban land is currently being used for grass and flowers, fruit trees and vegetable plots would be a much more beautiful use. Some urban farmers in Victoria are working warily with a developer to create a plan for a condominium complex with all-edible landscaping and its own farm and greenhouse.[10] Canada has an Office of Urban Agriculture, and, since 1994, a web page called Urban Agriculture Notes. Even the United Nations has got on board this movement, issuing a 1996 book on urban agriculture, which found urban food production increasing more rapidly than urban population, at an incredible rate.[11] Urban gardeners in New York and many other cities are experimenting with rooftop vegetable gardens. Some gardens are devoted to producing healthy food for people with AIDS.

In the USA, an organization called Chefs' Collaborative 2000 (founded in 1993), now has over a thousand members pursuing the concept of 'sustainable cuisine', which 'celebrates the pleasures and aesthetics of food while recognizing the impact of food choices on our health, environment, and the preservation of cultural diversity'. It also asserts that 'good, safe, wholesome food is a basic human right'. Chefs in Los Angeles, Boston, San Francisco and Berkeley, who had been involved with soup kitchens and other approaches to hunger, began to experiment with urban agriculture. They organized donors, acquired urban land and brought in organic farmers to train low-income urban residents in agriculture. Chefs ensure the economic viability of urban farms by committing to purchase their vegetables there.[12] Chefs who admit they were attracted to organic agriculture mainly because of the improved taste of the produce comment: 'I will never again look at a glass of wine or a plate of food and not wonder how it was grown.'[13] They are educating themselves and others about agricultural practices, building urban gardens, and changing their menus to be regional and seasonal. A related development is the European Slow Food movement, which recognizes the importance of small-scale producers in high-quality and diverse food options.[14] Its 1989 Manifesto challenges the 'machine' as a 'life model' and the slavery of speed, and proposes the 'firm defense of quiet material pleasure [as] the only way to oppose the universal folly of Fast Life'.[15]

One of the interesting aspects of chefs' involvement is that it provides a clear indication of the cross-class nature of this movement. While farmers' markets are important to food security movement in low-income communities, they are also a means to draw an ever-increasing share of food spending from high-income people and the chefs of exclusive restaurants. Stable contracts with restaurants increase the financial security of small farms. The health, food quality and environmental issues that organic agriculture takes on are cross-class issues.

The movements emerging to reclaim communities' relationships with food are precious for first worlders because we have the documentation about how to reverse the corporatization of the whole food system, not only technically but in terms of institutions, policies and social organization. While we have alternative techniques for housing, health, energy and transport, we do not have an understanding of the political economic systems that would be necessary to support de-corporatization of those systems.

Around the world people are motivated by ecological concerns and indigenous cultural visions to maintain or recover ecological habitats and livelihoods and the communal social forms and economies that can sustain communities. Indigenous communities suffering cultural invasion are developing systems based on traditional practices and knowledge, and third world countries are returning to simpler economic approaches having experienced the multiple failures of industrialization. First world environmentalists are seeking to establish sustainable low-consumption communities. Low-income communities, including urban and communities of colour, are drawing on communal knowledge and regional resources to develop urban gardens and relationships with farmers. As Wendell Berry and others argue, sustainable development also promises to enhance the quality of work (Berry 1996). Sustainable development advocates point out that projects like reforestation and low-tech sustainable organic agriculture would provide plentiful jobs for all. Grassroots sustainable development is committed to the elimination of both poverty and ethnocentrism.

In 1987 the United Nations held a conference on environment and development, and the World Commission on Environment and Development produced what is known as the Brundtland Report on sustainable development, which defined it as: 'Development that meets the needs of the present without compromising the ability of future generations to meet their own needs' (WCED 1987). The idea that sustainability can coexist with growth-style economic development co-opts the radical political economy proposed by the grassroots movement. This approach is echoed in official versions of sustainable development put forth by governments and NGOs. For example, the Centre for Environment and Development for the Arab Region and Europe defines its major objective as 'capacity building of national institutions within the region to enhance environmental management and influence *accelerated development*'.[16] The Gulf of Mexico Business Council for Sustainable Development, founded by Mexican and American corporate executives, builds partnerships, policy and sustainable development projects 'to support sound and sustained economic growth'. Suddenly what is sustainable is not the ecosystem, but the rate of growth! Moreover, institutions (including corporations) are accorded the same survival rights as ecosystems. This co-opted vision is what was promoted as Agenda 21 at the 1992 Rio de Janeiro Earth Summit. In contrast, grassroots sustainable development movements consistently repudiate growth and the rights and rationality of corporations to participate in economic decision-making.

The conference recognized the profound need to transform the industrial economy and to create a sustainable economy guided by the ethical values of social equity, economic prosperity, environmental responsibility, and cultural authenticity. Particular attention was given to human rights and to the challenge of building a sustainable economy in the context of social justice. (Concluding Statement, Conference on Ethics and the Culture of Development: Building the Sustainable Economy, 31 May–5 June 1998, Havana, Cuba)

Sustainable development emphasizes the resources and needs of the locality, and focuses production almost entirely on local basic needs and simple pleasures, delinking from larger economies. To implement such development, a great deal of knowledge about agricultural, economic and social techniques is needed. Once delinking is accomplished, there is no need to mention corporations. However, when sustainable development is discussed, the corporate economy is a major barrier to national sustainability and the integrity of localities. The seriousness of particular national and international sustainable development organizations can be judged by the extent to which they work to get corporations out of localities. Sustainable development impressively documents that people already have the relevant knowledge, and arrogant scientists are nearly always wrong about the things that matter. Not only do scientists have much less experience than traditional people who have been refining their agricultural and social systems for upwards of ten thousand years, but they often see no need to modify theories and techniques in response to the place to which they are applying them.

Small Business

A variety of movements can be categorized as defence and celebration of small-scale entrepreneurship. These include informal enterprises, institutionalized public markets, small business associations, campaigns against malls and corporate retail, community currency and punk 'Do-It-Yourself'.

Related to the redevelopment of farmers' markets as discussed in the section on sustainable development is the defence of informal sector vending, open-air markets, flea markets and public markets. They are sources of low-cost fresh food and goods, survival economies, business incubators, human-scale, sustainable and safe. Public markets are sustainable because they assist small farmers and entrepreneurs, require little infrastructure, and recycle goods and materials. Paris provides an annual US$4 million subsidy to support public markets. However, as documented by OpenAir Market Net, street-vendors are threatened by police harassment and are outlawed in many places. They are also regularly swept aside out of sight of international guests. In Mexico City and elsewhere, informal vendors' associations are organized. One such has a dues-paying membership of 5,000. The forbidding of street-vending in São Paulo, Brazil, provoked a huge march in July 1997. In Lima, Peru, 'the street-vendors' struggle' has become a social movement and is embraced by other movements. Women street-vendors in Durban, South Africa, have organized the Self-Employed Women's Union.

In the USA, UK, Puerto Rico and Canada small businesses are organizing to challenge mall and 'big box' retail developments. A satirical web page, 'The Big Box', invites webbers to 'find out what we're doing to the environment, and ... what happened to our competition ... (If We Don't Sell It, You Can't Get It!)'. The website is maintained by an owner of a hardware store that 'serves the community, providing the things they want or need at a fair price and in a convenient location ... employ[ing] people from the town and surrounding communities ... [and] reinvest[ing] locally'. Sprawl-busters is a consulting firm that 'help[s] communities stop the big box bull-dozers'. Its web page boasts having assisted 51 communities to 'reject megastores (at least once)'. Another web page, 'Us against the Wal', presents the story of Gig Harbor WA in four chapters. In Chapter 3, 'The Fight', townspeople figure out how many different ways to tell the corporation that they do not want it to come. But the politicians say: 'We can serve the community better by working *with* the huge corporation and perhaps try to convince it to paint the big-box a pretty color ... [and] negotiate that the huge corporation be required to at least leave a few trees.' (It was replacing a 20-acre wetland.) The fourth chapter posed the question of local autonomy, asking 'Does a community have this right? Can a village protect and preserve its "quality of life" by saying "NO" to a huge corporation or any other threat to its essential nature?' WalMart eventually withdrew. The Council of Canadians provides information about Big Box WalMart stores, critiquing their misleading low-price strategy, union-busting tactics, environmental impact and brutal treatment of purchased/converted stores. A local group encourages citizens to critique the 'seductive vision where convenience, rather than community, is the center of our daily lives'. Resistance to WalMarts has been mounted in Argentina, Brazil and Britain, drawing on the economic effects documented in the USA and Canada.

Another small business approach that attempts to strengthen the local economy against corporate invasions is community or local currency. Local currency facilitates barter and other local economic relationships. These systems go far beyond supporting local businesses. They actually create micro-business by assisting people in marketing skills and products that they would not otherwise sell. Ithaca, New York is home to Paul Glover's brainchild 'Ithaca HOURS' a currency system based on the hour (of labour) instead of the dollar, which since 1991 has added over $1.5 million of trading to the local economy. Another 40 communities are copying this system. HOURS express (but do not enforce) the idea that people should trade their labour on an hour-for-hour basis. In Ithaca, 300 local businesses accept HOURS. Use of HOURS benefits service professionals like masseurs and hairstylists whose business increases, lower-middle-class people who sell a few extra hours of their a week doing something that they enjoy and thereby managing to afford goods and services normally beyond their budgets, and working-class people, for whom HOURS income increases their buying power and makes affordable goods they would never have ordinarily consumed, such as art or music lessons for children. Because of HOUR-augmentation, Ithaca farmworkers are relatively well paid. Over 300 communities in France (those where unemployment is 12 per cent or higher) have implemented a similar system called 'Grain de Sel' which pays for organic produce, rent, cheese, cakes, plumbing, haircuts, and so on.[17]

The other major community currency system is the Local Exchange Trading System, or LETS, which was first developed in 1983 in Canada and was quickly copied in 20 other North American communities by 1988. By 1996, Britain had 200 systems and several hundred exist in Australia and New Zealand. LETS works with computerized debit/credit accounts instead of with actual paper currency, requiring centralization of the system and reporting of transactions. Landsman publishes an extensive guidebook and provides software for use in setting up LETS. The following quote is from the introductory section:

All over the world communities suffer from a shortage of money, simply because there is only so much of it, it's gone elsewhere and they can't print their own. When you think about it, this situation is nonsensical. Money is merely a means of exchange ... It is a measure of value, like an inch measures length or a ton measures weight. There need never be a shortage of the measure. Imagine a carpenter not working because he has run out of inches! ... The problem suggests the solution ... creating local money to finance local needs, to generate wealth and protect us from poverty. A local currency can't leave the community it serves, so it ensures connections between people exchanging skills, goods and services. With a local currency, the community is less affected by fluctuations in the external money supply.

Local currency systems are not just a way to improve the economic fates of local people. They explicitly oppose corporate retail encroachment, environmental degradation and overconsumption. They describe themselves as attempts to achieve sustainability and community. 'They are inherently ecological, since they are needs-oriented and local' (Meeker-Lowry 1996: 449). Much attention was given to local currency at the 1997 The Other Economic Summit. Eminent economists, including Bernard Lietaer (repentant designer of the single European currency system), have published statements supporting this approach to protecting local economies:

Greed and fear of scarcity are in fact continuously created and amplified as a direct result of the kind of money we are using ... we can produce more than enough food to feed everybody, and there is definitely enough work for everybody in the world, but there is clearly not enough money to pay for it all. In fact, the job of central banks is to create and maintain that currency scarcity. The direct consequence is that we have to fight with each other in order to survive.[18]

Lietaer writes that money should operate as a standard of value and a medium of exchange and monetary policies should limit its role as a store of value, a tool for speculative profit and a tool of empire. Lietaer encourages the use of demurrage policies with local currencies. These policies discourage saving and encourage reinvestment by levying negative interest on money that is not spent. This increases circulation and values repair and improvements over speculation. Community currency mobilizes unused resources and links them with unmet needs. Frente Democratico Campesino from Chihuahua, Mexico, is experimenting with 'demonetized' barter relationships, attempting to develop direct exchanges with Latino communities in the USA.[19]

Another development that supports small businesses is alternative credit, through rotating and community credit organizations – also known as 'micro-lending'. The Grameen Bank in Bangladesh is one of the most famous instances, and builds solid financial institutions with extremely high repayment rates (over 98 per cent) with very poor borrowers and no collateral. Grameen provides loans to groups, which it trains and 'conscientizes'. Borrowers are 'encouraged to accept a sixteen-point programme for social justice, group solidarity and women's emancipation' (Ekins 1992: 124). It also has strong policies to pursue these goals: 'The bank is 75 percent owned by its borrowers ... Only borrowers may own shares; no-one may own more than one share; female shares may not be sold to men' (ibid.: 124). Micro-lending is an excellent example of approaches to development in which first world low income communities can look to third world communities for models (Starr and Rodgers 1995). Micro-lending reforms banking practices by asserting the bankability of the poor. It also brings traditional forms of collective social responsibility into modern credit institutions and into the capitalist economy. It enables people (particularly women) to start their own small or micro enterprises. (Micro-lending has recently been co-opted, with international conferences devoted to increasing the indebtedness of the third world poor even further.)

A less well-known form of anti-corporate entrepreneurship is Do-It-Yourself, a punk movement that proposes a particular mode of economy: explicitly anti-corporate and usually anti-profit small business. Initially developed as a critique of the corporate music scene, punk DIY has evolved into a self-conscious enclave industry of bands, independent labels, zines, e-zines, publishers, arts venues and small businesses. One small business owner, Srini Kumar, says about his company, Unamerican Activities:

> My enemy is a conspiracy of boredom, bad jobs, shitty t.v., crap music ... designed to anaesthesize us from the horrors of the working week and the truth about our exploitative economic empire ... This is a land

... bounded by our painful, STUPID history ... And ownership, owner-ship, ownership. Every bit of which is stolen, stolen, stolen – from the raw power and ingenuity of those who dreamed it, designed it, built it, maintained it, and cleaned up after it ... This company exists for one reason – to overturn, overturn, overturn ... You are SO MUCH MORE LIKELY to have a 'political' conversation within ten feet of one of our products.

The products include t-shirts, mugs, and stickers, 'low-tech solutions ... ready to turn you into a billboard for treason', with texts like:

whitey will pay	drugs help alot	
fuck work	fuck school	don't get caught
bored	broke	
bomb the mall	darn the gov't	warm the globe
I hate the rich	racism is typical	

The owners of Angry, Young and Poor of Lancaster (USA) have day jobs in order to be able to support their shop because 'all of us believe in the scene and what punk stands for'. The purpose of the store is 'to sell all stuff for punks made by punks ... kids just like us'. In order to encourage 'the DIY way of doing things' they 'sell stuff as cheap as possible'. A DIY web page calls itself 'anti-corporate' and states 'as long as we're losing money, we might as well do our best to serve the anti-corporate community'. Australian, French, Chilean, Scottish, Swedish and German bands announce themselves as DIY: 'No profit taken!!' 'Disgruntled red heads ... form rebel hardcore outfit in an effort to further the multicultural DIY conspiracy, make noise, ride bikes, and constantly criticize industrialized capitalist society.'

What is important about the anti-corporateness of DIY? Not only do practitioners decry specific aspects of corporate practices, they also recognize and organize explicitly against the cultural effects of corporations, the 'boredom' of the totalizing corporate culture about which Marcuse wrote. They are teaching young people about alter-natives to corporate-dominated economies and building theory and community around youth alienation.

Ethnic enclave economies are an omnipresent version of small-scale entrepreneurship. While some enclave entrepreneurs are enmeshed in global production lines managing sweatshop production on contract, not all enclave entrepreneurship is of this type. Enclaves are important sanctuaries for people of colour. Enclave merchants provide culturally specific goods and contribute to institution-building in their communities. One of the theorists of African American entrepreneurship is Tony Brown, who, when accused of being a capitalist, explained:

> I am *not* a capitalist ... I'm not interested in proving capitalism ... that this system is better than that system ... I'm trying to pay my rent and keep the phone working ... I don't know what you call that. Whatever you call that, that's what I do ... I am simply interested in this. There are 30 million of us. We earn $300 billion ... equal to the 14th richest nation in the world. We're 12 percent of the population. We buy 18 percent of the orange juice, 20 percent of the rice, 26 percent of Cadillac cars ... We have 350 black organizations [of] middle class blacks, one million [members] of which go to white hotels each summer. They spend $16 billion discussing white racism and black poverty ... We spend 6.6 percent of our money with one another, 93 percent with other people. I'm simply interested in creating structures so we can transfer that money back and most of all, not to any black person in this room, but to poor black people.[20]

Brown articulates a form of nationalism that draws on the diasporic traditions of self-determination (Franklin 1984), survival as a revolutionary act (Reagon 1982), sense of nationhood (Gwaltney 1980), and duty to 'uplift', not on the ideologies of capitalism. Particularly important ideas are *collective responsibility* for passing on human capital, an economic system *organized* to distribute wealth among the community, and establishing a basis from which to resist oppression.

What are the political economic implications of small-scale capitalism? Small business advocates are not socialists and do not articulate the ecological principles that sustainable development theory attributes to them. Will small business be willing to stay small? Will the re-attainment of economic security convince small business people to stay closely linked with their local community and to consider the ecological limits that sustainable development advocates insist will naturally become more obvious to them? (These issues will be discussed further in the concluding chapter.) The discourse that is available suggests that small business people under pressure are developing a critical consciousness that includes values of community and environment that go beyond capitalist values. They explain how corporate economic advantages (some provided through policy, others, like group insurance rates, through corporate collaboration) make it hard for small businesses to provide the working conditions they would like to provide.

Small business owners offer a diverse constituency. They are also extremely valuable members of a social movement because they know how to produce food and other needed goods with little capital and narrow profit margins. However, participants in the various versions of this movement do not recognize one another as allies. Sustainable development activists have linked up with local currency activists, but ethnic enclave economies and DIY punks have not been recruited.

Sovereignty Movements

Colonialism, the devastating political economic system of invasion and appropriation, is not over. Many territories are still held under 'protectorates' or outright imperialism; they include the nation of Hawai'i, the Commonwealth of Puerto Rico, Guam, East Timor, the Philippines, and indigenous peoples' lands throughout the world. Explicitly anti-colonial struggles continue against imperial states, dams, corporate mining, oil and forestry projects. While many of these movements have internationalized their struggle and act in solidarity with one another, their newly globalized struggles are to maintain a local way of life.

Indigenous peoples' regional and international conferences and public statements present their needs with great consistency as: halting genocide; reclaiming community lands and securing their possession for future generations; honouring the authority and autonomy of indigenous leadership and decision-making; protecting sources of sustenance, which requires ending forestry and other exploitative practices that destroy sustenance resources; replacing Western cultural invasion practices, including Western health practices, with indigenous ones; and transforming educational institutions into culturally nurturing ones that teach and support indigenous languages, culture, and history. As stated by Julio Tumiri Apaza, indigenous struggles are for 'land, culture, and autonomy' (IWGIA 1989). Increasingly, third and fourth world struggles to achieve food security, environmental sanctity and control

over education and health institutions confront the international structures that constrain them with the accusation of genocide. They
compare the economic, political, military and cultural operations of
these structures with the mechanisms of colonialism, which decimated
indigenous communities.

The 1991 Covenant of the Unrecognized Nations and Peoples'
Organizations emphasizes the right to self-determination, insisting that
individual and collective rights are 'inextricably linked' and that control
over the natural environment is crucial to the exercise of self-
determination. The Declaration of the Rights of Indigenous Peoples
(composed under the auspices of the United Nations Commission on
Human Rights) asserts the right of self-determination, collective rights
and 'distinctive and profound' relationship to the total environment
of the lands, territories and resources.

In May 1997 Junin communities in Ecuador demanded government
intervention in Mitsubishi mining plans; receiving no response, the
affected communities removed and inventoried all Mitsubishi goods
from the mine site and then burned the mine to the ground.[21] In
February 1997, 4,000 U'wa threatened mass suicide if oil exploration
was undertaken on their land. The movement in opposition to the
Narmada dam in India has been so successful in bringing international
attention to the destruction of indigenous lands that first Japan and
then the World Bank pulled out as funders. When the central government and one of the participating states attempted to forge ahead, the
Supreme Court issued an injunction against further construction and
that state's government fell. In early 1997, the Tribal Areas, which form
about 7 per cent of India, partly in response to the WTO, declared that
the village is the highest form of government. Seed patents and other
things corporations are trying to control will require adjudication
village-by-village, through local decision-making bodies.[22] A town in
the state of Morenos, Mexico, disengaged from the state, declaring
itself a free democratic municipality, in part to oust a Japanese golf
course development. Mapuche people in Chile are refusing to exchange
their land to make way for the Ralco dam, a project of the Endesa
corporation. The Indigenous Unification Council of the Central Jungle
of Peru confronts the French oil multinational, Elf.

Indigenous people question politically the value of 'modernization',
'progress' and pragmatic politics that are artefacts of colonial culture.

They practise traditional forms of decision-making, such as councils of elders and chiefs. Haunani Kay-Trask, member of Ka Lahui Hawaii, the leading nationalist organization in Hawai'i, explains that she is not grateful to the USA for bringing 'democracy': voting doesn't deliver justice. Indigenous people are able to recognize the lie of export-oriented national development because their land and society are already ravaged by export-oriented development in service to international markets. Indigenous peoples' anti-colonial movements reach out to connect with people who suffer the same economic effects in other parts of the world and explicitly target corporations as the colonial enemy with which third world comprador states collaborate. Indigenous perspectives and values provide an important foundation for seeing corporations for what they are and for realizing that they are not beneficent.

The idea that colonialism is the problem and sovereignty is the solution is an analysis also made by public intellectuals in first world communities of colour. Cynthia Hamilton explains that local environmental justice efforts clarify the need for economic democracy on a larger scale. What is needed is a 'reconceptualization of evolution that would include decentralization of power' (1993: 63). Even in the USA, separatist struggles based on economic issues are recognizing who their enemies are. African American activists frequently describe their communities during segregation as more healthy culturally, socially and economically. Similarly, French Jews criticized their 'emancipation' from the ghettos as a means of destroying their culture, 'whereas within the walls of the ghetto this identity had flourished' (Kepel 1991: 7). A few of these movements have resulted in urban 'incorporation' struggles. East Palo Alto was successful in forming a separate city so that Black people could be self-governing. The contiguous communities of colour in Boston, calling their territory 'Mandela', have also been organizing for incorporation. Their referendum was defeated by a concerted attack that claimed Mandela did not contain sufficient tax base and know-how to run a city.

There are a number of extant and new Black Panther organizations in the USA, now allying as the New Panther Vanguard Movement (NPVM). The Ten Point Platform of the NPVM demands reparations and '*independent* community-based economic, social, cultural, and political institutions that serve the collective needs of our communities'. In Milwaukee, one of the groups calls itself the Black Panther Militia.[23] For now, the emergence of sovereignty themes is a growing whisper, whose consequences are yet to be clarified.

In Eastern Europe, as cultural communities shape new political formations, we can observe the 'current revival of communal identity' (Boulding 1993: 213) as a reaction to cultural homogenization and to de-colonization's unfulfilled promises of cultural autonomy and authority in first and third world alike. In contrast to the ruling paranoia that endorsing people's rights will lead to infinite fragmentation, institutions like the Unrepresented Nations and Peoples Organization invite newly articulated peoples to their membership.

Not only indigenous peoples but third world nations, and particular communities within all nations, also struggle for sovereignty and territory. Sovereignty enables barriers to be raised against outsiders' projects. Bangladesh exercised sovereignty by banning 1,700 dangerous or useless drugs in 1982. At that time, national sovereignty was challenged with 'colossal pressure from foreign governments and multi-nationals' (Ekins 1992: 173). In the face of the WTO, such sovereign moves are untenable. Politically sovereign peoples face with increasing starkness the decision of having to eschew international loans and trade because they must maintain economic independence to maintain political sovereignty. The economic and political options modelled by indigenous peoples' struggles may soon be recognized as important to other sovereign entities. Peter Berg of the Planet Drum Foundation suggests slogans like 'US and NAFTA out of Shasta Bioregion'.

Religious Nationalisms

> ... undeniable evidence of a deep malaise in society that can no longer be interpreted in terms of our traditional categories of thought ... They are true children of our time: unwanted children, perhaps, bastards of computerization and unemployment. (Gilles Kepel 1991)

Religious nationalist movements are portrayed as authoritarian movements unallied with democratic humanism that reassert traditional social formations, including patriarchy. Supposedly, they essentialize their own racial and cultural identity and that of neighbours (sometimes brutally). They use violence as a social movement strategy. Worst of all, religious nationalism is irrational. It lives permanently outside the bounds of reasonable, democratic dialogue and is fervently committed to its positions. People wish there were some way to contain religious nationalism, to rescue people from its socially backward projects and to protect ourselves from its inexplicable, unpredictable eruptions of violence. These movements are a shunned other.

More recently, religious studies scholars have defended the rationality of religious nationalist thought. But even sympathetic readings do not consider the possibility that they have a message for seculars, that what they are saying has meaning, value and importance for our own lives. What if religious nationalists are more than rational in the context of their own local cosmology, what if religious nationalists are rational in the context of the global forces that are reshaping our worlds alike? Is it unthinkable that religious nationalism could offer a contribution to humanitarian struggles for democracy and equity?[24]

What is religious nationalism? According to Mark Juergensmeyer (1993), second and third world religious nationalist movements reject secular nationalism with its continuing ties to European economic and ideological hegemony. What does it mean to reject the modern secular state? It means to reject the 'moral order' – or, more accurately from a religious nationalist perspective, to reject the lack of moral order of the existing state and to assert (even violently) the urgency of the re-establishment of possibly reimagined but nevertheless promising old and supposedly eternal values and ways of living. Gilles Kepel proposes that it is the sudden visibility of 'human misery', wrought by both 'liberal and Marxist secular utopias', that has produced a number of movements that 'demand ... a link with religion as the foundation of the social system' (1991: 5). As described by Kepel, beginning in the mid-1970s, Islamic movements developed a new approach based on the conclusion that in the final analysis 'the modernism produced by reason without God has not succeeded in creating values' (1991: 2, 4). Religious nationalist movements are trying to gain control of institutions and/or territory so that they may regulate the main agents of invasion of their culture, and their social and moral order.

Most scholars of religious nationalism dismiss the possibility that these movements have a basic political-economic dimension. To document Iranian fundamentalism's lack of political-economic concern, Martin Riesebrodt (1990) shows that the multi-class movement is not based on 'economic interests' – instead it is about 'common values and ideal ways of life' threatened by 'nationalization and inter-nationalization of the market' (184, 189). The movements were made up of the following groups: clergy who find their 'upward social mobility' curtailed; urban migrants with 'hope of rising from their slum or shanty milieu'; 'traditionalist middle class ... independent business people, merchants, and artisans ... now regarded as un-modern and backward' who increasingly face 'economic insecurity and an enormous loss in cultural prestige' with the coming of foreign enterprise; educated children of traditionalists whose 'striving for upward mobility ... is either disappointed or denied altogether'; and 'the uprooted' and 'dislocated masses' (ibid.: 186–90).

These groups shared 'sociomoral' concerns that were expressed by challenging 'the willingness of others to violate hitherto established rules', 'structural discrimination, exploitation, and impoverishment', increasing 'influence of "foreigners" [who] import their culture and economic enterprises and increasingly take over political power', and the state's collaboration with 'foreign' influence (1990: 195). Protest was directed at symbols of 'economic immorality', including big industrialists, war profiteers, banks and supermarkets (competing with the bazaar). Riesebrodt concludes that 'Not material interest but moral implications of changes in the economic structure and economic ethics were in the foreground of fundamentalist mobilization' (ibid.: 196). Fundamentalism's 'patriarchal moralism' is expressed through 'the defense of ... small enterprise organized along personalistic–patriarchal lines as the cornerstone of an economy regulated by religious moral-ism'. This form of economy is explicitly contrasted with 'large-scale depersonalized enterprises, whether state run or privately operated' – an approach 'distinct from both capitalism and socialism' (ibid.: 180–1). Inexplicably, Riesebrodt and many others conclude that because these movements are not explicitly anti-capitalist, or movements of the lowest classes exclusively, or articulated solely around material issues, they are therefore not political-economic movements. On my reading, there is plentiful evidence for political economic grievances.

John Foran's massive 1993 study of Iranian social movements provides excellent material through which to make a more complete analysis of the political-economic nature of religious nationalist struggle. He documents that historically cross-class populist alliances emerged in resistance to foreign economic domination and Shahs' ongoing collaboration with it. Islam was consistently used as the ideological and organizational basis for these movements. In the 1891 tobacco rebellion (against the Shah's granting of a monopoly concession to a British company), shopkeepers gathered at mosques, and religious leaders announced a consumers' boycott by suddenly declaring tobacco 'unclean' (1993: 64) and legitimizing political economic goals with statements such as 'How do you dare to sell to unbelievers the means of livelihood of the Muslims?' (ibid.: 167–8).

During the 1961 Oil Nationalization Movement, again meetings were held in mosques while workers went on strike (ibid.: 284–5). The movement was again urban, multi-class and focused on breaking 'Iran's external dependence on the West' (ibid.: 283). Likewise in building the 1978 revolution, a diverse array of merchants, secular democratic intellectuals, destitute urban marginals, workers and leftists recognized the institutional, moral and populist power of Islam as an organizing to further their goals. The merchant class funded religious leaders to build the movement because they perceived 'the shah and foreign capital ... clearly ... as threats to their livelihood' (ibid.: 376–90). Religious leaders 'activated a religious political culture of opposition to tyranny and foreign domination' (ibid.: 385) while the movement as a whole gathered Muslims and Marxists into a collective vision by linking 'true Islam with revolutionary activity'. According to Foran:

> *intertwined* economic, political, and ideological crises in the Iranian social formation ... [were] caused largely by the effects of *dependence* ... Most classes and groups ... had grievances as a result of a century of increasingly intense contact with the West ... the vast majority of medium and small traders had lost much of their standing. Artisans had suffered the collapse of their livelihood in many sectors, especially the formerly central handicraft textile one ... Peasants saw their standard of living inexorably decline as cultivation shifted from food staples to export crops ... Tribespeople witnessed the circumscribing of their economic activity by the new value placed on urban and agricultural production. (ibid.: 175–6)

Roger Friedland and Richard Hecht's ethnography and cultural analysis in *To Rule Jerusalem* also provides suggestive material for analysing religious nationalism. The anti-Zionist Israeli *haredim* oppose planners, big hotels, swimming pools, archaeologists, autopsies, disinterment, cinema, missionaries, national sports and pro-development banks. They defend non-market housing programmes and traditional livelihoods in modern institutions, such as prayer and blessing food. Their activism has scared off 'investment' from Jerusalem (1996: 191). Whatever we may think of their projects, the *haredim* show that religion can be used as a tool to defend territory.

Benjamin Barber's 1995 *Jihad vs. McWorld* imagines religious struggles for nation in several dialectical relations with a corporatized 'McWorld'. He sees that *jihads* are efforts to protect community and culture from corporate depredations. In *The Future of Islam in the Middle East* (1997), Mahmud A. Faksh explains that religion and politics are traditionally united and these movements insist that they do not need anything from other cultures.

In the USA there are two quite different religious nationalist movements. The one that is making a serious attempt at seizing state power is the moral majority/Christian coalition force, newly politicized fundamentalists and evangelicals who were reeled into politics by a couple of northeastern Catholics in order to swell Republican ranks (Stan 1995). More recently they have been transformed by public relations into a front for the corporate agenda of deregulation and tax cuts (Sklar 1995: 163). The other one is the radical fringe, which I call, as they call themselves, the Christian/Patriot movement. While portrayed in alternative media as part of a scary and well-connected new right continuum, Christian/Patriots are neither embraced by nor interested in the mainstream religious right, which violates many of their primary concerns. Like religious nationalism elsewhere, this movement has been a subject of political and media panic from both the mainstream and left. This discourse has lumped several quite different movements into one irrational, violent, racist package.

Like religious nationalism elsewhere, the Christian/Patriot movement is far from homogeneous in its relationship to religion, and many parts of it should not rightly be called religious at all. It is not seeking a simple institutionalization of religion into the state, as the mainstream religious right claims to.[25] The movement has a number of legitimate political and political economic concerns about local economics and politics. Like religious nationalism elsewhere, the Christian/Patriot movement has racist elements, and, like movements elsewhere, panicked accusations of racism are being used to delegitimize core concerns and proposals, which are democracy, populism and the rights of locality.

Both the Freemen and the militias subscribe to conspiracy theories that not only are not anti-Semitic but differ little from left-wing analyses, emphasizing the Trilateral Commission, the New World Order and GATT. 'Conspiracy theorists' are denigrated by the left for focusing on individuals rather than 'the system'. Their analyses of elite manoeuvrings echo no less revered a scholar than William Domhoff, author of the 1967 classic *Who Rules America?* Conspiracy analyses contain the theory that (capitalist) elites systematically network to protect collective interests. According to a critical analysis by Joel Schalit: 'Reviving nationalist sentiment by targeting international capital as responsible for the decline of American life has led the white working class to take up arms for the first time since the post-Civil War Ku Klux Klan.' Attorney-General Joe Mazurek says of the Montana militia movement, 'it's hardly a mystery why an increasing number of Montanans – and Westerners in general – have embraced the radical right. Threatened with the loss of jobs and traditional uses of the land, they fear they are losing control of their lives.' Mazurek explains that the Freemen have been successful at organizing farmers who are at risk of losing their land to banks.[26]

Although this exploration of religious nationalism is quite preliminary, it does suggest that these movements should be considered within the scope of options for political economic struggle. Scholars' dismissal of a fundamental political economic element in religious nationalist movements on the basis of inadequate evidence of relative deprivation or recent increases in inequality takes a far too narrow view of even the material aspects of political economy. Certainly in the USA: it is not about relative deprivation or about inequality compared with other countries. The political economic dimension is about national myths, the American Dream, mobility expectations, and so forth. Examinations of the political economic dimensions of religious nationalist movements in other places need to be less economistic and more fully political economic by incorporating colonialism, corporate imperialism, cultural and livelihood encroachments of capitalism, and symbolic promises. Moreover, the presence of religious and cultural concerns in the movement does not invalidate basic political economic concerns; it is quite likely that a damaging political economic regime will also affect cultural and religious realms.

Samuel Heilman explains that religious nationalist rigidity of life, practice and faith is not only about rigidity, or even only about loyalty to the cosmology it represents. When that rigidity is chosen and fought for against opposition, it takes on a further meaning. It is a liberation struggle: 'But we fought back by not disappearing, by not giving up our ways. We did not all cower' (1992). On the basis of this preliminary analysis, I hypothesize that religious nationalism may be a rejection of an imposed political economy that is not working for most people and, thereby, is wreaking moral chaos by disrupting traditional social patterns and the meaning-making power of culture. 'Getting rid of foreign imperialism' is a necessity for a religious nationalist movement in proportion to the degree to which the movement seeks to regain moral order over social life. A fight for moral order is necessarily a fight for political sovereignty over culture and morality. A fight for political sovereignty is necessarily a fight against invasion of the political economy. When religious nationalists or sovereignty movements say 'we want our culture back' or 'we want our moral order back' they are saying that someone else has control of it. And world-systems theorists know (even if religious nationalists only see part of the picture, such as: 'it's the Trilateral Commission', 'it's Western corporations', 'it's planners and hotels') that what is invading national and local political economies everywhere is multi-national corporate capital. But economic globalization, the expansion of a centralized economic system with its values (or lack of values) expressed through its products and its labour and environmental abuse, wreaks havoc with every aspect of local social structure and practice.

What is a political-economic struggle, after all? It is a struggle that seeks to rearrange the nature of material economic life on a structural (political) level. To say that the struggle of the *haredim* is not a political-economic struggle because it is, *instead*, a struggle to 'maintain cosmic order' (Friedland and Hecht 1996: 140) or to re-/assert meaning is to misunderstand why people wage political-economic struggles; which, per Marx himself, are rearrangements made necessary because human beings cannot be fully human – not rearrangements for their own sake.

Charlie Kurzman (1996) notes that as postcolonial people have felt that regular civil politics are not working, they have returned to pre-democratic institutions (or sought to meld the power of those institutions with the process of representative democracy) in order to assert moral order. Religious nationalist movements may be using religious institutions to 'extend the democratic imaginary' (Laclau and Mouffe 1985) by reasserting populism against political-economic oligarchy (both national and international) that disrupts traditional economic moralities, cultural integrity and anti-colonial visions of sovereignty. The US Civil Rights Movement and liberation theology as practised in Central and South America have shown that religious practice can be agentic: people will use culture or religion or whatever they have to confront colonialism in all its new guises (Juergensmeyer 1993: 143–5). The Iranian revolution demonstrated that political-economic struggles gain from culture-based criticisms of the full range of dangers posed by recolonization.

> So that the resistance to economic exploitation has also become a resistance to political hegemony, initially expressed in nationalist and cultural terms. Hence the revolutions in these countries are not necessarily class, socialist, revolutions – they do not begin as such anyway. They are not even nationalist revolutions as we know them. They are mass movements with national and revolutionary components – sometimes religious, sometimes secular, often both, but always against the repressive political state and its imperial backers. (Sivanandan 1990: 167)

Discussion

The Non-Governmental Organizations' meeting at Rio alongside the United Nations Earth Summit in 1992 issued the People's Earth Declaration, which conveyed 'broadly shared consensus' on a series of principles, including 'organizing life around decentralized relatively self-reliant local economies'. Leading grassroots organizations, working through a consensus process, insist that sustainable development is to be achieved through delinked relocalization (rather than through an improved corporate economy). Not only do such groups see corporations' logic as illegitimate, they insist that corporations have no place in the future.

Like movements in the other modes, one tries try to re-embed the economy in a socio-moral framework. Obviously, religious nationalism is not the only movement crying out for moral order. It is not the only movement that calls out to people to rediscover their most basic values, to cherish tradition and community and to refuse the goodies of modernity. In the small business movement, business people are turning against larger capitalists, using moral terms, emphasizing externalities, defining business as in service of a community, eschewing convenience and low prices and denying the legitimacy of corporate acts. Their ideology amounts to an attempt to change the rules (cosmology) of capitalism without actually resigning – yet it certainly goes beyond reformism. As the diversity of movements explored in this study shows, there are several different paths to the vision of a small-scale economy. All of these movements point to existing models that provide technical and institutional tools and on this basis insist that small-scale economies are eminently realistic. Defending an independent economy will require political autonomy. 'Separatism ... carries the threat of xenophobic nationalism – but it may also carry the hope of returning economic and political structures to human scale' (Weinberg 1991: 168–9).

Taking this mode seriously as a social movement immediately raises concerns about a number of feared meanings and consequences of local autonomy. Because first world social justice and social equity struggles have long been focused on universalist legislation and jurisprudence, the left often responds to both national and local autonomy with panic. Indeed, leftists seem to panic more about local autonomy than they do about the destruction of national politics as a site for civil rights. Religious nationalism is a particular flashpoint for left concerns about autonomous movements. Like indigenous sovereignty movements, it seeks to reassert moral order over the political economy, and requires local political autonomy in order to protect cultural integrity. Like these movements, with which the left is more sympathetic, it is anti-colonial, questions the notion of 'progress', and prioritizes local social life over capitalist goals. These issues will be explored more fully in the final chapter.

Notes

1. All unattributed quotes are from primary data collection.

2. The people who participated in property crime were very well organized and strategic about their transnational corporate targets. They have disseminated their philosophy about property crime as protest in a document entitled 'N30 Black Bloc Communiqué by ACME Collective', which is available at www.zmag.org and elsewhere on the worldwide web.

3. Environmentalist Randy Hayes at the Tropical Rainforest Conference, 18 October 1987, New York City, in Weinberg 1991: 158.

4. 'News and Updates', *Boycott Quarterly*, 13, Winter 1997: 34.

5. J. Michael Kennedy, 'A healthy crop', *Los Angeles Times*, 19 April 1996: E1–2.

6. Ibid.

7. Joel Malkin, report on the four panels at the 3rd International Public Market Conference, Philadelphia, 8–11 February 1996.

8. Andy Fisher, co-founder of the Community Food Security Coalition and author of the policy paper that led to the development of the 1996 Congressional Food Security Act.

9. Michael Abelman, 'Lessons from the past: inspiration for the future: a journey to the world's farms, gardens, and markets', lecture on 27 April 1994 in the Santa Barbara Community College's Continuing Education Division Lecture Series, 'From the Good Earth: Perspectives on Food, Farming, and Community', 1994, Santa Barbara, CA.

10. James MacKinnon, 'A future in farming: urban farmers working with a condo developer?', *Monday Magazine*, 1 February 1996.

11. UNDP, *Urban Agriculture: Food, Jobs and Sustainable Cities*, Habitat II Series, 1996. The book examines 18 third world countries and 12 first world cities.

12. Nina Simonds, 'Body and soul, nourished with pride', *New York Times*, 21 July 1993: B1, B5.

13. Suzanne Hamlin, 'A culinary Woodstock celebrates the garden', *New York Times*, 6 July 1994: B1, B6.

14. Dahlburg, John-Thor, 1998, 'Cooking up a reply to Big Mac: the slow food movement', *Los Angeles Times*, 18 November 1998: A1, A24.

15. It has a quarterly journal, *Slow*, via Mendicità Istruita, 14–12042 Bra (Cn) Italy. www.slowfood.com, international@slowfood.com.

16. My emphasis.

17. Bernard Lietaer interviewed by Sara van Gelder, 'Beyond greed and scarcity', *Yes!*, spring 1997.

18. Ibid.

19. Josette Griffiths, Tanya Hayes and Rachel Hays, 'Rural coalition develops alternatives to globalisation', *BorderLines 15*, 3(7), July 1995.

20. Ibid.

21. Rainforest Action Network, 'Ecuador forest communities shut down Mitsubishi mine – for now', RAN *Action Alert 130*, July/August 1997.

22. Vandana Shiva, at IFG Teach-In 3.

23. 'LA summit launches national panther movement', *Black Panther International News Service*, Summer 1997: 1(14).

24. This section draws on scholarly texts for analysis of second/third world religious nationalism. It also includes my empirical work on US religious nationalism. Note that Islamic movements in the USA are nationalist/separatist, in that they seek independence, but they are not religious nationalist because they are not making claims on the state.

25. Indeed, most Christian sectors refuse state authority because the church is supposed to be the highest authority; they call IRS 501 churches 'harlots' because accepting a government licence is recognizing a secular power to be higher than the church.

26. Todd Wilkinson, 'Home, home on the range ... where neo-Nazis and skinheads roam', *High Country News*, 26(12), 27 June 1994.

CHAPTER 5

PopCulture v. AgriCulture and Other Reflections on the Anti-Corporate Movement/s

> A healthy local community cannot be replaced by a market
> or an information highway ... The neighborhood, the local
> community, is the proper place and frame of reference for
> responsible work. (Berry 1996: 414)

§ THIS chapter explores the possibilities, promises and perils suggested
by the movements discussed in the last three chapters. Returning to
the theoretical questions raised at the beginning of the book, the first
section of the chapter explores the premise that movements are naming
corporations as their enemy. How do they do so and what does it
accomplish? This is not the only contribution the movements make to
social movement practice; the next section presents these other contributions. Turning from the movements' mobilization to their visions
of rebuilding the world, the third section discusses the possibilities
they present for an 'alternative political economy'. The fourth section
analyses another important aspect of their vision, their relationship to
democracy. Finally, movements that pursue sovereignty are seeking to
be somewhat autonomous. But social justice theorists have become
quite wary of both the nation and the very idea of sovereignty. The
final section attempts a thorough examination of issues raised by the
possibility of autonomy.

Figure 5.1 reviews the major movements and sub-movements and
shows the abbreviations that will be used in the figures throughout
this chapter. Since each major movement is composed of diverse
organizations, groups, and sometimes sub-movements, these charts
cannot be perfectly complete. Still, they provide a schematic of differences between movements and modes.

Contestation and reform	Globalization from below	Delinking/relocalization
Fighting structural adjustment [fSA]	Environment [Env]	Anarchy [An]
Corporate welfare reform	Environmental justice	Sustainable development [Sust]
Peace and human rights [PHR]		Agriculture
Land reform [Lan]	Labour [Lab]	Urban
Rural land reform	Socialism [Soc]	Small business [SmB]
Urban squatters	Parties	Public markets
Anti-growth	Alternative institutions	Anti-big box
Explicit anti-corporate [A–C]	Anti-FTA [FTA]	DIY
Anti-genetic engineering	Zapatismo [Zap]	Local currency
Cyberpunk [Cyb]		Sovereignty [Sov]
		Religious nationalism [Rel]

Figure 5.1

Naming the Enemy

> The global house is on fire and we have the facts and moral authority.
> They only have money and guns. (Kevin Danaher)[1]

This section explores the issues of knowledge which shape the possibility of recognizing an enemy and the closely related social movements questions about how the movements wield discourse.

The first question raised about discourse and its knowledge base in the theoretical inventory in Chapter 1 was whether it is possible to see the enemy through the veils of ideological illusion artfully arranged by the structure's hegemonic discourses. Of course there is no way to know for sure if this is happening without historical perspective. The independent NGOs' activities at the 1992 Rio Earth Summit seem to be evidence that ideology is not totally hegemonized. NGOs and social movement organizations forged a Treaty on Alternative Economic Models, which challenged the positioning of corporations as 'partners' in sustainable development and named them instead as enemies of sustainable development:

> The neo-liberal State uses its power and violence to enforce and expand this oppressive economic system under the coordination of the author-itarian Bretton Woods institutions, particularly the World Bank, International Monetary Fund (IMF) and the General Agreement on Tariffs and Trade (GATT), for the benefit of transnational corporations' growing monopoly and their control over the world's resources. The [official] Brundtland model of sustainable development will perpetuate this situation.

Movements seeking to decommodify land, housing, seed, food, the internet and elections have remembered what capitalism most wanted them to forget, their right to 'an abundant, self-yielding nature' (Scott 1990: 81). By challenging the logic of commodification, they have broken through the false choices presented to them. Similarly, labour movements challenge 'international competitiveness', peace movements challenge inevitable conflict and the logic of self-defence, anarchists challenge the necessity of centralization, and sustainability activists reject the necessity of modernity/technology/progress.

The second question is whether the movements believe it is *useful* to name a single enemy. All the movements studied here are confident in their analysis of the structure. They see the structure as constraining, if not determining, the conditions of life. It threatens much of what they need and care about. Do they theorize the enemy as partial in order to preserve spaces of empowerment? No. Every single movement here triumphantly accuses a totalizing world. Knowledge of the multiple oppressions effected by globalization is not disempowering; movements are inspired by the belief that so many people are being screwed in so many ways that the global plebiscite will refuse this system.

The third question is *how* they conceptualize the enemy. Few of the movements criticize capitalism as such. The exceptions are the socialist and anarchist movements. The Zapatistas use some Marxist language, but are not limited to Marxist analysis. Some sustainable development advocates are Marxists, but sustainable development logic does not depend on explicit criticism of capitalism. Third world movements criticize 'neoliberalism'.

	Contestation & reform					Globalization from below					Delinking/relocalization				
	fSA	PHR	Lan	A-C	Cyb	Env	Lab	Soc	FTA	Zap	An	Sust	SmB	Sov	Rel
Does the movement criticize: capitalism?				–	~			•		•	•				
Neoliberalism?	•		•	•					•	•				•	
Globalization?	•		•	•		•	•	•	•	•	•	•	•	•	•

Key: •   criteria are present
     –   weakly present, or only among a sub-group
     ~   could be interpreted to be present

How do the movements understand globalization? If few of them are concerned about capitalism, it follows that they will not define globalization as just part of capitalism. Instead, they tend to see globalization as a repeat of colonialism, or as a 'new strategy' (People's Global Action). As described in Chapter 1, scholars of globalization lay out several aspects of an effective critique of globalization: growth, consumption, dependency and colonialism. These critiques are quite popular among anti-corporate movements in all three modes, with the third mode having the most instances.

Contestation & reform					Globalization from below					Delinking/relocalization				
fSA	PHR	Lan	A-C	Cyb	Env	Lab	Soc	FTA	Zap	An	Sust	SmB	Sov	Rel
Does the movement criticize: growth?														
	•	•			•			•	•	•	•	•	•	
consumption?														
		•			•		•	•		•	•	•		•
dependency?														
•	•	•	•					•	•	•	•	•	•	•
Does the movement see corporations as colonial														
•	•		•		•			•	•	•		•	•	•

Key: see p. 151

The labour movement does not use any of these critical concepts to analyse economic relations. This could explain why even in South Korea, labour leaders decided to go along with IMF structural adjustment programmes including massive layoffs, announcing that 'we signed the agreement because we wanted to help the country attract foreign investment'.[2] The US National Labor Committee explains that they want to 'join' Disney 'in an attempt to improve conditions'.[3] The labour movement is one of the diverse and international 'globalization from below' campaigns, yet it is not confronting the corporate political economic model.

The critique of *consumption* is very important for first world movements, as they must change their relationship to privileged consumption in order to delegitimize depredation of the third world and in order to reclaim the noton of citizenship from the reduced conception of consumership. It is equally important to third world movements' efforts to reject the modernization model.

Colonial analysis is useful for a number of reasons. It can handle the many forms of domination (multiple oppressions) effected by corporate hegemony (economic, political, cultural, ideological, alienation of land). It clarifies how dependency is produced and reproduced.

It resolves the burble of contradictions between the seeming relativism of multiple epistemologies and the coherence of their joint conclusions about the structure. It can account for racialization and gendered and sexualized intersectionalities (Nandy 1983). It explains the comprador class in political economic terms that incorporate an understanding of the internalized effects (identity). It proposes a vision of how to address the problem (decolonization and sovereignty) with the understanding that decolonization must include education as well as political economy. It acknowledges that colonized people use a variety of cultural systems to critique, reject and confront that system.

The analysis of corporations as colonial theorizes them as extractive, reveals their actions on behalf of the 'public good' as manipulative and paternalistic, reminds us of the uses and genocidal consequences of cultural invasion, and articulates dependency (as workers and consumers) as an intentionally produced situation. Martin Khor of the Third World Network suggests that corporate 'economic pariahs' should be seen as 'threats to national security'.[4] The colonial analysis also clarifies how corporations are constraining and redirecting third world peoples' 'choices', not serving them.

The fourth question is how movements come to their critiques – what tools do they use? As mentioned above, some movements have access to Marxist analysis or other political economic frameworks, such as colonial analysis. Farmers and small business people have a lot of clarity based on their experience about how corporations achieve market control. The peace and human rights movements, third world debt relief movements and labour movements use humanitarianism. The environmental and sustainable development movements use the notion of ecological limits and 'ecocide' to challenge the rationality of the economy. Another set of mediating tools are moral frameworks. The peace movement argues that nuclear weapons are 'blasphemy ... they should not exist'. Religious nationalists see the economy as 'propagating immorality'.

The environmental justice movement is an excellent example of how moral frames operate. Racial justice traditions bring a human moral dimension to environmental discourses. In various ways, these movements subject the 'neutral' logics of corporate capitalism (such as 'risk assessment') to other criteria of rationality. 'The compromise between a healthy baby and a dead baby is a sick baby,' say the Mothers of East Los Angeles, and that compromise is not an 'acceptable risk'; it cannot be justified by the needs of capital-intensive growth (Hamilton 1990: 219–22). Legal scholar Patricia Williams explains that such understandings of justice are based on negative recognitions, which she describes as 'I do know what it isn't' (1991: 109). Lois Gibbs explains how moral epistemology shapes political strategy: 'We bring the authority of mother – who can condemn mothers? – it is a tool we have. Our crying brings the moral issue to the table. And when the public sees our children, it brings a concrete, moral dimension to our experience' (in Krauss 1993: 113). The movement is constrained neither by existing protest channels nor by economic orthodoxy. It insists on the prioritization of life, 'cessation of production of toxins', 'detoxification and containment at the point of production', and democratic citizen participation 'as equal partners at every level of decision-making' (Environmental Justice Principles 3, 6, 7, 1991).

Supporting Laclau and Mouffe's (1985) hypothesis of 'extensions of the democratic imaginary', many of the movements use some sort of democratic framework. The Zapatistas justify their uprising by explaining that: 'We did not count ... in the accounts of big capital.' Resistance to structural adjustment and land reform movements demand citizens' entitlements to be prioritized over corporate interests. Sovereignty movements and Religious Nationalists also insist on their right to survive (with cultural integrity) as an invocation of democratic pluralism.

All the movements of the third mode have critiques strongly informed by their knowledge that they have a workable alternative. Alternative (non-Western or non-modern) epistemology is an important resource and strength for these movements and contributes to structural critique by redefining the realm of possible and impossible.

Does the movement use alternative epistemology?

Contestation & reform					Globalization from below					Delinking/relocalization				
fSA	PHR	Lan	A-C	Cyb	Env	Lab	Soc	FTA	Zap	An	Sust	SmB	Sov	Rel
~		–						~	•	•	~		•	•

Key: see p. 151

What is the status of alternative epistemology *vis-à-vis* structuralism? The academic acknowledgement of epistemological variance played an important role in the emergence of poststructural theory. But as Sandra Harding points out, this move need not end in relativism: 'feminist inquirers are never saying that sexist and antisexist claims are equally plausible' (1986: 27). Alternative epistemology and cultural tools result not in fragmented, contradictory, incomplete understandings of the world, but in quite sharp and consistent namings of the enemy. In terms of planning the future, there is recognition of the diversity of traditional farming practices, but the celebration of multiplicity does not extend to industrial agricultural techniques. The multiplicity espoused is principled and bounded.

Are these Michel Foucault's 'new subjectivities' and Alberto Melucci's 'new cultures' at work? Foucault's 'new subjectivities' are ways of knowing woven from interiorized oppression. Melucci's 'new cultures' are a little more forgiving. Since the movements are using traditional culture or some hybrid of it, it seems that 'new cultures' would be a more accurate description than Foucault's notion of how subjectivity is formed. But these theorists' recognition of the importance of what we now call epistemology is obviously important. Notice that the movements of the third mode, which have managed to articulate visions of the future, are most likely to have access to alternate 'cultures'. In the sustainable development movement, archives of traditional practices and extensive experimentation enable people to believe in the possibility of alternatives.

There is yet one more route to oppositional knowledge here. Terry Eagleton proposes that 'active political struggle' is a crucible in which 'political and ideological discourse' will 'go to work upon' people's 'material interests' in a non-'arbitrary' direction (1991: 224, 212–13, 210–11) – meaning that while the outcome is not 'natural, automatic or ineluctable' (as the postmodernists claim about reductionist Marxism), it may well follow the structural interests of the oppressed. Celine Krauss explains that when women in the environmental justice movement petition what they assumed to be a benevolent government and find it 'indifferent' to their communities, they 'develop a broader analysis of ... power as shaped by gender and class', become activists, find ways to expose government's favouritism for business, and struggle to 'make the system democratic' (1993: 109–12). This was certainly the pattern of mobilization for NGOs and farmers *vis-à-vis* GATT. José Bové explained that he first travelled to Paris to ask his government to deal with the trade sanctions hurting his Rocquefort sales to the USA. When they shrugged their shoulders saying 'WTO', he returned home to take direct action against the McDonalds in his town.[5]

The fifth question is how they engage in discursive forms of struggle. All the movements use discourse in the form of truth as part of building the movement and in the process of presenting themselves to outsiders. None proposes that truthful speech has no power. Most of the movements are wielding discourse in a struggle for hegemony. This means both hegemony of interpretation among allies and also hegemony in the larger social discourse. Exceptions are those movements mostly involved in direct action against corporate interests or for survival.

The movements studied here are fighting for ideological hegemony. They are not fighting to have their truths acknowledged *alongside* dominant truths. Their namings do not hide behind partiality; they claim the status of truth – the truth of Hegel's and others' slaves. These new efforts to name enemies are made possible not by the entry of multiple truths into the public arena, but by the assertion of populist truths about structural, colonial, institutional enemies. Religious nationalism is the most successful struggle for ideological hegemony via an insurgent discourse. It would be interesting to examine this process more closely as a model of struggle.

Contestation & reform					Globalization from below					Delinking/relocalization				
fSA	PHR	Lan	A-C	Cyb	Env	Lab	Soc	FTA	Zap	An	Sust	SmB	Sov	Rel

Struggling for ideological hegemony

•	•		•		•	•	•	•	•	•	•	•	•	•

Interested in transformative dialogue with the enemy

		•					•					•		

Key: see p. 151

Only a few movements believe that discourse might have transformative power in achieving social consensus with the enemy. The rest of the movements insist on the possibility of justice without compromise, suggesting that Habermas' faith in transformative dialogue may be misplaced. Sustainable development has such faith in its accomplishments that it still imagines the possibility of corporations seeing the light. Peace and human rights movements work with the idea of common moral frameworks in attempting to transform enemies.

Indeed, it is dangerous to position corporations as partners and allies. Coming to the table to negotiate often means accepting the corporate project, therefore negotiation tends to benefit corporate interests. Negotiation brings activists into a process of collaboration with the company, gets them invested in a non-oppositional process, and changes the issues of 'salience' from siting (or not) to technical issues of operation, safety, and so on. As Reinhold Niebuhr recognized over fifty years before the environmental justice movement, the idealism/liberalism emphasis on negotiation ignores the different moral positions of the two sides. The 'glorification of co-operation and mutuality' actually means accepting 'traditional injustices and the preference of the subtler types of coercion to the more overt types' (1932: 233). Rather than presenting themselves as respectable, rational, legitimate organizations, anti-roads groups in Britain avoid dialogue because it legitimizes the state's process.

> As this epic struggle unfolded the campaigners recognised that to be drawn into a polite debate was to take the road-lobby and the Department of Transport more seriously than they deserved ... Stern's advice is don't waste energy making the case against the project. If the forces of 'progress' were susceptible to reasoning they wouldn't be trying to build it in the first place ... The campaigners saw that the only way of redressing the awesome imbalance of power between the two sides is to keep the bureaucrats guessing as to what will come next ... Looking at officials/inspectors through binoculars is good. (Field 1999: 70–1)

Most of the movements eschew negotiation, seeing it as unnecessary. They feel no need to acknowledge corporate rights or to include their concerns in the process. For movements of the second and third modes, corporations are expendable. Within the anti-FTA movement, some sectors believe that the WTO agreements could be rewritten and improved, according to the ideology of 'fair trade'. But many third world movements opposing the FTAs refuse absolutely the WTO and insist that it be dismantled.

Will discourse become more or less important as the ravages of corporate globalization hit home? As DuBois (1940) pointed out before Foucault, the power/knowledge concatenation has no interest in the truth. Now that knowledge of environmental crisis has achieved hegemony with negligible effect on industrial activity, we see that truth does not transform power. Is the struggle for ideological hegemony a sufficient response to the problem that power does not care about truth? Ideological hegemony may be useful to organizing people, but it alone will not cause a shift in power relations.

Structural projects are viable today, are being chosen by activists, and are only strengthened by multiple epistemologies. Their ideologies are expanding through new connections with each other. 'Turtles and Teamsters – Together at Last!' While naming the enemy is a powerful part of the accomplishment of the movements studied here, there are a number of other social movements concerns to which they contribute interesting findings.

The Movement

New, quite structurally focused movements are being taken up in unprecedented alliances by the very people who were expected to only be interested in particularistic, identity-based organizing. This section explores the possibility for a 'unity of many determinations' and also examines the movements' uses of identity and culture in their organizing.

'Unity of many determinations'? Each of the movements explored in this work makes an important contribution to building an international anti-corporate movement. Some provide logics of delegitimation, others provide new allies or tactics. The first world–third world anti-structural adjustment mobilization shows the ability of diverse people to agree on a major structural analysis and plan of action (debt cancellation). The corporate welfare reform alliances build new ideological bridges by showing that conservative premises can be used to address environmental and social equity concerns. The peace and human rights movements have long revealed government collusion with industry and have established first world–third world connections through humanitarian work. Land reform movements insist that people want self-sufficiency and that commodification of everything is simply

not working for the poor. The explicit anti-corporate movements provide explicit naming of the enemy, reinvigorate praxis strategy, strengthen first world solidarity with the third world through critical development perspectives and develop new legal strategies ('three strikes and you're out' for corporations, revoking corporate charters, Seventh Generation Amendment), and have initiated celebratory modes of protest.

The labour movement is creating mechanisms of legal responsibility between legally separate enterprises, asserting a proactive stance in establishing the rules of the game, developing analyses that challenge the consumption privileges of first world workers, and working out ways to raise standards for working conditions for all workers. The movements challenging FTAs have built tremendous cross-class first world–third world alliances, a 'global carnival against capital'. Environmentalism's diversity is leading to a proliferation of useful economic critiques and strong alliances with a wide range of social struggles. It is becoming hard to distinguish between environmental and human rights organizing, which is evidence of tremendous ideological growth on the part of environmentalists, but indigenous struggles deserve the credit for crystallizing these connections. Socialist parties insist that revolution is possible and that socialist alternative institutions provide models for democratically run enterprises.

Anarchy and cyberpunk are nurturing critical youth constituencies. Cyberpunk contributes expert critiques of technology and also develops tactics that are already widely in use. Anarchists offer their long-term work on the relationship between delinked communities and equity and an alternative form of organization. Sustainable development activists worldwide have articulated systems for materially abundant communal life – a transformative political economy.

Small business movements may be cracking capitalist cosmology by forging themselves into constituencies for sustainability and equity. The Zapatistas and other sovereignty movements invite people of all oppressions into their vision and struggle – modelling multicultural internationalism. Sovereignty movements model the seriousness of the relationship between people, land and culture in repeated non-negotiable 'No!'s to corporate and government projects. The anti-FTA movement and its surprise victories are made possible by all these movements, by an insurgent political economy, its popularization, and

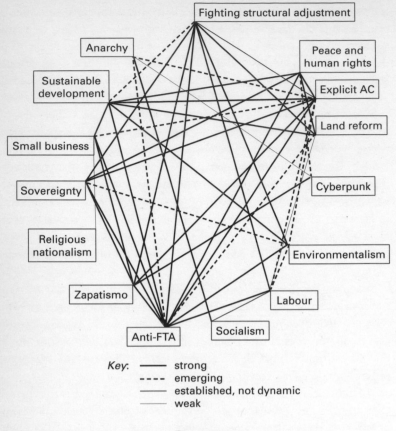

Figure 5.2

strong solidarity across class, race, national and ideological borders. And religious nationalists *may* be modelling an effective strategy for enforcing moral order over the economy. As discussed above, alternative and moral epistemology contributes to developing both delegitimatizing discourses and 'alternative political economy', as will be discussed below. If the 'politics of difference' can produce multiple strengths and strategies, the 'unity of many determinations' may emerge. It is important to note that just as the most powerful multicultural politics are alliances among people of colour, the most important international alliances may be among third and fourth world peoples, perhaps organized as debtors' alliances.

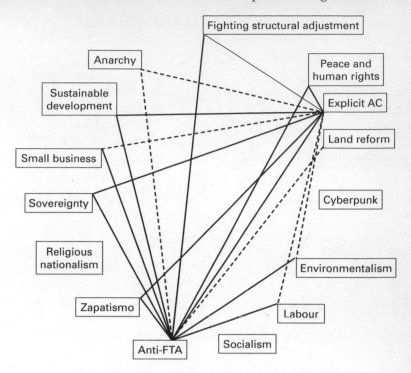

Figure 5.3 A-C and anti-FTA connections only

Anti-corporate critiques and practices are emerging from different classes, nations, social systems, ethnicities and religions. Is this the 'unity of many determinations' (Marx 1873)? Since I was focusing on discourse, I did not gather data on actual cooperation between movements; Figure 5.2 is based on collaborations mentioned in the materials I did collect. Having a connection is here defined as a public embrace of each other's ideology and/or projects. In analysing the chart, a 'link' is a line, a 'connection' is one end of a line.

Movements involved in four or fewer connections are anarchy, cyberpunk, socialism and religious nationalism. The isolation of anarchy and cyberpunk may be a function of youth and/or perceived involvement with illegal activities. Religious nationalism, like socialism, is an ideological pariah. It is important to keep in mind that the 15 major movements contain diverse sub-movements. Some

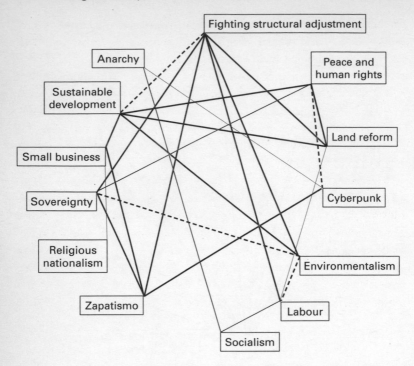

Figure 5.4 All connections except A-C and anti-FTA

sub-movements are also less well connected (DIY) and some are better connected (e.g. local currency) than small business movements as a whole. Simplistic counts indicate that the first and second modes have the most connections, 31 each, while the third mode makes 23. Total connections can be broken down into connections within mode (10, 10, 4) and connections outside of mode (21, 21, 19). The number of connections outside of mode suggest the strength of ideological resources available to anti-corporate movements through their alliances.

Out of 44 total links, 21 connect with either the explicit anti-corporate movement (10) or the anti-FTA movement (11). These movements appear to be important contributors to the appearance of a densely connected set of anti-globalization and alternative-developing social movements. The multiplicity of threats produced by FTAs produced a movement of multiplicity which forged alliances across established barriers, including: first world–third world labour, labour–environmentalism, labour–people of colour, and scholars–activists. Indigenous peoples' organizations and religious and secular human rights organizations find new solidarity with anti-FTA organizations. The 1999 Seattle WTO Ministerial protests were the first indication of anarchist youth being valued by these other sectors, although they have been active in anti-FTA protests in Europe for some time. Figures 5.3 and 5.4 show the network created by those two movements alone and the network that exists apart from them.

The next best connected movements are fighting structural adjustment (8) and sustainable development (7). Indigenous sovereignty movements have made strong connections (6) with many first world movements. Sustainable development advocates, although primarily focused on building systems, are well versed in other struggles. Environmentalism, labour and Zapatismo have six each. Perhaps more important than the existence of connections is the question of whether these connections cross boundaries of identity, ideology and national status.

Has the movement made linkages across identity or ideology?

Contestation & reform					Globalization from below					Delinking/relocalization				
fSA	PHR	Lan	A-C	Cyb	Env	Lab	Soc	FTA	Zap	An	Sust	SmB	Sov	Rel
ideo	1/3	rural-	1/3		1/3	1/3		1/3	4/1		class	class	4/1	class
1/3		urban	ideo		1/4			ideo	4/3		race			
		1/3			3/4						1/4			

Key: ideo = links across ideological boundaries
1/3, 1/4, etc. = links between first and third world, etc.
class, race, etc. = intranational links across class or race

Many of the movements are making important links across identity (first world/third world, class, race) and ideology. Those that are not are the same movements that appear generally less well-connected in Figures 5.3 and 5.4.

The anti-corporate roster suggests a multi-class alliance. Issues of food quality and health attract multi-class interest. For example, the organic farming movement is increasingly being organized by its intelligentsia in ways designed to address the political economy of food. As Hilary Tovey argues, 'alternative agriculture movements demand that we somehow overcome this consumption/production divide in our thinking about food' (1997: 23). Anti-consumption movements of various kinds insist on a solidarity between the health and welfare of the consumer and that of the workers or residents. The people on the front lines of the pesticide industry are farmworkers and DuPont's neighbours, not consumers (Bullard 1994). The *petit bourgeois* Mexican debtors' movement, El Barzón, is allied with the Zapatistas (Ross 1998). Such recognitions of commonalities *cannot* be seen postmodernly as 'political interests which are by no means necessarily tied to *class* situations' (Eagleton 1991: 210) – instead, they expand the meaning of class to incorporate a wider framework of dispossession.

In addition to anti-FTA, other movements show groups coming together from very different ideological positions around the same basic critique. The US corporate welfare and corporate finance reform campaigns are multi-ideological in very surprising ways. They have discovered that they need not agree theoretically on the benefits of free markets in order to organize together against international enforcement of a free market. Sustainable development activists have worked with small business people to build local currency systems, public markets, food policy councils, market-protected community supported agriculture, and other institutions that localize the economy in hope of making it sustainable. These alliances present a corrective to an interesting oversight shared by postmodernists, neoliberals, and Marxists – the tendency to ignore small capital-holders (and their effective job engines and culturally specific production) in their analysis of globalization and responses to it. In fact, small businesses are among corporations' prey (via market competition, exploiting niches developed by small businesses, exclusive agreements with distributors, refusing to give patent licences, and so on).

The promise of anti-corporatism is its ability to develop a diverse and unified constituency mutually threatened by the corporate hijacking of economy and politics. Many possibilities for alliance have yet to be explored. It seems that we should be careful not to jump to conclusions about social movements' goals, particularly when apparent enemies (like religious and other nationalists) are being demonized by neoliberal elites. Obviously, people interested in 'globalization from below' must work as hard within national borders as across them, and also across generations, class and ideology within nations (see Moore 1997).

Can PopCulture deliver us from capitalism?: the struggle How do the movements conceptualize their own agency? Where do they struggle? Do they use identity? Is culture a medium of struggle? PopCulture?

Environmentalists note that when the movement focuses on legal actions, the mass of supporters demobilize because they have nothing to contribute. Rather than depending on judicial and legislative procedures, French and Canadian citizens, empowered by a sense of entitlement conferred by socialist political traditions, took to the streets to refuse structural adjustments to their social welfare. The figure below explores the sites utilized by various movements in the course of struggle.

Contestation & reform					Globalization from below					Delinking/relocalization				
fSA	PHR	Lan	A-C	Cyb	Env	Lab	Soc	FTA	Zap	An	Sust	SmB	Sov	Rel

Site of action: street

•	•	•	•		•	•		•	•	•	•	•	•	•

legislative/judicial

•	•	•	•		•	•	•	•				•	•	~

direct pressure on corporations

	•	•	•	•	•	•				•	•	•	•	•

party politics

•	•	•	•		•	•	•	•				•	•	•

Key: see p. 151

Seven movements (about half), spread through the three modes, use all four of these sites (street, legislative/judicial, direct pressure and party politics). This shows the strength and diversity of anti-corporate mobilization, whose tactics range from the exercise of direct democracy through mass mobilization, to working with formal institutions, to economic democratic practices of boycotts and protests against corporate activities. El Barzón uses mass mobilization (barricading banks, refusing to pay loans), judicial defence against foreclosure, and legislative action.

IDENTITY As identity has come to be seen by social movements scholars as the prime mover of social movements, unity has seemed less possible. Groups are fragmented because their unique identity experiences make it hard to relate to and trust one another. At the same time, both postmodernists and neoliberals privilege identity as one of the most crucial aspects of responses to globalization. Both decry 'reactionary'/'backward' nationalisms and celebrate new global identities.

Meanwhile, the empirical realities of corporate hegemony suggest promising possibilities for a shift beyond the difficulties of identity politics. The empirical work of critical globalization scholars shows how corporations are using all possible opportunities to exploit women, people of colour, workers, poor communities, discrete cultures, health, environmental quality and people's natural and scientific commons. Women of colour are preferred as light manufacturing operatives (because browns are cheaper and women are thought to be more docile) by corporations who also poison nearby communities (including workers and non-workers, men, women and children) because they are also brown and poor. How can these experiences of Maquilladora be separated? Perhaps the experience of multiple oppressions no longer requires multiple theories of oppression because corporations multiply oppress. Women organizing against sweatshops are doing so as women, but their enemies are not only women's enemies and threaten them in ways that are both gendered (hiring only women workers, using sexual harassment as a means of control) and not gendered (taking land, poisoning communities).

While few of the movements organize on the basis of identity, many of them address the problem for which identity was the solution. Contrary to expectations, anti-corporate movements do not deny the idea of multiple oppressions, but centre it in their analysis of the enemy and in their visions of rebuilding the world. Similarly, as anti-corporate movements have moved beyond the boycott perspective that aimed to reform particular corporations (one at a time) to a general anti-corporate frame, they have embraced a critique of corporate logic that is thoroughly multi-issue. In addition, most of the movements appear to incorporate the idea of difference into their theory and most manage to nurture diversity within the ranks ('internal inclusivity').

In becoming anti-corporate, identity-based movements neither abandon their identity nor adopt a new one; they oppose corporations from their identity-based stance, while also making connections outside of an identity-politics mode. They have redefined enemies in ways that do not depend on identity as the basis of understanding and allies in ways that do not depend on a subtle and fragile 'politics of difference'. Neither the Zapatistas themselves nor their supporters understand their movement as a movement of identity, although identity is part of their discourse. What is at stake is political economic: indigenous lands, corn, NAFTA and the purchase of the Mexican political system.

Panellists at the First National Conference of the Community Food Security Coalition, held in October 1997 in Los Angeles, insisted on the need to work to 'systematically cultivate allies', and spoke about their successful experiences in bringing together rural white small farmers and urban people of colour. Of course 'at first', said one panellist, there was racism, but 'it didn't take long' before people recognized their economic commonalities. They saw race as an organizing barrier that could be overcome by organizing people around their common relationships to the food system and the global economy.

This study suggests that identity may no longer be the most important organizing principle for social movements as they embrace multiple oppressions, confront corporations on many fronts at once and recognize allies who cannot be contained by an identity politics framework. The international invitation to be a Zapatista mirrors the invitation to be queer – it is a moral solidarity around a political economic critique, not any kind of claim about interiority or essence. Despite movements' commitments to multiculturalism, they do not propose that there are multiple truths about the world. They speak with clarity about the enemy and build diverse alliances.

CULTURE Current ideas about social movements combine fun culture, the everyday and individualism to propose 'subversion' through
personal cultural performances or 'repetitions' (Butler 1990). Given
people's fragmented identities and infatuation with media imagery,
this seems to be the only possibility for building social movements.
Celebrating individualism enables movements to appeal to fragmented,
complexly identifying cosmopolitans.

Discussing the limits and possibilities of an effective anti-Nike campaign, activists articulate the shortcomings of campaigns that fail to
confront consumerist culture. Adolf Reed argues that 'We have a youth
movement that collapses so completely into adolescent consumption
that the movement's adherents often seem incapable of recognizing
any other notion of politics.' Tina Bartholome explains that youth are
not mobilizing politically because 'you are told that [material goods]
will give you whatever self-worth or image that you don't have because
it was either stolen from you or denied you through your education.
It's almost like you have an empty soul.'[6] Anti-corporate movements
challenge such identity by rejecting important aspects of consumption.
Even small businesses insist on limits to a consumption-based economy: healthy local economies come first, not infinite choice and
cheapness.

When PopCulture appears as a medium of struggle among the
movements it only does so weakly. AdBusters, part of the explicit anti-
corporate movement, produce hip magazines and 'uncommercials'
deconstructing corporate messages. Their attempts to buy advertising
space are usually refused. They have provoked, internationally, guerrilla
uncommercials in the form of poster campaigns and repaintings of
billboard ads. The anti-FTA movements use street parties, dancing,
theatre, and 'mobile lounges' to make protest celebratory. Zapatista
messages may be carried on the internet and may include poetry and
sophisticated writing (including savvy jokes on postmodernism) but it
is always focused on political economic concerns and physical mobilization. I was surprised to observe that the Convergence Center at the
WTO protest in Seattle did not have a bank of computers; apparently
computers were not seen as where the work was to be done, despite
the important role of the internet in the months leading up to the
action.

Contestation & reform					Globalization from below					Delinking/relocalization				
fSA	PHR	Lan	A-C	Cyb	Env	Lab	Soc	FTA	Zap	An	Sust	SmB	Sov	Rel

PopCulture as medium of struggle

			–	–	–			–	–					

The everyday as a medium for struggle

•	•	•			•		•		•	•	•	•		•

Key: see p. 151

A number of movements act in the cultural and lifestyle spheres, acknowledging the importance of everyday practices alongside post-modern theory. Notice that the globalization from below movements are least likely to incorporate this approach and that movements of the third mode (which also make a strong showing in traditional modes of struggle) also consistently work through everyday practices. Foucault and Melucci hoped that nurturing new subjectivities and cultures would create critical consciousness and real alternatives. What I have called 'alternative epistemology' may be the emergence and embrace of such new forms of consciousness that facilitate reinterpretation of the world. Do these new cultures give rise to alternative spaces, oases of possibilities for new ways of living?

Contestation & reform					Globalization from below					Delinking/relocalization				
fSA	PHR	Lan	A-C	Cyb	Env	Lab	Soc	FTA	Zap	An	Sust	SmB	Sov	Rel

Create alternative spaces

	•	•	•				•		•	•	•	•	•	•

Traditional culture as critical lens

	•						•	•	•	•	•	•		•

Key: see p. 151

The movements most likely to build strong alternative spaces are those with strong connections to traditional culture.

For most of the movements in this study, culture means material culture, whose purposes are traditional, carrying intergenerational information about survival – growing food, raising children, language, cosmology, medicine, and traditions of self-governance. The work of recognizing the objective superiority of traditional knowledge for producing food in a particular place is the foundation of a more general critique of modernization and a path for moving towards other models. First and third world scholars alike are urgently documenting farmers' traditions and supporting them in valuing their knowledge. Farmers themselves are rapidly coming to the conclusion that imported agricultural technology does not work and are recovering pre-Green Revolution methods. Alongside revaluation of traditional culture, people are recognizing the social and community wisdom contained in traditional systems.

The real test of PopCulture as a social movement medium is what content it carries. It does not carry intergenerational information about physical, social and spiritual survival. It does not help the next generation understand how to live. (AgriCulture, on the other hand, does carry this vital information.) Jameson describes the condition of postmodernity as 'obliterat[ing] traditions of the kind which all earlier social information have had, in one way or another, to preserve' (1998: 20). Armand Mattelart (1993) proposes that international anti-corporatism has produced a 'revenge of culture' that insists on pluralism and 'a relocalization of communication' – a revenge on behalf of traditional culture, it seems.

What makes anti-corporatism a really interesting case through which to think about Laclau and Mouffe's replacement of socialism with democracy is that we're looking at an emerging movement that reasserts democratic autonomy at a community level not merely to protect identity (which some Marxists begrudgingly accepted in hope of swelling the ranks) but to assert control over and protect a local political economy. This is not the expected democracy – or the expected political economy.

Alternative Political Economy

As discussed earlier in this chapter, movements in all three modes share important political economic critiques of growth, consumption, dependency and colonialism. But these critiques alone do not tell us about the kind of economy they would rebuild. This section explores the differences between and implications of the three modes' political economic visions and the possibility of the third mode as an 'alternative political economy'.

The first mode assumes that states can be held accountable to regulate rather than facilitate corporate operations or, alternatively, that consumer demands can hold corporations accountable. A strict regulatory environment could force corporations to internalize social and environmental costs. Anti-monopoly law could be extended and enforced. Corporate subsidies could be cut and public resources and policy turned to support small business development. Citizens' groups could use boycotts (as unions use strikes) to force corporations to the bargaining table, where agreements on consumer concerns (including social issues) could be negotiated. This approach is Lockean and Keynesian; it presumes that some form of state or civic governance system can establish and enforce a social contract in the interests of people. It also presumes that the purposes of social contracts are social. The alternative explanation is that the social contracts are ameliorative. They pacify the working class temporarily to facilitate relatively undisrupted pursuit of capitalism and are rescinded as soon as politically possible.

> The liberal ideal of democratic participation ... [has] many faces, including 'liberal' ... 'social democratic' and 'authoritarian' ... dissolves into a pluralist social contract ... an institutional framework of social bargaining ... in which the state ... mediates social conflict ... No conflict is tolerable that challenges the supreme requirements of capitalist rationalization – economic growth, profit maximization, productivity ... held together by a productivist ideology, which stresses ... the struggle for material advantage ... Qualitative issues inevitably get deflected or submerged ... unruly forces yield to the 'pragmatic' requirements of technology and bureaucracy. (Boggs 1986: 25–7)

One of the best-intentioned of the experiments with social contract might be the Mondragón complex, the Basque cooperatives established to provide justice and empowerment for workers. They have recently abandoned their commitment to worker ownership because they needed 'a more dispensable sector of the workforce' in order to 'compete in ... the global market'. The Mondragón Cooperative Corporation now employs non-member labour in low-wage havens like Thailand, China and Morocco.[7] The lesson here is that an economy (even a socialist one) that secures welfare for its citizens by relying on productivity (export) is subject to laws of capitalism that undermine democratic and egalitarian goals. Evidence from the European social democratic experience suggests that as long as employment and consumption are dependent on corporations, they will be able to undermine the social contract by threatening fearful outcomes if productivity is lost.

A productivist approach does nothing to interrupt imperialist extraction from the third and fourth worlds. Increased productivity demands the creation of new markets – accomplished by colonial procedures. Even land reform, if it stays within an export model, will be subject to many market hazards; it just democratizes opportunities for export entrepreneurship. To the extent that land reform decommodifies resources and re-establishes the 'sacred right of property' (Marx 1867: 361) for purposes of self-sufficiency, it can resist the necessities of export.

Within the liberal model, we must be wary of corporations' hegemonic discursive powers. They have the power to shape the terms of the debate in their interests. As an example of this dynamic, Shiva points out that the politicization of the idea of 'cheap food' has been used against the poor by legitimizing toxification of food and mal-treatment of agricultural workers. The right to cheap food manifests as the right to poisoned food and workers. 'Cheapness' does not even guarantee that food will be distributed equitably and ultimately facilitates concentration in the food industry and growing profits. Thus pseudo-concern with poverty justifies more cost externalization and more profit.[8] (In the USA, ironically, cheaper food actually inhibits appropriate adjustments of federal estimates of the cost of living because the poverty line is a multiple of food costs.) Relying on the market to deliver basic needs enables corporations to mobilize the legitimizing framework of the social contract in their own interests, to facilitate cost externalization and dangerous practices.

The second mode would subordinate corporations to people's collective will. States (or international governance bodies) would charter corporations for specific tasks under limited terms. Corporations could be unintegrated vertically or horizontally and/or limited to a small proportion of market share. The economy could be analysed sectorally, with some industries left in the hands of corporations and others protected for small or cooperative businesses. Also consistent with this mode would be the socialization of corporate decision-making in keeping with goals of democracy and/or full employment. This mode emerges from the Marxist tradition, which recognizes that the only way to control capital is to internationalize people's authority. Such a system would presumably be vulnerable to the problems of bureaucracy, rationalization and elite manoeuvring articulated by Weberian analysts. How would control from below be maintained?

The goals of globalization from below require centralization. Centralization makes the new system vulnerable to many of the problems of corporate globalization. It is a setup for logics of comparative advantage that would, again, subordinate localities to priorities set at the centre, denying them control over their own resources. Extraction of resources, with devastating effects on localities, has been a problem shared by free market capitalism command capitalism, and state socialism. Centralization also reproduces dependency for basic needs on a distant and massive system. And centralized production and distribution are hard to govern democratically, partly due to the necessities and proclivities of bureaucracy and partly due to the requirement of an objective and universal operationalization of 'the public good'. Not only does universalism steamroll cultural diversity, it also insists on standardization, which uses resources less efficiently than local technologies. After witnessing the destructive impact of the arrival of the global economy in a remote village, Helena Norberg-Hodge became an anti-globalizationist of the relocalization variety. She argues that 'communism and capitalism are both centralized, colonial, ruthless. Both exerted pressure on people to stop producing a range of products for local consumption and instead to monocrop for export.' In her view, it is centralization that caused the fall of Eastern Bloc state socialisms and will cause the fall of the WTO.[9]

The third mode would elevate local epistemology and priorities over corporate rights. Localities or regions would permit (or not) limited corporate operations. They would be unlikely to permit extractive forays by outsiders. Communities could re-establish commons regimes to regulate use of natural resources and land. They might issue local money to keep value within the community. They might prioritize particular kinds of production and socially enforce particular business practices. Relocalization defends small-scale entrepreneurship while working to undermine the bases of corporate capitalism. This mode draws on the traditions of Jean-Jacques Rousseau, Henry Thoreau, Mahatma Gandhi, Mikhail Bakunin, Peter Kropotkin, E. F. Schumacher and indigenous scholars, who argue that local economies (partly because of their access to local knowledges) use resources more efficiently, are not extractive, and provide conditions for equity and democracy. Various sects of anarchism have been insisting for nearly a century that localized non-governmental communism would provide far more secure democratic opportunities than would nation-state formations.

This approach raises concerns about a number of *social* implications, which will be dealt with later in this chapter. *Economic* concerns include inadequate provision (perhaps some localities cannot meet needs with available resources), the loss of economies of scale, the reduction of available goods (and thus standard of living) to what can be produced locally, how self-sufficient localities would survive natural disasters that threaten subsistence resources, and cost externalization and abuse of commons by small enterprises determined to grow. A somewhat vulgar critique of localization insists that modernization, industrialization, high-tech and global trade are now inevitable. Small-scale economies are seen as romantic, undesirable or absurd. Regulation and socialization of the economy, both of which are premised on large-scale production, are generally considered to be the only possibilities.

Summary of the modes' political economic assumptions

	First Mode: Contestation/ reform	Second Mode: Globalization from below	Third Mode: Relocalization/ delinking
• how material needs get met	market	central planning & distribution	local production w/ local resources
• how administered	social contract	bureaucracy	community based decision-making
• how system changes	bargaining	large-scale democratic processes	highly participatory local analysis & modification of technique

Movements of the first two modes tend to assume the continuation of a global economy, while the third mode emphasizes limitation of the economy to a small scale based on production for local consumption. Some parts of the environmental, anti-corporate, land reform, anti-FTA and Zapatismo movements envision a local economy. Religious nationalism is articulated at local, national and regional scales.

Progress and technology In addition to the scope of trade, other aspects of economic vision are informative. As explored in the discussion on religious nationalism, orientation to the notion of progress varies among movements. (Is development possible? Is there anywhere to go? Does solving social problems depend on development?) Another important question is whether the movements' visions of economy presume ecological limits.

Contestation & reform					Globalization from below					Delinking/relocalization				
fSA	PHR	Lan	A-C	Cyb	Env	Lab	Soc	FTA	Zap	An	Sust	SmB	Sov	Rel

Seeking progress/industrial-style development?

fSA	PHR	Lan	A-C	Cyb	Env	Lab	Soc	FTA	Zap	An	Sust	SmB	Sov	Rel
~	•		−	•	•	•							−	•

Presume ecological limits?

fSA	PHR	Lan	A-C	Cyb	Env	Lab	Soc	FTA	Zap	An	Sust	SmB	Sov	Rel
•	−	•	−		•			•	•	•	•	−*		•

* community currency
Key : see p. 151

Notice that faith in progress and awareness of ecological limits often have an inverse relationship. This makes sense, since modernization-style progress tends to depend on extraction of unlimited resources. Notice also that those movements which take ecological limits seriously tend to include visions of local-scale economies, rather than national or global ones.

An important aspect of progress is technological development. Modernization theory and neoliberalism insist that technology will solve social problems and lead to abundance, perhaps even a social Utopia free of drudgery. The stance on technology is one of the significant differences between approaches to anti-globalization. Most of the anti-corporate movements studied here do critique technology. Scholars from Karl Polanyi (1944) to Jeremy Rifkin (1995) argue that production technology drives wages down and displaces labour. A given technology can have radically different effects on people with different relationships to the means of production. Polanyi argued that 'machine production' causes commodification of 'the natural and human substance of society' and results in a market-regulated economy (1944: 40–2).

While technology is very efficient for displacing labour, it may not actually be efficient for provision. Shiva (1991) compares Green Revolution 'high-yield' monocropping with traditional systems that produced food, fodder for animals, and house material. The Green Revolution varieties produce more grain, but that is all they produce, resulting in decreased efficiency. The short stalks are too tough for animals to eat (and full of toxic chemicals), and are useless as house material (the water runs right through). Tractors require fuel while bullocks provided it (two-thirds of India's total use) *and* fertilizer, both now being replaced by imports. Bullocks also provided baby tractors. Shiva says 'the mystical world of high tech justifies any amount of destruction'.

Agriculture scholar Marty Strange (1988) concurs, explaining how high levels of capital investment in technology reduce unit profit ratios, requiring productivity growth. This can lead to overproduction and price collapse. Technology's inefficiencies include its specialization, which constrains production flexibility while indebting the farm, and standardization and centralization, which displace potentially more efficient local systems. Norberg-Hodge points out that 'We're told that technological development is a natural, inevitable, intelligent process', while 'knowledge is being lost every day' as technology rapidly displaces agricultural, social and cultural systems that were socially and environmentally sustainable for thousands of years. One of the differences between genetic engineering and the ancient practice of hybridization is that genetic engineering is centralized, displacing the farmer as the source of knowledge and decision-making. In contrast, sustainable development relocalists, indigenous sovereignty movements and some religious nationalists insist that low-tech economic, social, political, communications and material techniques met needs with local resources and lower levels of waste, pollution and stress. Elegant technologies are dependable, transferable, inexpensive, straightforward, easy to fix and sensuous. David Morris (1996) draws on one of the major theoretical themes of anti-corporatism in suggesting that we choose technologies that make people more independent and secure, rather than dependent.

Another important consequence of the relationship between political economy and technology is that current rates of technological advancement are burning up resources at a rapid rate due to resource-intensive products, environmental toxification, rapid obsolescence and highly dispersed/individualized use of gadgetry. Tons of hazardous chemicals are used in the production of silicon chips, with devastating effects on workers and communities. Even reduced rates of consumption and technological advancement would still require centralized, often toxic, production and large-scale trade. Thus decentralist visions cannot defend economic/ecological independence *and* high tech. Morris makes a distinction between technologies that require small-scale production and use (such as solar cells) and those that require large-scale production (such as computers). Legitimizing centralized technological development means legitimizing continued obsolescence, technology as an arbiter and symbol of social status, and unsustainable rates of consumption.

Much of the left imagines that technology is 'neutral' and could be made to serve social justice. 'Internet organizing' and the www are being used as mobilization, networking and information tools, and sophisticated high-tech media products are seen by movement activists as important vehicles for communicating alternative viewpoints, particularly to young people. In contrast to claims that technology will enhance organizing strategies, scholars at the International Forum on Globalization's 1997 Teach-In criticized high tech for *enabling* globalization and the centralization of power. Simply because a technology is useful does not mean it is socially beneficial. Its development and use amounts to legislation, but it is not governed democratically. Technological development is naturalized, producing a corresponding naturalization of the economic changes it ushers in. By allowing technological development to proceed unchecked, we are re-engineering life forms to be more compatible with technology, rather than the other way around (for example, saving endangered species by genetically engineering eagles to survive an environment contaminated by heavy metals, and programming salmon to breed without having to go upstream).[10] Technology has become autonomous and totalitarian, detached from human well-being.[11] In response to the idea that computers can facilitate democracy, Jerry Mander points out that corporations use computers far more effectively than do activists, with devastating effects: 'Someone forgot to tell the corporations about "virtual democracy".'

One of the crucial arguments made by Shiva and other technology critics (including cyberpunks) is rejecting the idea that technological 'progress' is inevitable and akin to natural evolutionary processes. Shiva summarizes high-technology hegemony as follows: 'Every act is constructed as a success. Technology has always been a means, now it is an end. Human questions about technology are systematically wiped out.'[12] People's Global Action argues that Western science and technology have 'swept away very diverse and valuable knowledge systems and technologies based on centuries-long experience'. They go on to note that the 'reductionist scientific method has an extremely limited capacity to produce useful knowledge about complex and chaotic systems like agriculture'. In contrast, 'traditional knowledge systems' are more appropriate because they draw on 'generations of direct observation of and interaction with unsimplified complex systems'. Peoples' Global Action is working with a 'globalization from below' approach, but seems to endorse local autonomous economies rather than centralization as a long-term vision.

There is an alternative Neither wresting justice from corporations, *à la* the protest and confrontation movements, nor a massive populist revolution, *à la* 'globalization from below', provides a clear vision of liberatory political economy. As mentioned at the beginning of this study, several scholars of globalization have called for the articulation of an 'alternative political economy'. While the first two modes' proposals have been fully debated by scholars under the rubrics of reform, liberalism and socialism, the third mode has been largely ignored by scholars as a viable (and, unlike the second mode, existing) approach to political economy. Therefore, I devote space here to an exploration of the economic possibilities of delinking and relocalization. (I will not review the ecologised arguments presented in Chapter 4.)

Development discourse offers a theoretical basis for an alternative political economy consistent with the third mode – self-reliance. Urban areas can implement systems analysis and import-substitution strategies to generate employment around local needs while building on strengths and sensibilities of locality. Jennifer Wilkins (1995) suggests the idea of 'foodshed' to analyse a community's carrying capacity. Karl Birkhölzer (1996), arguing that grassroots self-reliance efforts compose a 'growing international movement', recommends urban policy that 'systematic[ally] promot[es] all forms of economic self-help and grassroots initiatives'. Summarizing a series of cases, he explains that a variety of movements with different emphases seem to have the common goal of discovering 'how a given population can secure the existence of its community in a particular place, in which and from which its members live [securing] local work for local people using local resources'. While small businesses may not be paragons of progressivity, they do a lot of important things much better than corporations, such as culturally specific production, the maintenance of crafts, husbandry of natural resources and interdependence between other local economic sectors.

David Imbroscio (1995), concerned with how cities' dependency 'biases both the form and substance of urban democracy', suggests that cities analyse 'resource flows' and foster indigenous economic development with a high degree of local ownership and interindustry dependence. Such an economy would be 'dynamic, diversified, innovative, and, hence, resilient ... capable of withstanding exogenous shocks brought about by capital disinvestment'. Such an approach to urban economic development would 'liberate' cities from competition for 'corporate-centered urban development efforts', whose failure has been well-documented. An economy with only locally owned businesses creates the possibility for community accountability.

According to J. Ann Tickner (1986) Jean-Jacques Rousseau's theory of self-reliance as a political economic strategy was focused on citizens. Believing that growth and organic solidarity 'increased inequality', he envisioned 'a relatively simple, non-progressive subsistence economy with a minimal division of labor'. The nation-state in such an arrangement would be 'small, poor, agrarian and self-sufficient', attributes that would minimize its own 'expansionist ambitions' and be unattractive to 'predatory' neighbours – thus enhancing the possibility of peace.[13] Gandhian development follows this path, emphasizing the benefits of 'decentralized political institutions' through which 'people [could] be protected against exploitation', alleviating unemployment through 'complementary small-scale industry', prioritizing 'solving the problems of poverty' rather than 'compatibility with the world market', and avoiding 'commercial rivalries' and 'power politics' (470–1).

Kumar (1996) adds that Gandhian development, known as *swadeshi* (home economy), is a vision of 'self-governing, self-reliant, self-employed people' living in 'village republics'. These republics would have 'maximum economic and political power – including the power to decide what could be imported into or exported from the village'. In the course of redefining development, third world scholars are recovering indigenous visions. Some first world movements are drawing on these sources to assist them in reimagining communities, economies and communal cultures. Anthropology has documented a huge variety of local economic systems involving private ownership. Third world studies show multiple or mixed modes of production. Industry-specific analyses reveal the possibilities for small-scale enterprise.

Relocalization is a promising political economic project for several reasons. There have been thousands of successful models of local political economies (including both indigenous peoples' societies and more recent first world experiments). The scale of governance is one we know to be appropriate for highly participatory democracy. Localized economies by necessity recognize ecological limits. Locality protects diversity (biological, cultural and social). While local economies benefit less from economies of scale and will be vulnerable to natural crises of the resource base, in many ways they have more security than an integrated global economy. They are independent of global prices and transport, and thus of fads, production priorities and technologies originating elsewhere. Knowledge about how to produce basic needs is archived locally. Economic priorities are determined by the affected community.

As Laxer (1999) points out, the immobility of labour raises important issues for the appropriate scale of political activity. Of course labour is not entirely immobile and is not even limited to a nation, but its mobility (at whatever range) is often involuntary. Autonomous communities make possible political space appropriate to the immobility of labour, as well as appropriate cultural space for diversity.

Martin Khor argues that the third world poor need two things: the 'right to non-development' and appropriate development that serves human needs and is not 'useless, harmful, or leisurely'. Appropriate development would be organized around equitable access to land,

Postcard from a Post-Corporate Relocalized Economy

Goods that serve basic needs are produced locally with local materials and labour. Labour-intensive methods ensure full employment. Decentralized production of diverse foods ensures community food security. Use of local materials, natural resources, and reused/reclaimed processed materials requires recognition of limits of local ecosystem and the protection of that system for the future. (No more dependence on the resources of other places; no more access to other folks' stuff.) Elegant low-tech designs utilize local resources for easily replicable and easily learned tools. Production uses plant-based materials and small-scale renewable fuels produced locally, and rebuilds durables. Places are unique. Trade occurs only in non-necessities or in emergency situations. Nearly all transport systems became unnecessary due to local employment and intermittence of trade. With the preservation of local environmental quality, travel as escape to more pristine landscapes is no longer necessary (and might be restricted by destination communities). Internationalism is no longer exploitative (resource extraction, cheap labour, tourism) but is a means of humanitarian relief in emergency situations and for sharing of techniques for rebuilding communities. Redevelopment of communal distribution systems ensures zero poverty (sharing of surplus, availability of commons resources to all, e.g. fruit trees on public land). Enterprises have no larger market than the local community. Care for community, workers and place becomes part of their work and community standing. Work itself, rather than implying a job, means a livelihood and is 'necessary, good ... satisfying and dignifying to the people who do it and genuinely useful and pleasing to those for whom it is done' (Berry 1996). Less time spent at work and travelling to work frees time for family, social and cultural pursuits, and (vigorously debated) community governance. Community is the highest political authority and has absolute sovereignty. Leadership is dependent on approval of the community in all cases. Communities control their own land.

credit and local markets. Technology and production processes would be under the control of the community. Diversity of products and of social economies would be protected.[14] Both nationalist and localist approaches will require serious changes in consumption practices for first worlders, as necessities and pleasures will be limited to what is available locally. This is important because social equity and social justice organizing have not traditionally acknowledged these limits.

One of many models for moving away from monetarized economies, back to community-based and managed economies, is provided by John F. C. Turner. Since the 1970s, he has been working on housing issues with third world poor. His work makes the important move of decommodifying housing by defining it as an activity and a process ('housing' as a verb) as opposed to an object ('housing' as a noun, and therefore a commodity, to be profited from even when it is built for the poorest of the poor) (Ekins 1992). Permaculture projects in the third world aim to decommodify food by rebuilding food forests and commons regimes to manage them.

We will find other models once we start looking. And people will re/create them when they get the chance: during the Iranian Revolution, community structures emerged organically to address political and economic needs: 'shuras ... were grass-roots decentralized strike committees organized at factories, offices, and schools ... (which) took over production and distribution in their factories as the strike came to an end' (Foran 1993: 387). Similarly, 'Islamic komitehs (committees) in neighborhoods throughout the country ... though loosely co-ordinated and locally rather autonomous ... provided strike support, welfare, food, and security ... (and) constituted parallel governments with economic, political, and military functions' (ibid.: 385–6).

Scale and place (and Marxism) Relocalization movements propose that neither corporations nor a globalized economy can be fixed because they are fundamentally flawed by the *scale* at which they operate. Large-scale economies that require communities to export their produce to buy necessities create dependency and too easily permit colonialism. Most first worlders are actually monocroppers: we spend most of our time and energy producing a single crop that must be exported in order to purchase things with use-value. In response, movements of locality promise that limiting the economy to a region would provide full employment, security in basic needs, economic stability, social diversity, cultural strength and political dialogue. By ceasing trade on the basis of 'economies of scale', the first world could cease extraction of third world resources and thereby facilitate third world localities' ability to re-establish traditional economies and ecologies. This is a radical political economy that does not look like Marxism in that it is neither permanently industrial nor primarily proletarian or aimed at collectivization or universalist.

While relocalist analysis sees scale as a crucial issue, Marxist commentaries published on the work of the International Forum on Globalization (IFG, which advocates both globalization from below and relocalization) maintained that 'fighting the trend toward globalization through the pursuit of local economic development and the re-assertion of the rights of marginalized peoples mistakenly leads to the adoption of a capitalistic focus on markets and government' (Sandler 1995). Doug Henwood, editor of the *Left Business Observer*, called the conference 'nostalgic' and 'market apologist', and described the 'dream of local self-sufficiency' as 'suffocating and reactionary' (1996). While critiquing an article by John Clark, Joel Kovel sideswipes (1998), writing that assessments of economic globalization and corporate power 'stop short of a crucial level of abstraction: that it is not corporate power so much as *capital* – that power of which corporations are an expression – which drives the crisis onward'. (It is only fair to note that the IFG assiduously and rather inexplicably eschews Marxist analysis.)[15]

What does it mean for Marxism that people are critical of corporations but refuse to use proper political economic terms and are just not interested in the Western socialist tradition (or even alienated by it) while being radical in other ways about political economy, using odd concepts like 'place'? What about those who imagine small business as a sustainable and healthy economic form? Must they be either apologists for capitalism or hopelessly beguiled by it? The disdain of the intellectual left extends beyond the IFG scholars to the populist conspiracy theorists. Of course there are a few voices of dissent from this tendency. In 1997 labour activist Michael Moore chastised American intellectual leftists to get with the 'real populist progressive movement taking shape'. The anti-'whitist' journal *Race Traitor* is one of the few American left voices to validate the sentiments expressed by right-wing populists (Winter 1996).

The 1997 Conference of the Community Food Security Coalition provided several valuable insights into the meaning of a radical movement at this historical conjuncture. Neither the food conference nor the IFG's 'Teach-In on Globalization' included explicit Marxist or socialist analysis. But at the food conference, the sanctity of private property was questioned (by both audience and panellists) during the opening panel discussion. Panellists acknowledged small farmers' need for 'secure land tenure' but denied that corporations should have the right to control land. Environmental justice activist Carl Anthony challenged the audience to think about land in the context of a social system in which African Americans and women 'used to be property'. This radical discussion occurred at a conference at which panellists and audience members were continually joking about how conservatives loved their movement because it is self-help and mutual aid, and is 'non-ideological'.

Yet at the IFG's much larger conference, both conservative populism and Marxism were thoroughly excluded, while levels of anti-corporatism and anti-FTA critiques were equivalent between the two conferences. Food security activists evidenced complete clarity about Cargill's behaviour and intentions. Shayam Shabaka of the Strong Roots Program (an Oakland, CA intergenerational garden project) explains his relationship to his work as: 'I'm not interested in fighting any battles that aren't about changing structures.'[16]

The divisive issue at the Community Food Security Conference was not Marxism or race, but a bitter battle between charity/hunger/ social service advocates and food security organizations. Food security activists have apparently approached hunger organizations, many of which have redefined their work along Community Food Security lines. However, some hunger organizations have felt that Community Food Security meant abandoning their urgent day-to-day work and have felt attacked and put down by the approach. So here are humanitarian leftists joking about how fond libertarians are of them and naming their enemies as corporations and the liberal charity tradition. Small-scale production and the informal economy are celebrated as 'liberated territory ... free from corporate rule' – a very different model from the liberal defence of the welfare state or the Marxist accusation that small business is 'reactionary'. Building a liberated territory was described as 'friend-centered strategy' that not only 'holds enemies at bay' but also makes sure you don't turn into them through the processes of negotiating with them or playing by their rules.

Community Food Security and other relocalization movements are neither escapist nor apologists for capitalism. They are also not liberal. They speak with clarity about enemies and also determinedly build alternatives. One might even say that these low-tech, material movements are postmodern, because they address daily life with an integrated vision of change that addresses the episteme. This is why it was so important to co-opt sustainable development, to enfold it back into the economic growth paradigm.

In analysing anti-corporate movements in the context of Marxism, it is important to stay focused on what kind of emancipation Marxism is really after. As Arendt points out, Marxism can be understood as the desire to return to family-based enterprises in small-scale communities and to a form of labouring that is pleasurable instead of professional (1958: 230–3). Marcuse (1964) suggested that capitalism has the whole human being oppressed – more than just our labour. Anti-corporate movements are concerned about the quality of the air, the quality of the food, the relationship with nature, the quality of the moral order, the falseness of the freedom to consume things like Western film, the autonomy of the community to operate on the basis of its own culture. Immiseration is being articulated in ways that go beyond traditional Marxist categories by people in a whole range of relations with the economy, all of whom feel that the capitalist political economy is dehumanizing them in some way. So their analysis is basically Marxist and their answers are both classically Marxist in terms of challenging the relations of production and Marxist in a broader sense of trying to reimagine and reconstrain the economy to deal with the many ways this economy is oppressing us. Writing about indigenous resistance movements in Mexico, John Ross argues that their struggle 'is a class war as much as it is a war of national liberation' because it is 'their very specific defense of place that pits them against the greed of globalizers' (1998: 239).

Marxist critique raises two very important questions. The first is whether scale makes a difference within a market economy – are small businesses baby corporations, bound to grow up? The second is whether the economy can actually be embedded within other social institutions/priorities/cosmologies.

SCALE Marxists insist that all small businesses (and their owners) naturally tend towards corporate growth. Do they? In a local economy, what good would it serve to outgrow your market? And do they really have no choice? Examining the Russian peasant economy, A. V. Chayanov concluded that family-based farming must be 'taken as a whole in all its works', could not be subsumed under capitalist economic theory, and 'required a different economic theory'. Crucially for the purposes pursued here, Chayanov found that on peasant farms investment decisions are *subjective* (Thorner in Chayanov 1966). Scholarship on family-owned farms in the USA shows that, contrary to capitalist predictions, families defy economic rationality in their devotion both to farming and to their lands, working off-farm to avoid losing it (Strange 1988). A Kansas farmer told an interviewer 'I just wish you could tell us how to get smaller' (in Mason and Singer 1980). Chayanov challenged the then hegemonic assumption that peasant economies were 'inferior'. Apparently, farmers do experience the farm subjectively and holistically. 'Get big or get out' was a recent (1970s) addition to farm ideology, neither a law of capitalism nor an agricultural tradition (Berry 1977). Marx's defence of artisans' economic autonomy expressed his concern for unalienated labour in a form quite like small businesses – could it be that he recognized the possibility for owners of small amounts of capital to have a diversity of interests that do not lock them into growth?

Even if owners of small businesses have regressive social beliefs, they have much less money to implement their preferences undemocratically than do Shell and Monsanto, which will also profit from race if they can. We have little possibility of political dialogue with them. If we are willing to do the work, we can dialogue with a local businessman about his business and political practices. 'But it's much more likely that a large corporation will unionize than a small local one,' critics will argue. Communities concerned about the plight of the workers should be able to pressure small business-owners to improve working conditions. Another popular argument against small business people is that they 'were the constituency of fascism in Germany'. But at *this* historical moment, due to institutions of economic globalization which threaten their existence, small businesses seem to be developing an anti-corporate consciousness and involving themselves in alliances which impart humanitarian perspectives. As reported by Peña and

Gallegos (1993), small businesses eventually joined an environmental justice struggle, disaffiliating from corporate interests. 'But local retailers carry corporate sweatshop products,' the critics go on. That is what reduction of consumption is for. The crucial difference between local elites and corporate elites is that their *locality* makes them vulner-able to social pressure.

Environmental 'trade-offs', destruction of local livelihood, cultural homogenization, bureaucratic dehumanization, food insecurity, hege-monic health practices and discrimination would not necessarily be solved by socializing today's large enterprises. Is scale a 'new' material category that Marxism must understand if it is to speak radically and meaningfully about our time? Can there be 'new' Marxist categories? As I understand it, historical materialism is confounded by the 'failure' of the working class to play its revolutionary role and by its own failure to generate effective mediative tools. Attempts to explain these failures emphasize the way Marxism is stuck in the moment of history that gave rise to it and has thereby ceased to do historical materialism. In order to speak to today's material realities new categories may be needed. In addressing the 'failures', Adorno (1972) pointed to two mirroring possibilities. The totalizing powers of capitalism infect every gesture of emancipatory practice (much as, according to Ashis Nandy, colonialism inhabits *every* gesture made in India *and* Britain, including those who understand themselves to be in opposition to colonialism [1983]). At the same time, Marxist visions can exert totalizing powers (negating the negations), an outcome that Adorno feared. To the extent that Marxists to some extent prohibit Marxist innovation, we are already exerting that closure of criticism.

Is the defence of small business a symptom of an infection or a historically specific expansion of Marxist theory? Several theorists have pointed out the necessity of adding scale to Marxist theory (Trainer 1989; Daly 1993). In Bill Weinberg's words, which bring this critique to the socialist states alongside of the capitalist ones, 'Revolutionary movements which fail to profoundly reevaluate modern industrial civilization's obsession with mega-scale development and top-down planning may find themselves depleting their nations' resource bases and alienating their own populace to the same degree as the repressive oligarchies they sought to replace' (1991: 161).

RE-EMBEDDING   Karl Polanyi (1944) opposed the theoretical tendency to separate economy from society and the accompanying reduction of people to self-interested producers and consumers. His political economic vision encouraged 're-embedding' the economy into the community, which would require the decommodification of production and consumption and their governance within a framework of social and cultural goals. Similarly, Muto Ichiyo argues that:

> Economic activities should be reintegrated with the life of the people – people in the community. Production and consumption should be organized as material aspects of communities ... Here, people-to-people relations regulate the economy, and not vice versa ... This is what we mean by 'taking back the economy.' (Ichiyo 1993: 153–8)

One of the things alternative moral epistemology could provide is a way of constraining economic forces within social ones (since neither social contracts nor regulatory bureaucracies seem to work). This possibility of embedding is crucial to the approaches of the first two modes, which insist that democracy can forcefully embed the economy. If the Marxist vision of the world is accurate, mode of production strongly shapes the other institutions of society. Polanyi argued that this is only so when economic exchange is market-driven (a political choice about how to organize economic exchange, which could alternately be made in the form of reciprocity or redistribution). But if the Marxists are right, embedding the economy is impossible because mode of production has always been and will always be the base. In Marxist terms, Polanyi's claim would be that mode of production becomes the base only under capitalism. What could explain the incredible diversity of economic systems among indigenous societies if they were not embedded in diverse cosmologies?

There are other arguments for the possibility of embeddedness. What if our particular historical condition gives rise to something that was impossible before – a conscious small-scale entrepreneurship that will *stay* small because it has *learned* that it has other interests than M' and is committed to them? (Having joined together to fight the predations of corporations, small businesses embed themselves, transforming the mode of production in some way?) A post-corporate political economy might entail new entrepreneurial goals (such as the internalization of costs), a changed set of acceptable forms of rationalization, new social rules (a new moral order to contain the political economy) or the lack of large-scale market discipline. The return of barter-based systems suggests political economic systems with private ownership and enterprise reorganized around goals other than M-C-M', and may signify an emerging political economic distinction on the basis of scale that suggests some kind of yet-to-be-articulated ethic of small business. Could this be an evolution in mode of production, therefore consistent with Marxist theory?

AbulHasan Sadeq argues that the Islamic economic institution of Zakah embeds entrepreneurship in a moral system that systematically alleviates poverty and distributes wealth equitably. By supplementing the buying power of the poor, Zakah 'increases effective demand for basic needs and thus helps production of socially desirable goods and services' (1996: 50). The US Black Power movement has been in part socialist but (like the organic farming movement) has also pursued a bounded entrepreneurship that is committed to community-based goods provision and unwilling to trade off human, cultural and environmental values in favour of profit. In Islamic economic thought, 'objectives such as optimisation, maximisation and minimisation ... can only become useful if they contribute to the attainment of Islamic objectives. In this sense, value-judgements lie at the roots of the Islamic economic system and its economic theories' (Nomani and Rahnema 1994: 43).

Often concerns with scale develop out of the defence of a particular place as economic globalization homogenizes places and alienates people from their placed histories. Challenging corporate scale is necessary to protecting qualities, particularities and sovereignty of a place. Defence of place is a moral framework. The dream of the re-embedders is that some social structure would be so overarchingly powerful that it could leverage the power to embed. Could place be it? In *God Is Red* (1972), Vine Deloria, Jr., articulates place-based epistemology and contrasts it with the Western European time-based one. Sustainable development teacher Bill Mollison, founder of permaculture, berates sub/urban first worlders for 'having no idea where you are'.[17] Farmer Wendell Berry (1977) emphasizes the length of time it takes to actually get to know a piece of land. Kirkpatrick Sale and other bioregionalists explain the ecological uniqueness of every region, which dictates a customized economy. Sale defines bioregionalism as the process of becoming 'dwellers in the land', emphasizing that our 'crucial and perhaps only and all-encompassing task' is understanding the specific capacities, limits, timing and possibilities of our places (1996: 472). It is Smithian and at the same time anarchist (and sustainable) to insist that 'ownership must be rooted in place' (in Korten).[18] Since places come with communities that can enforce their values on the operation of local businesses (prohibiting cost externalization), another of Smith's propositions becomes feasible: the market allocates efficiently as long as all *costs are internalized*.

There is a *material* force that could re/embed economies. The abundances and limitations of locality and region gave rise to particular modes of production, which may then have given rise to cosmologies, political and social systems, and so on. Limiting an economy to an ecological region could create leverage over mode of production without abandoning the recognition that mode of production is somehow still the base (see Harris 1974). Ecology is not a social structure, but the choice to limit an economy to an ecological region is still a political choice – therefore evidence of social/political embeddedness (which we're not sure can happen). What if the decision to constrain an economy geographically were made not from within the social structure of that economy, but by the colonized places on which it arrogantly feeds (whose mode of production, dependency, shapes the necessary political response, repatriation of resources)? That could force embedding without presuming that social institutions can escape their structural conditioning.

All three modes of anti-corporatism ultimately seek re-embedding. They take different theoretical and logistic approaches. If re-embedding is the task, we face a social movements question for which the field is hardly prepared: what might be the approaches for leveraging re-embedding? By what various means can communities retake ownership over 'productive capacity' (Morris 1996: 437)? After spending a lot of time wrestling with religious nationalism, and why it made sense to me to include it in the study, I realized that religious nationalisms' attempt to assert what Mark Juergensmeyer (1993) calls 'moral order' over the economy appears to be one of the most effective methods for re-embedding. Are there things to learn from religious nationalist strategy? Democracy is seen to be one of the most important such frameworks. The next section attempts to discover how the movements think about and use democracy. This is important because some of them do so in ways that may not be immediately recognized as such. If we are interested in using democracy as a tool for re-embedding, we must think about all of its possible permutations.

Democracy

> Therefore, if we wish to construct the hegemonic articulations which allow us to set ourselves in the direction of ... radical democracy ... we must understand in all their radical heterogeneity the range of possibilities which are opened in the terrain of democracy itself. (Laclau and Mouffe 1985: 168)

This section explores how the movements use democracy – or, in Laclau and Mouffe's terms, what the 'surfaces of emergence' look like in all their *heterogeneity*. It is here that the uncomfortable inclusivity of this study may bear fruit. What are the opportunities and necessities for radical democrats who seek new allies? The discussion is organized around a series of critical discourses on democracy: formal democratic structures, social democratic values, bureaucracy and political order.

Modernization theory proposes that with economic growth and industrialization *formal democratic structures* will arise. Despite the fact that for the most part it does not happen (with the remarkable but explicable – and hardly egalitarian – case of South Korea), it seems useful to at least articulate the kind of democracy that was supposed to happen: the Western European centralized statist variety in which while the people vote, the elites still manage to rule. It is only this particular variety that the USA and UK are willing to support (and only so long as they approve of election results). Less centralized and oligarchic nationalist democratic movements are generally suppressed militarily by the 'leaders of the free world', particularly the USA. It is presumed that within such systems channels exist for the expression of dissent and for the articulation of citizens' concerns and priorities. However, for the most part, peaceable citizens' movements are permitted to gain hegemony only when their concerns do not conflict with elite priorities (Zinn 1980; Glasberg 1990). Extensive attention has been devoted to the nature, practices and possibilities of nation-scale formal democracy. Both within formal democracies and in countries that do not (yet) have democratic states, social movements often find it necessary to use extra-democratic tactics in order to give voice at all.

Almost all the movements studied here are critical of such democracy. They are aware of internal contradictions of liberal democracy and the hypocrisy of American democracy, in particular. Such critique is absent from the sustainable development movement, which does not have a critique of liberal capitalism, often believing that it is possible to coexist with it as long as corporate depredations can be sidestepped. While sustainability activists often have little interest in formal 'politics' as they understand them, concentrating their energy on protecting and expanding sustainable spaces despite whatever it is that government is up to (which certainly is not seen as supportive of sustainability), they do fantasize that governments will see the light, and therefore tend to wax eloquent about official proclamations on sustainability.

While they see the contradictions of formal democratic systems, movements of the first and second modes try to make them work. The first and second modes attempt to get liberal democracy to work properly, demanding that it deliver on its democratic promises. These movements exercise democratic participation through protest, judicial and legislative efforts, and citizens' campaigns against corporations. They demand that states and international agencies live up to their egalitarian promises. In essence, while not directly challenging liberal democracy, they try to strip it of its liberal proclivities, insisting that secular civic democracy can constrain capital and serve the interests of the people. The environmental justice movement draws on democratic logics forged in the civil rights movement, a sensibility of right and wrong that is accustomed to living in the margins of hegemonic ideology. In the third world, states are also called upon to deliver the postcolonial promise. At the same time, they are wary of electoral politics in the liberal democracy: 'The closer to parliament the further from the people' (in Petras 1998).

The difference between the first and second modes is that the second mode, while still using formal democracy as a mechanism for achieving social justice, aims to surpass existing nation-states. Movements of the first mode tend to use already existing formal, institutionalized, legalistic channels as a means to confront and change corporate practices and reassert citizen sovereignty (whether for liberal or socialist purposes), within a liberal democratic framework. Second mode movements espousing global democracy envision that all people will gain far more powerful, direct and dignified relations to governance (direct democracy) while new global institutions are formed to protect the public interest. Kevin Danaher of Global Exchange proposes to begin 'people's globalization' by holding 'global plebiscites' in which billions of people would vote on basic economic and human rights issues.

Globalization from below movements insist on the possibility of super-participatory, accountable, inclusive democracy, but it is unclear how this is to be achieved. What happens the day after the revolution? How is the new power managed democratically on a global scale? How can massified democracy be participatory and inclusive of difference? The unrepresentativeness of labour unions participating in social contract negotiations is a good example of the difficulty of implementing democratic practices at such scale. I worry about the ability of 'people's globalization' to develop mechanisms of international democracy; we simply haven't had much practice. In 1999 we witnessed in Eastern Europe the horrific results of having endorsed the powerful to righteously 'intervene'. Not only were humanitarian principles invoked deceitfully, but also the 'intervention' outstripped the brutality, and indeed criminality, of the highest estimates of precipitating events.

Much of the third mode has little interest in existing democratic structures. Rather than struggling to control the nation, delinking movements do their best to ignore it and build their own bases of power. They do some international work – sharing techniques, for example – but do not build new governance organizations. Various political theories inform such practices, including Rousseauian/Leveller defence of the rights of citizens (limited and equal private property as basis of independence and freedom), and the idea of sovereignty as a practice of deep democracy. There is support both for the idea of independent holdings as the basis for political equality and for the notion that limitations would have to be placed on the size of holdings in order to preclude excesses of political power. The current liberal civic secular setup seems to hold little promise, and far-away governance institutions are not seen as legitimate authorities. Anarchist theory includes well-worked-out approaches to local governance, social equity and regional coordination (through 'federalism').

With the unusual exception of Hannum (1990), democratic theory pays scant attention to self-determination and demands for sovereignty as democratic practices. Yet survival is certainly a prerequisite for a system like pluralism. Indigenous and other oppressed peoples' demands for sufficient land and resources for survival expands Rousseau's understanding of the basis of democracy to a group level. Sovereign communities are best able to participate in pluralism. Independent community sustenance could be understood as the foundation of democracy.

Supporting communities in their demands for sovereignty and autonomy would in effect defend spaces ruled by alternative epistemologies, values and economic systems. Community autonomy might thwart liberal capitalism because liberal promises would always be tested against community integrity (and would often fail). Through a federalist system, distinct communities would engage in dialogue about common concerns, drawing on the strengths of many knowledge and social systems. Ensuring that every community had what it needed to survive (land base, natural resources, control over institutions and local decision-making) would enable pluralism, not threatening to impose majority lifeways on smaller or weaker communities. Drawing on an extensive review of case studies, Hannum suggests that we see sovereignty as a flexible tool to deal with complex political situations, rather than seeing it as a threat to existing nation-states. Positioning the massive secular nation-state as the only political structure limits our ability to solve problems. In local autonomous zones, people would have the opportunity to ensure justice around issues of race, class, gender and sexuality without waiting for laws, rulings and enforcement funding from the liberal state or the flaccid United Nations.

Somewhat by definition, the most interest in sovereignty appears among movements of the third mode. However, there is also interest in issues of self-determination among movements of the other modes. In the first mode, Rousseauian democracy eschews distanced institutionalization in favour of more direct democratic practices, but still assumes existing nation-states as the unit of governance. Only the third mode proposes actual alternative models for democracy, drawing on historical instances that emphasize how small-scale communities enable democracy to work.

Long before reformulations seeking to respond to new social

movements, democratic strivings were crucially constitutive of the soul of Marxism. Unalienated labour that maintains human relationships between production and use is labour with voice and autonomy. Distorted as such strivings have sometimes been (by 'correct' theory, controlling organizers and hierarchical organizations), workplace democracy remains a staple of socialist vision. Marxist concerns with democracy have inspired friendly critiques of communist states. The movement for 'economic democracy' is a US attempt to popularize socialist principles with reference to a democratic framework. Instead of using explicit socialist ideology, economic democracy combines populism with social justice concerns and workplace and union issues. Popularized in the 1970s by Tom Hayden, this was one of the early anti-corporate movements, which also was 'incubating a longer range vision of decentralized, radical democracy' (Boyte 1977).

Despite its commitments, Marxist democracy has often suffered from a lack of interest in the 'raw and powerful connection' made possible by inclusion of potentially theoretically incorrect differences (Lorde 1984: 112). Marxists less hampered by correct theory have gone off in many directions – most notably into anti-bureaucratic alternative organizations – that address well-founded fears of socialist state centralism while exploring more humanistic and creative aspects of Marx's vision.

Marxist concerns have been updated into 'social democratic' values. It is primarily in the second mode that we find movements aspiring to all three of Philip Green's (1985) social democratic criteria (achievement of greater material equity, equal rights, and fuller participation in decision-making). In other modes, the only movements that aspire to all three of Green's criteria are the anarchy, punk DIY, and sovereignty movements. However, it is important to note that one or two of these social democratic goals are held by all sorts of movements in all three modes. The second mode's social democracy comes in the form of reliance on bureaucratic approaches to achieving justice. The second mode is also most devoted to workplace democracy. Interestingly, movements of the third mode show commitment to unalienated labour, but believe this can be achieved in non-statist ways. The first mode is least likely to take on the issue of workplace democracy.

Throughout all three modes, movements show interest in and commitment to multicultural equity (the social democrats of the second mode have no monopoly), but only the third mode actually has a theory of how diversity is to be valued and treated democratically. Since third mode movements do not rely on centralized, universal control, diverse communities will be able to develop their own economic and political systems. Sovereignty movements point to a long history of diversity and social technologies for integrating it. Sustainable development theorizes human diversity as a tremendous resource, consonant with biological diversity. Unlike mainstream Marxism, anarchism insists that a community is stronger for all the different approaches people have to solving problems and for their different interests in various community responsibilities (Ward 1982: 57).

Built from a critique of formal state democratic practices and then applied internally within social movement organizations, the *anti-bureaucratic* tradition militates against the seemingly benign anti-democracy of hierarchy. Atilio Boron (1995) articulates the concern with the deadening effects of statist bureaucracy, as did Martin Buber, who explained how a democratic system which invests in bureaucratic operations empowers the state to self-importantly invent work for itself; this 'political surplus' becomes an excess of state power, which the state then defends and defines as necessary (in Ward 1982: 24). Political reflexivity of the 1960s prioritized the articulation of alternative organizational forms, eventually to include businesses, social services, meetings and conversational style. Feminist concerns made important contributions both to the elaboration of the problem and to new models. Feminist theory and ethnic studies scholarship together brought epistemological variances to the table, which brought both strength to the critique and a rich (and as yet hardly explored) source of alternative decision-making systems (Collins 1991).

Concerns with the effects of bureaucracy appear scattered through all three modes. Despite this, movements of the first mode tend to rely on statist and bureaucratic methods for the implementation of social justice. An excellent example is the peace and human rights movement, which relies heavily on statist approaches while also containing a strong social critique of bureaucracy, which is part of the culture of the movement. Movements of the second mode claim to avoid bureaucracy, but it's hard to see how they will manage that. The third mode's abandonment of statist structure and bureaucratic administration is not a harbinger of lack of interest in social justice (it scores well on

Green's criteria) but a belief that social justice can be achieved with other means. Internally, within their organizations, movements of the first and second modes are far more likely to be bureaucratically organized than those of the third mode, but there are movements in every mode which eschew bureaucratic organizing. While relocalization speaks to many of the strivings of traditional social justice movements, its repudiation of centralized governance frightens leftists. These concerns will be explored further in the next section.

In his 1980 *Terms of Order*, Cedric Robinson suggests that democratic logics are structured by the Western notion of *political order*, which infects not only the political realm, but other aspects of society as well. Anthropologist Pierre Clastres (1987) concludes similarly that the very idea of a state is totalizing and leads to essentialism by proposing that society is 'one'. Robinson's claim that political order is 'the dominating myth of our consciousness of being together' casts a shadow on Laclau and Mouffe's (1985) celebration of the extension of the 'democratic imaginary'. To what extent is the 'democratic imaginary' a statist vision?

Are there movements that use the democratic imaginary but might not be adopting notions of political order? Those movements that do not merely *use*, but work to be entirely structured by non-Western epistemology, may escape the mythical structures of secular political order. Investigating and investing in non-Western, non-modern epistemology could be a way to 'subvert that way of realizing ourselves' (Robinson 1980: 218). Third and fourth world epistemology is used frequently throughout the three modes. This takes many different forms, from techniques shared by farmers in the sustainable agriculture movement, to spiritual appropriations practised by members of the peace and human rights movement, to analytical models and political solidarities pursued by scholars in the anti-corporate movements, to religious cosmologies embraced by religious nationalists. Certainly movements that support extreme social diversity, including conflicting systems of order, might be those closest to achieving Robinson's vision. Those would be indigenous sovereignty movements, Zapatismo, DIY, cyberpunk, and the agricultural component of the sustainable development movement.

In the USA, a set of ethnic studies and activist projects have already organized around the deconstruction of French/American democracy.

Reasserting the historical fact of and exploring the significance of the Iroquois Confederacy's contribution to US democratic systems has been one such project. Another has been questioning the liberatory potential of American democracy in light of Constitutional exclusions of the nation's people of colour, women, and other propertyless peoples. A third project has been to privilege the material history of the USA so that genocide, exploitation and imperialism are exposed as the 'real' principles of the nation, rather than mistakes in the perfectible democratic inheritance (Zinn 1980). Democracies, then, are resited as collective and world-historical heritage (known by other names), and the French/American arrogation is delegitimized by its own material contradictions.

Use of non-Western and non-first world epistemology creates openings for alternate political frameworks (and alternate conceptions of democratic practice). Clearly, fourth world epistemology is one of the aspects of 'radical heterogeneity' that will expand the 'terrain of democracy'. Its implications, however, are challenging. It will be hard for human rights advocates who have seen centralized, secular, formal processes as crucial to question universalism. Only by doing so can the 'radical heterogeneity' of potential allies and systems be explored. For example, populist movements raise important questions that should be considered in the context of Marxist politics. Interestingly, leftists who notice the rhetorical similarities between far right decentralism and populism and our own respond by working hard to find some difference between us. Typically, a US left analyst collapses Christian/patriot ideology into that of Posse Comitatus (a racist group) and then argues that the sovereign claim for county sheriff as highest authority is authoritarian and anti-democratic. But there have been all kinds of systems in which a local chief was kept accountable to some kind of democratic process.[19] Even the Islamic imams deserve obedience only if they protect the rights, happiness, harmony and prosperity of the people (Mernissi 1992: 27, 33). Christian/patriots express a great deal of interest in one form of democracy (local sovereignty) instead of another form (the national centralization we have come to rely upon in the search for social justice and equity).

Opposing the elite who benefit from the corruptions of liberal democracy, populism traditionally champions the common people and simple life, presuming that democratic majoritarianism will be an unproblematic agenda (McKenna 1974). Anti-intellectualism and nativism alienates leftists from populist movements in both the USA and Europe, which otherwise might be recognized as proletarian revolutionary movements. Interestingly, despite their wholesale rejection of populism, advocates of 'globalization from below' make similar assumptions about the will of the majority and the ease of implementing it. Rather than abandoning the notion that there is such a thing as common interest among the common people, globalization from belowers might question their assumption that populists are pursuing some *other* kind of politics, irreconcilable with the goals of self-identified social justice movements. The problems of majoritarianism might even be a productive framework for dialogue between populists and globalization from belowers.

If, as Laclau and Mouffe argue, the 'alternative of the Left should consist of ... expanding the chains of equivalents between the different struggles against oppression' (1985: 176) then we must pursue dialogue with those democrats who do not seem immediately to be 'radical' and we must push ourselves to see the value and potential 'power' in our difference (Lorde 1984). Finally, we must believe in the capacities of community, most importantly its capacity to be organically democratic. Doing so will be much easier if we recover pre-modern forms of democracy rather than seeing it as something only made possible by modern organizations, university education and Western cosmopolitan philosophy.

Who are our democratic allies? Let me again remind (the first world intellectual left) to be clear about the enemy. Who or what does the left name as the other? Let it not be the enraged unemployed, desperate for explanations and a sense of self-determination, currently recruited by the right. How could right-wing populists expand visions of democracy? Is local sovereignty under a yet to be named local government system more or less democratic than a sham elected government beholden to corporations? Is the United Nations, whose every decision is manipulated by the weapons and economic power of a small number of nations, more or less democratic than a society in which hundreds of local mullahs vie for followings on the basis of the power of their ability to make meaning of the world? Is the first election in a newly democratic country ('assisted', of course, by colonial powers) more or less democratic than Cuba's many forms of neighbourhood self-governance and neighbourhood and workplace-based policy contributions to the national government? Is a nation that perpetrates racism and sexism in its explicit and implicit policies democratic? Is economic equality such as that ensured by the Islamic system of *zakah* more or less promising as a basis for democracy than an electoral system in a capitalist economy?

Shall we begin by acknowledging the limits of secularism? The limits of state enforcements of civil rights? Of the civil rights project itself? Of the universalism of human rights? Of its antagonistic relationship with place and culture – the very culture now embraced by so much of the left as a liberatory combustible? Can the left's 'struggle for hegemony' even be a democratic process? Perhaps an easier way to begin, rather than with angry street youths, would be to consider the consequences of our valiant struggle for hegemony in the context of indigenous peoples' demands for cultural autonomy. What does it mean that the humanitarian left wants them to participate in plebiscites? Can we de-Christianize the statist democratic agenda, humble it? If we could just manage to grow our own food and incorporate our shit into our own soil, might that open more possibilities for others to be themselves than some universalizing, inevitably bureaucratic 'participatory democracy'?

Political systems, whether democratic in some way or not, need vessels. The question of the basis of political authority is perhaps one of the most important questions facing would-be re-embedders. Concerns about political legitimacy often focus on problems with nations and assume that surpassing them would better enable global democracy to exist. Not all the movements here take such an approach, which demands a new analysis of possible bases for political authority. The next section examines issues of autonomous political authority under the rubric of 'nation', exploring its potential contributions to resisting globalization as well as its implications for larger social justice projects.

Nation

Each of the three modes articulates a different political vessel: civic nationalism, internationalism (without the nations) and community 'sovereignty' (in Western political terms it's anarchism or anarchist federalism). For the purposes of this discussion, I use the word 'nation' to refer to political autonomy / sovereignty at any scale (including both the first mode's existing nations and the third mode's autonomous localities). More important than debating which is the best approach to political formation is exploring what is at stake in autonomy. This section first reviews established critiques of nation and nationalism. It then problematizes in more depth suspicions of three elements of autonomy – community, essentialism and traditionalism. Finally, it presents the movements' relationships to nation and nationalism.

Simply put, nation is not an unambiguously good thing. Sophisticated critiques of nationalism have been articulated around a number of interrelated problems associated with the ethnocentrism of the national concept, its rather recent, mostly imperialist origin, and its questionable epistemological foundations. Historically, the nation-state was imposed by European colonial powers over the top of existing tribes, territories, kingdoms and ethnic groups. One consequence of this is that nations can be critiqued as all about imperialism. Another is that the artificiality of nation-state boundaries has in many cases created territorial conflict. The resulting nation-state, even when freed from European control, has a colonizing political relationship with pre-existing social / political units, some of which overlap more than one nation. This is sometimes used to explain why the nation has not 'worked' in Africa. Other scholars point out that the 'failure' of postcolonial nations to deliver to their peoples is instead a function of recolonialism at the hands of transnational corporations and international 'development' agencies (Khor 1993).

Second, the modern liberal democratic nation is based on the idea of similar sovereign citizens – a homogeneous society. This individualization of the basis of political power forges a particular essentialized notion of the self, which is culturally peculiar. Moreover, the ideology of direct, rationalized individual relations to the state, political power and democracy distorts both the appropriate pluralism of social movements and the undemocratic powers of elite organizations. Florindo Volpacchio points out that liberal democracy insists on an individualistic universalism, in which rights are given to individuals. He argues that 'rights can only be exercised in a community' (*Telos* Staff 1995: 87). But if nations artificially elevate the status of the individual, communities lose their political status.

Third, the legitimacy of the nation is tied to the sovereignty of a people. In order to make the claim that 'the people ... constitute a socially integrated body, a meaningful whole' (Calhoun 1997: 77), arguments for cultural homogeneity seem necessary. Once established, in order to make coherent national meaning over a cacophony of other established meanings and/or ongoing conflicts, simplified notions of politics, leadership, citizenship and peoplehood have been hegemonized. Hobsbawm (1990) and others argue that national traditions are mythical inventions, 'imagined communities' (Anderson 1983). A classic example of the success of such myths is France, which remembers as French heroes speakers of different languages who died claiming independence from that homogenizing nation (Calhoun 1997: 53). To assert independence, the nation must naturalize its already existing peoplehood, a process that requires both myths of 'ancient roots' (ibid.: 58) and 'forgetting' heterogeneous and contradictory pasts (Renan 1882). The result has been essentialized notions of the citizenry, which have led in some cases to nativism, exclusion, forced assimilation, discrimination, denial of actually existing ethnic, language and other diversities, and the imposition of unitary identity on complex social systems. Again, even the freed colonial nations pursued such identity in an attempt to be 'modern' participants in the world system (Nandy 1983). Unfortunately, much discourse on nationalism focuses on identity, rather than on political economic/anti-colonial motivations for autonomy (*Telos* Staff 1995; Kofman 1998), treating identity as a mysterious, independent social phenomenon. This leads to distorted perception of why those identities are formed.

A fourth set of critiques is organized around the relationships between nations, capitalist imperialism and liberal democracy. Secular national governments exist to serve commerce and industry (capital accumulation), not for the public good (Horkheimer 1947). Liberal democratic states offer the possibility of reform only to mollify workers; capitalism cannot be voted out. Domestic and international relations are consistent; liberal democracy pretends to provide freedom for all citizens (and sovereign nations) to realize their capacities, but in reality protects the ability of the 'stronger to do down the weaker' (Macpherson 1977). This reinforces nations' tendencies to eliminate heterogeneity. Partha Chatterjee explains that modern nations 'seek to obliterate the fuzziness of communities' with the use of 'mechanisms of normalization' (1993: 227) because capitalism needs marketable-to consumers who desire standard products. This requires the reduction of human diversity and the quelling of all non-capitalism-serving disputes that might disrupt commodification and marketing. 'The modern state, embedded as it is within the universal narrative of capital ... must therefore subjugate, if necessary by the use of state violence, all such aspirations of community identity' (ibid.: 238).

A fifth set of critiques focuses on modern statehood. While the state apparatus can be distinguished from the nation and is sometimes treated entirely separately, it is important to acknowledge that national-ist demands claim that an already existing national people deserve a separate and matching state (Calhoun 1997: 103). And it was the rise of the modern state as a new structure that made the unitary aspects of nation possible. Nations were centralized, administratively know-ledgeable, monopolized legitimate violence, and were thus capable of ruling everyday life (ibid.: 68). This approach to politics replaced a diversity of other methods, which were for the most part less totalizing. One of the crucial results of this setup is that liberal social justice struggles have fought to be articulated as state projects. Some of the failings of justice via the centre are obvious: social welfare programmes are never safe within capitalist states and the world system, people bridle under colonizing rules that come from somewhere else, bureau-cracy is deadening, centralization produces an 'excess of political power' that emerges in the form of self-important invented work (Buber in Ward 1982), and there is an essentializing effect of making rules at the centre and assuming that all peripheries need them and/ or will benefit. Other commentators point out that the removal of responsibility for social welfare from the community results in apathy and a loss of community skills (McKnight 1995).

But there are positive aspects to the nation as well. The flip-side of the homogenizing peoplehood that nationalism seems to require is the idea that *peoples* have the basic right to sovereignty, to *not* be ruled from outside. Such sovereignty delegitimizes external/imperial rulers and imperialist projects. Ernest Renan described this as a 'spiritual principle' of continual 'consent, the desire to live together', which produces a 'moral conscience' that eschews 'seizure' of provinces against their will. Along with this comes an international political order in which nations are equivalent political units (Calhoun 1997:

93), leading to a democratic internationalism, which many countries strive for despite elite nations' incessant thwarting of it. As Patricia Williams writes about civil rights in the USA, 'blacks believed in them so much and so hard that we gave them life where there was none before' (1991: 163). Likewise, third world nations have created international democracy in the interstices of the arrogant powers.

Gord Laxer (1999) argues that the nation is of democratic origin, and thus is a special and important site for 'civil' politics. Laxer also argues that essentialism is not an essential part of nation, pointing out that anti-fascism of the 1930s and 1940s mobilized nationalism as the basis of its opposition. Laxer might argue that it was the discursive civil nature of the nation that gave rise to its use as a defence against the very essentialism for which it is blamed. Laxer retells the drama of nation as the struggle between civic nationalisms that strive imperfectly for democratic polities and ethno-cultural nationalisms that are often (but not always) essentialist.

Indigenous peoples have adopted the idea of nation as a legal basis for defending their territory and sovereignty. In the process of using it, they have articulated other visions of nation. While their national identity sounds similar at first to oft-criticized Western nationalist identity ('We are the people ... This is our land ... We are proud of who we are') there are also important differences. Indigenous ideas of nation include taking responsibility for the land, caring for the people / community, and providing for the next generation(s). Indigenous people have no doubt that their sovereignty and authority over their territory, economy, education, culture and community life is crucial to their ability to meet their responsibilities. Westerners who seem to want to dismantle the nation-state in service of social justice deny the necessity of community authority over territory and social life for indigenous peoples' survival and justice needs.

As Bhabha points out, study of the 'ambivalent tension' of the nation tends to focus on it as a 'system of cultural signification' and on its role in shaping 'social *life* rather than ... social *polity*' (1990: 2) The critiques just summarized raise many important points about this new, odd and forgetful institution, the Western nation, fast coming to be seen as one of the 'dark corners of the earth' (ibid.: 6). These critical discourses, however, come from a context of assuming that nations have the right and power to self-rule. In that context, 'nationalist' movements are indeed about social *life*. Globalization's attack on that right and power, and the very possible loss of it, decentres those questions and brings new (or perhaps older) ones into sharp focus. These questions are less social and again political. Can national governments surrender the sovereign rights of their citizens? What space is there for sub-national political units to defy the nation-state without seceding? What forms of political organization are best for resisting colonialism? For resisting liberalism?

The nation-state involves three basic components: the monopoly on legitimate force, the legitimacy of pursuing the 'public good', and its relationship with capitalism. What will happen if the corporate globalization project is complete and the public good is no longer determined from within the state? How will the ensuing evacuation of bureaucratic legitimacy change the meaning of the nation? In the short run, the bureaucracy will simply change clients (from the ever-compromised state to the new rulers, corporations), but what will happen when corporations no longer need the state to facilitate their activities? More specifically, what will happen to the meaning and practice of nation when it can promise neither to provide public goods nor even to facilitate operations of the jobs- and commodity-providers? Presumably, severe changes in the political status of nations will also change the social expressions of nationalism, but probably in new ways.

Community, traditionalism, essentialism As mentioned above, the proposal of community autonomy raises serious concerns about social justice. As promised, I will at last explore these concerns. Autonomous communities, it is commonly held, will tend towards stultifying, homogeneous identities, which will enforce backward traditions on people and, moreover, are prone to fascist essentialism. As outlined above, these charges are often levelled against nations; national sovereignty is seen to facilitate essentialist definitions of community, legislates traditional rigidities and tends towards fascist rule. The third mode aims for a pre-modern economic formation protected by the modern technology of (national) sovereignty. Community control over territory amounts to national sovereignty.

Western/ized elite cosmopolitan culture celebrates detachment from place and community and defines modernization, urbanization and anonymity as freeing. At the same time as they reject nationalism, they see the achievement of universal human rights as dependent on strong, centralized, secular political structures.

At the same time, we have some contradictory knowledge about community. We know that oppressed people use the word 'community' constantly, referring to a whole range of meanings, from the local population with which they identify, to a national community that shares experience, culture and striving, to a vision of spiritual human community. This community is enacted, making place, home and politics. Native American (Okanagan) Jeanette Armstrong explains that community is 'as essential to our survival as our own skin ... I know that without my land and my people I am not alive. I am simply flesh waiting to die' (1996: 467–8). At the same time, we have a variety of first world 'communitarians' decrying the loss of community among privileged classes (Bellah et al. 1985; Etzioni 1995) and attempts to strip it away from working-class people through the imposition of professionalized social services (Worms 1982; McKnight 1995). We know that the freeing cosmopolitanism argument is particularly persuasive in the case of gays and lesbians, yet their struggles also demonstrate the crucial role of community in survival and liberation (D'Emilio 1983). Finally, it seems to be the same folks who are calling for a renewal of community-scale responsibility ('think globally, act locally') who tend to see centralized political structures as necessary to enforcement of human rights.

The value of community was even acknowledged by Marx and Engels in *The German Ideology* (1846):

> Only in community [with others has each] individual the means of cultivating his gifts in all directions; only in the community, therefore, is personal freedom possible ... In a real community the individuals obtain their freedom in and through their association.

Perhaps it was this concern that led Marx to question his life's work when he started to study indigenous peoples' economies. In his last and unfinished work, a set of ethnological notebooks, Marx questioned his assumptions about industrialization, economic scale, historical stages and the value of culture (Marx 1972). The claim that community is always false, always exclusionary, always repressive, tends to be made from a particular historical position – by people who don't live in communities. Those who reject community are the first people in history to attempt to live without that institution.[20]

Autonomy movements often make claims to *tradition*. As discussed above, these claims are sometimes mythical and often at least forgetful, a tendency that scares humanists. One of the most popular forms of this concern is traditional patriarchy, or what Riesebrodt (1990) calls 'patriarchal personalism'. Mary Mellor writes 'one's heart sinks when the examples … heap praise upon … the "independent" Swiss cantons that did not give women the vote' (1998). Cosmopolitans are also wary of tradition because they associate it with suffocating isolationism. A similar critique of movements claiming 'traditionalism' is that they are not accurately traditional. These two critiques could be taken to contradict one another – or to explain one another. Modernized articulations of tradition might indeed be more essentalist than the historic tradition being invoked simply because essentialism is the modern political technology.

What is traditionalism? Of course it looks different everywhere, but traditionalism sees answers to modern problems not in futuristic solutions but in social technologies that have already existed and been refined through many years of practice. Traditionalism also challenges the logics of modernity by positioning communal well-being as the highest goal of social organization. Traditionalist social systems are organized around the intergenerational conveyance of human society, including the means of survival, preservation of history, the meanings of social roles, and a particular cosmology. Survival techniques and cosmology enmesh traditional societies in relationships with ecology – relationships that, before the machines of the modern era, were observation-based and collaborative rather than dominating. In its contingent relationship with nature and fundamental commitment to human and community well-being, traditionalism is necessarily at odds with capitalism and imperialism. Gandhi, questioning the value of Western formal education, explains that traditional life provided honest work, food, understanding of the world, guidelines for social behaviour, and morality. He asks whether 'a knowledge of letters' will 'add an inch' to the happiness of a traditional person (1908: 89). What, then, does Western education provide? Psychological rejection of traditional lives, wage-workers and consumers desperate for symbols of modernity and Westernization (Norberg-Hodge 1991).

Norberg-Hodge's analysis of the effects of modern Western 'development' on the people of Ladakh lead her to conclude that the entrance of money and Western ideals of life systematically undermined a culture that had been affluent and abundant for at least a thousand years. Since understanding this process, she has worked with Ladakhis to question critically the Western development process and collectively to defend a communal economy. The Ladakhis offer a model of a sustainable non-monetarized economy that provides material abundance, healthy individual and social life, and, as Norberg-Hodge writes repeatedly, 'happiness'.

Clearly it is necessary to critique both traditional patriarchy and patriarchal reconstructions of traditionalism. Gandhi explained that 'Nobody mistakes [such defects] for ancient civilization.' Conflating patriarchalism and traditionalism is itself an essentialist error that delegitimates and dismisses traditionalism as a means of political, social and economic order – and does so on grounds contested by many indigenous women, among others. Indigenous scholars often insist that gendered roles were not about gendered hierarchy (Jaimes 1992; Gunn Allen 1986; also see Burke Leacock 1972 [esp. 29–46], 1981). Walter Williams has documented a number of indigenous systems that recognized the need for and managed permeable gender and sexuality boundaries (1986). In terms of stifling isolation, we know that indigenous peoples travelled extensively, had sophisticated trade networks and employed federalist political structures. Traditional systems were more than intermittently patriarchal, they were also communal, and, as traditionalists assert, they did manage to contain the economy within a moral order (until it was weakened by several hundred years of multi-faceted colonial attack). As Foran (1993) documents, revolutionary restoration of Islamic law was imagined and perfected *as a barrier against foreign economic and political domination*. It would be a distortion to imply that anti-imperialism was just a cover for patriarchal cultural enforcement – a distortion that suggests disregard for the anti-colonial tradition.

Does anti-patriarchy require modernity? Is modernity less sexist? Leila Ahmed explains that Arabic and Islamic feminists break out of the dichotomy of traditional patriarchy and Western feminism. They draw on indigenous feminisms, women as 'leaders and fighters' (1982: 167). Women then stake their freedom on the indigenous historical cultural elements of their own locality rather than on escape from the local via the alienating feminism of the colonizing West (which often relies on courts and state and national legislators – that is, on the institutions of the modern, secular, state).

Traditionalist movements are often accused of not really being traditional. Their impurity (use of cellular phones and fax machines) is used as a basis to delegitimize their claims to be *choosing* tradition over modernity and to dismiss their critical observations about modernity and their offer of alternatives. Among the anti-corporate movements, sustainable development, religious nationalist and sovereignty movements reject futurist solutions to human problems and instead seek to rebuild societies based on already established and practised social methods. In so doing, they must actually recover the past in a futuristic way, in that they must negotiate modern tools as means of championing and articulating pre-modern social techniques and values. The struggles to do so forge new practices. Riesebrodt calls such 'reformulation' mere 'reactionary modernism' (1990: 177). Heilman counters, explaining that what distinguishes the *haredis'* relationship with modernity is not their use of its tools and/or fruits, but that they do not accept the premises of progress and do not celebrate the future (1992: 359). Of course these movements will be modern, which in no way undermines their demand for another, better, 'older' way. He goes on to describe how people who 'live in a situation of modernity, surrounded by competing alternatives in life', understand traditionalism: 'To maintain tradition when all about you others do not, to define a world of sacred order when the profane is the order of the day, to assert that change need not occur when all around you everything has undeniably changed, is a fundamental transformation of the meaning of tradition, the sacred, and the past ... a new order under the cover of giving life to an old one' (1992: 13, 352). Traditionalist movements, like any other movement seeking to re-embed global economic forces, struggle for the right to make their own choices, rather than letting the market decide.

Just as indigenous people use legislation, courts and international bodies like the United Nations, traditionalists use some tools of modernity (technology) to defend and advance their claim for control over the material (land, political economy and so on) necessary to protect cultural integrity and sovereignty. Oppressed people using non-violent means of struggle often come on to the oppressor's territory, use his language and institutions in order to plead or argue their case. Would anyone suggest that since European-style courts of law are not indigenous to a particular tribe, that it should not defend its land in them but should be limited only to traditional rituals? Even the nation is such a technology. If, as Chatterjee (1993: 4–5) and others note, nationalism itself was an imposition, then nationalism is a way of speaking to the West on its own terms.

Kutty (1996) makes an interesting link between the modernity and essentialism charges. He argues that religious nationalist constructs of nation and politics require a self that was not available in the same way without modernity. Benjamin Barber (1995) can retort that the very 'self' that McWorld brings into being to exploit so handily must be used against it. Anyway, the identity theorists tell us that identities are 'multiple'. 'Of course they are modern', Ashis Nandy (1983) would say, for there is no going back after colonialism. Can modern identities (as citizens, as 'minorities', as mythical ethnicities, as individuals) be wielded in sophisticated struggles for alternatives and the sovereignty to pursue them without permanently supplanting traditional forms of self and community? I suspect that many supporters of the Zapatistas confidently expect them to put down the guns once their goals are achieved. They well may put down computers too, or they may continue to communicate with allies over the internet, perhaps *while* rebuilding traditional economic, decision-making, health and cosmological institutions. Already the Zapatistas have indicated their interest in recovering and defending communal landholdings while changing certain aspects of gender relations. Other sovereignty movements too may well *choose* a traditional life despite their strategic use of modernities.

The accusation of modernity should also be placed in the context of US and other countries' attempts to dispossess indigenous people by challenging their 'authenticity'. The imperial state reserves unto itself the definition of 'indigenous' (via blood quantum and other means) and positions artifacts of modernity such as clothing, culture, language and use of technology as violations of colonial criteria of authenticity (disregarding how colonial practices affected language use and cultural maintenance, how use of modern artifacts might be necessitated by poverty, or how they could be grudgingly used as part of political strategy). Reducing the numbers of official indigenous benefits the state. Meanwhile, third and fourth world movements' strategic use of essentialism to claim a history and to provide an epistemological basis for a firm rejection of secular modernity are dismissed as inauthentic, illegitimate or oppressive.

The main argument raised against autonomy movements (whether national or local) is that they are *essentialist*. Essentialism is a reductionist vision of identity, often described as 'monolithic' in its description of cultural traits. Some critics argue that even postcolonial ethno-nationalist demands for self-determination are based on contradictory and mythical ethnic histories, are themselves exclusionary, and merely manipulate the idea of self-determination (Dragadze 1996). Essentialism is frightening because it can be exclusionary; thus it is seen to be a precursor to fascism. Social justice movements have also learned to be self-critical about the limitations of essentialist notions of identity based on such lessons as the failure of liberal feminism. Women achieving high posts in business, government and the military have not carried with them 'essential' differences from men, differences that promised to transform those institutions.

It is important to distinguish who is afraid of what in essentialism. The right has no problem with its racism, but merely seeks to delegitimize any kind of populist movement, while the left confuses local sovereignty with fascism, rejecting both and championing strong federal powers to enforce civil rights. In the USA Pat Buchanan's presidential campaign aroused quite different fears among the left (of fascism) and the right (of protectionism) – both dismissed him as 'nationalist'. The right uses left critiques to further its projects, as has clearly been the case in intervention in the former Yugoslavia, a situation which at first found the left floundering. Without an appreciation of self-determination (outside cases of fourth world peoples) and with a thorough commitment to universalist humanitarian intervention (preferably peaceful), the left has had to do its own body count in order to expose the duplicity of NATO's offensive.

Ashis Nandy's recent work on religious nationalist violence in India suggests that fears of parochial, primitive assertions of racial purity are not well-founded: *ancient* Indian identity is fluid, fragmented, multiple, not homogenizing. The newly hegemonic BJP, famed for anti-Muslim riots, has never had a cabinet without a Muslim minister

– not to mention Jews and Christians, and condones Hindu–Muslim intermarriages, even among children of party leaders. According to Nandy, this party's 'traditionalism' is expressed in authentic religious multiplicity; its 'modernity' is expressed when some of the dispossessed and urban of its members *reach for secular power by rejecting multiplicity*.

Even as the BJP on one (secular) level practises mono-identity, its popularity and very success in secular politics lie in its ability to speak to non-secular traditional culture, which is a culture of religious and cultural heterogeneity. And this tradition of heterogeneity is not only a spiritual tradition, it is also materially grounded. Nandy (1997) interviewed the litigants in the 40-year Hindu–Muslim legal battle over the Ayodhya Mosque site. They travel to court in the same car. Why? 'Because petrol is expensive.' Community is the means of material interdependence and therefore must contain social technologies of heterogeneity – pluralism still exists, even in the practice of the paramount symbol of 'ethnic strife'.

Vandana Shiva is able to document that pluralism was always part of community and locality and that it was not a problem when most members of the community were organized around providing for subsistence and other community needs. But 'uprooted communities' will adopt the 'models of power presented by the nation state … carrying out a homogenizing project of development' (1991: 189–90). Daniel Kemmis (1990) explains the necessity of 'a good barn' to make it through the winter and how that necessity made community essential to survival. Community efforts to build and repair barns also required people to accept diversity. Disagreements exist within community, but community is plural and material, it is a solid, tangible structure within which disagreements may be managed. On the basis of his experience building the first 'rainbow coalitions', Mel King (1981) argues that the development of community brings ever-increasing social and psychological capacities for diversity.

Meanwhile, the secular state itself promotes essentialism. Shiva (1991) documents that the *pre-BJP* Indian state initiated 'communal' strife as a distraction from political economic demands: in the early 1980s, Punjabi peasants mounted resistance to the impoverization produced by Green Revolution and autocratic national agricultural policies. This resistance took two complementary forms: tens of thousands of farmers engaged in massive protests and Sikh religious leaders organized people to confront cultural degeneration brought on by the new 'culture of cash and profitability'. At the movement's height, farmers threatened to withhold their grain and Mrs Gandhi sent the army to sack the Golden Temple, massacring the Sikh cultural leader Bhindranwale and followers. The national government thus transformed 'discontent that ... was the result of centrally controlled agricultural production and the resulting economic and political crisis [into] communal conflicts ... treat[ing discontent] as only having a religious base unrelated to the politics of technological change and its socio-economic impact' (1991: 184). Where ethnicity has been *used* by civic secular states, it is likely that movements will articulate themselves through it. Such movements may or may not be inherently essentialist.

Examining the case of Bosnia, Craig Calhoun exposes a similar history. He explains that the idea of homogeneous cultures 'rooted in compact territories' was 'sharply at odds with the actual history of the region, which had rendered every country and especially every city multicultural'. This multiculturalism was maintained in part by rituals that were 'at once ethnically divided and mutually engaging' (1997: 60). The naturalized image of ancient conflicts is a powerful political image. Daniel Kofman (1998) points out that 'Balkan ethnic hatred', was 'manufacture[d] ... in order to rationalize our non-intervention' – as later it was used to justify brutal intervention.

The history of the relationship between ethnicity and nation has been contradictory. According to Rogers Brubaker, nation-building literature was articulated as part of the 'high noon of modernization theory' and understood ethnicity as parochial, disruptive, and soon to be homogenized into the civic state. Modernization suppressed ethnicity in postcolonial contexts while maintaining it in the first world. Simultaneously, however, ethnicity was constitutive of re-articulations of European (and US) nationalism. Critiques of third world ethno-nationalism need to be understood in context of both colonialism and Western European nationalism. Brubaker explains this well: 'Far from being vestigial or unmodern, the dynamics of ethno-cultural nationalization ... represented a distinctively modern form of politicized ethnicity, pivoting on claims made in the name of a nation to political control, economic well-being, and full cultural expression within "its own" national state' (1996: 415).

Nor is the liberal secular West free of essentializing tendencies: liberal integrationist racial politics and basic humanitarianism enforce a cultural essentialism that is secular, legalistic, centralized and governed by state-centred democratic procedures. Although I disagree with his defence of nationalism (as a 'dialectic of the finite and the infinite' that predates the nation-state), Russell Berman makes an interesting point about anti-essentialism. It is 'fundamentally indebted to the same universalism [anti-essentialists] imagine they reject' (1995: 55). We should carefully evaluate whether indeed nationalist movements pose as consistently racist, brutal and irrational a threat as do elite nations' secular governments. Even if ethnic communities are essentializing, is 'ethnic strife' worse than McDonalds' or Nike's essentialism?

Secular cosmopolitan consumer society is not culturally neutral. Moreover, violence is, after all, the dominant mode of international relations (arriving also in the forms of structural adjustment [Bello 1994], modern agriculture [Shiva 1991], and biopiracy [Shiva 1997]). Corporations take particular advantage of people of colour and women. It is the third world 'other' who can be dumped on, worked blind at 30, policed by his or her own nation's military in service of the corporate elite, and starved within view of export crops (Sivanandan 1989). Diasporic connections are obscured as one oil company pleads guilty to boardroom racism in California and another participates in the trial and execution of indigenous activists in Nigeria. Perhaps economic globalization is more essentializing than traditional communities were.

Other scholars make a substantive distinction between movements. At first, Haunani-Kay Trask's[21] claim that 'our nationalism is ... a genealogical connection to our place' (1993: 128) is hard to distinguish from fascist nationalist claims to land, soil, blood and kin. But Trask states that Hawaiian nationalism eschews both 'predatory consumption' and 'intolerance'. Harry Cleaver (1994) makes an important point in comparing indigenous peoples' nationalism with other current nationalist identity struggles, particularly in Eastern Europe. On the surface these movements appear to make similar claims to national self-determination and autonomy of language and culture. However, a comparison of their goals is revealing: the Central European movements' goals 'appear to be inextricable ... from the inherited structures of capital accumulation', while the same claims put forth by the Indian nations in the Americas pose an 'extensive critique of the various forms of Western Culture and capitalist organization which were imposed' and also affirm and 'aim to expand the space' for a 'wide variety of renewed and reinvented practices that include both social relations and the relationship between human communities and the rest of nature ... for the elaboration of their own ways of being, their own cultures, religions'.

Anti-essentialism imagines the capacity for heterogeneity as a child of cosmopolitanism. The glorification of secular cosmopolitanism as diverse, tolerant, and so on requires a concomitant description of small rural communities as utterly homogeneous, intolerant and anti-intellectual. It suggests that people's interest in and capacity for diversity emerges suddenly in the rarefied atmosphere of the city. The claim that people are only at home in homogeneous spaces may be both socially and historically awkward.

If evidence suggests that cosmopolitan stereotypes of small communities are mistaken, perhaps we should treat national communities as a different object, rather than imputing these stereotypes to them. This distinction enables a recovery of the local as a site for humane life, politics and economics, a site I then counterpose to the existing nations of the first mode and the global community of the second mode.

Recovering nationalism Calhoun (1997) argues that nation is employed discursively, as one of several available discourses for dealing with discontent (others include religion and communism). There are two ways of seeing nationalism as social movement strategy: the first is a struggle for power to shape the existing nation-state (I'll call it 'state nationalism'). Civil war and the movements that produce it are consistent with claims for governmental righteousness in the national and peoples' interests. Third world land reform movements are examples of this approach, as are fascist populisms, such as the anti-immigrant movements in the USA and Europe.

The second use of nationalism is towards secession or autonomy, in which the goal of a group is to separate from the existing nation and achieve sovereign control over separate territory. This approach is most obvious in indigenous movements for control over their territories. As practised by other internal minorities, these movements build and sustain separate institutions and ideologies as the foundation for their sovereignty. De-colonization is an important ideological component of these movements as they often arise in reaction to political economic expropriation.

Laxer (1999) proposes that current nationalisms can be distinguished from earlier essentialist nationalisms which are the foundation of left fright in that 'nationalisms in all their plurality are more and more returning to their roots as voices of non-elites'. Eva Geulen (1995) also notes that new forms of populism, federalism and communitarianism are 'non- and even anti-nationalist'. These movements' distrust of their nations, even embodied in their nationalisms, suggest a shift in the legitimacy of political vessels. Marta Fuentes (1989) explains that these movements tend to 'seek autonomy for themselves, and not state power'. She sees such autonomy as ultimately socialist because each attempt contributes to 'the reinterpretation of "de-linking" from contemporary capitalism'. The striving for sovereignty, then, can be seen as an anti-capitalist project even when the resulting nation is not a socialist one.

Another important aspect of secessionist nationalism is defence of identity and culture. This confirms Renan's vision of the nation as a group that continually chooses to live in common. John Langston Gwaltney documents the African American tradition of sovereignty nationalism, a tradition of consciousness that says: 'We are a nation primarily because we think we are a nation ... That man has got his country and we are our country.' (Not a claim on the existing government.) Brubaker describes this as 'citizens recognize one another as "belonging together" in a subjective, "internal" sense rather than as simply belonging to the state' (1996: 413). Martin Rady (1996) points out that the Badinter Commission expanded (or restored) the United Nations' principle of self-determination to also protect peoples 'not under colonial and alien domination'.

As de-Shalit (1996) argues, self-determination is ultimately a political, not cultural, demand. The problem with an emphasis on cultural survival and the development of criteria for legitimate cultural autonomy (Miller 1996) is the imposition of external adjudication. Outsiders' evaluations of movements' essentialism or authenticity underplay the driving force behind actual self-determination demands, 'political and economic inequalities or colonial relationships ... or [denial of] participation in the political discourse and representation in political institutions' (de-Shalit 1996: 914).

Only a few scholars take secession and local autonomy seriously. Some of these draw on the federalist tradition, explaining that many larger states exist only as convenient arrangements between autonomous smaller regions, who never meant to give up their self-governance. This approach questions the insistence on massive unitary states as the only possible and best political order. Political units have the right to secede if they want to – a subjective determination (de-Shalit 1996; Livingston 1998). Others argue on the basis of international law that secessions are entirely reasonable as part of the practice of human rights. This approach tends to place secession in a normative framework; under certain objectively determined conditions secession may be appropriate (Kofman 1998; Tiryakian 1998). The defence of 'objective conditions' is, in part, a way to deal with the controlling paranoia of recursive secessions or 'Balkanization'. If one believes that nations are the natural outcome of cultural identity and diversity is infinite, then it appears that the number of nations will be ever-increasing. Hirst Hannum takes a different approach, seeing autonomy as a 'creative attempt to deal with conflicts ... before they escalate into civil war' (1990: 473).

Drawing on an extensive review of case studies, Hannum suggests that we see sovereignty as a flexible tool to deal with various complex political situations, rather than seeing it as a threat to the nation-state. Positioning the massive secular nation-state as the only political structure limits our ability to solve problems. At the same time, some interpretations of the 1970 UN Friendly Relations Declaration insist that peoples 'cannot be prevented from choosing independent statehood' – whatever that may mean (Tomuschat 1993 in Hannum 1990). The secret trump word here is 'people', which, according to Rady, is given by the UN a civic and territorial, rather than ethnic, definition. Political self-determination rights, then, are not accorded to minority groups (although 'cultural self-determination' rights are) (1996: 381). How a group is supposed to self-determine its culture without political (and economic) autonomy is a mystery. Rady's analysis of UN arbitration concludes that consistency in application of international law is not a satisfactory basis for adjudicating self-determination claims. In the former Yugoslavia, the United Nations recognized new nations, but only along the borderlines of old sub-states, which contradicted the formations of the actually seceding groups.

Examining the relationships to nationalism among the movements studied here, we see that in the first mode, the problems caused by globalization can be addressed by demanding accountability from existing political vessels, whose sovereignty is crucial to their ability to respond and therefore must be reclaimed via some kind of civic nationalism. In the second mode, 'globalization from below', powerful new movements will work through new political vessels, driven by the concerns of the people. While these movements draw on 'inter-nationalist' traditions, existing boundaries and political vessels will be superseded. Some of these movements, such as Reclaim the Streets, ignore the nation while defending public, participatory, civic space and dialogue. They also practise the internationalism that Laxer describes as part of civic nationalism, but in a way that eschews formalized internationalism and seeks direct 'people-to-people' relations. Such relationships are seen as highly agentic, able to surpass the decrepit state both in building new liberatory structures and in improving social and economic conditions in local communities.

Wary of existing nationalism, 'globalization from below' scholars propose international structures that could secure justice and human rights. Muto Ichiyo draws on identity politics in proposing shifting identity away from the national state and to common 'transborder peoplehood' so that: 'People ... will move away from their identity as "Japanese", in the sense of identifying with the so-called Japanese national interest – which is synonymous with corporate interests.' How can this be done? 'We who live in Japan should refuse to contribute toward further increasing GNP and further increasing production ... slow down our activities and reduce the productivity and efficiency of the most "advanced" sector of our industry' (1993: 157). Elaine Bernard proposes the development of 'charters', agreements 'among move-ments and people, not ... governments' (1993: 211). Denis MacShane (1993) points to the emergence of international company-specific unions that ignore national boundaries.

Laxer (1999) points to a number of problems with these 'global-ization from below' approaches. First, he emphasizes 'the relative immobility of labor', pointing out that 'capitalists are the true globalists and cosmopolitans, not workers'. Therefore peoples' movements are inherently localist and particular, not internationalist. The 'detached cosmopolitanism' of intellectuals, lacking 'commitment to place', cannot forge the kinds of solutions that will really work for the workers of the world. He argues that existing nations are 'the most effective means' for fighting globalization, and we know this in part because we know that corporations have organized to eliminate national sovereignty as a barrier to their operations. If we reject the nation utterly, we throw all peoples into dependency on the wisdom and benevolence of international governance, whose anti-democracy, ethnocentrism and collaboration with capitalism are only too well known.

In the third mode, sovereignty is crucial because the ability to say 'no' to corporate predators depends on a bounded and autonomous political vessel. The focus in the first mode is on the capacity of citizens and other constituencies to compete with other interests for the loyalty of their states. In contrast, the third mode focuses on the actual autonomy of that vessel. The third mode pursues local autonomy and sovereignty over territories not now defined as national, or, in the case of religious nationalism, for reasons not currently considered legitimate forms of civic nationalism. Laxer describes localist movements as 'anti-nationalist' while I see them as providing models for a smaller-scale, more independent nationalism. Importantly, such a nation must not be economically dependent and it must be willing and able to say 'no'.

What do these potential nationalisms look like? Since the second mode, 'globalization from below', attempts to supersede nation-states as currently understood, this analysis only examines the first and third modes, which do work with notions of territorial sovereignty. At the same time community makes a strong showing in all three anti-corporate modes and is held as an important value by all of the movements in the second and third modes.

Somewhat by definition, the first mode tends to a 'civic' form of nationalism while the third mode is secessionist. (The exceptions in the third mode are sub-movements that show interest in civic dialogue within the existing nation.) While the first mode relies upon it, the third mode shows little interest in empowering the state.

I operationalized essentialist national identity and narrative as invocation of a notion of peoplehood prior to the existing political formation, mythical traditions and authoritarian definitions of nation-hood. It turns out that the nationalisms articulated by the first and third modes show little interest in mythic traditions (essentialism) and authoritarianism (fascism). None of these movements has a clear commitment to all three components of essentialist nationalism. Interestingly, there is a disjuncture between invocations of identity and interest in the state. Those first mode movements that are particularly interested in the state are not interested in mythical peoplehoods at all.

Using Laxer's (1999) criteria for 'positive nationalism', I looked for respect for diversity within the nation (a combination of several of his criteria), respect for the self-determination of other countries, and whether the civic nationalism proposed is internationalist. I found that movements of the first and third modes have widespread commitment to inclusivity within the nation, other nations' self-determination, and international solidarity, which should alleviate concerns about homogeneity and hostile or stultifying insularity.

For third and fourth world movements, multiculturalism arises out of the horizontal development of allies and the recognition of the many faces of oppression. Within the sustainable development movement, issues of race are not frequently addressed, but one of its most important practices is sharing knowledge all over the world in the effort to rebuild sustainable communities. In the case of permaculture (one of the most widely practised form of sustainable development), this relationship is anything but extractive as permaculture practitioners do as much work in the third world as they do in the first world. Third mode internationalism means interest in the epistemologies and living systems of third and fourth world peoples, appearing in the form of enthusiasm for abandonment of first world ethnocentrism and epistemology as well as solidarity struggles.

The extent to which various nationalist movements prioritize essentialism in their projects is an important area for further research. Is there internal debate about race and gender constructions within the movements? If so, then do we trust the democratic processes within the movements to work these issues out? What resources are available to do so?

The logics of social justice and social equity projects have become totally dependent on civic nationalisms and internationalisms to provide legislation, adjudication and enforcement of civil rights. First world structural adjustment rollback of civil rights, environmental and other regulations, and social welfare policies reveals how humanitarians are dependent on centralized structures for their projects. Aronowitz (1996) points out that liberals are trapped in a model of the welfare state and social contract that elites long ago abandoned. Critics who see the contradictions and limitations of liberal civic nationalism are often the same activists who urge other nations to develop centralized state-dependent civil rights structures, accepting this mode for achieving safety, equity and justice for internal minorities.

In the same way that destruction of locality (specifically local crafts) enabled modern industry to benefit from the totalizing powers of the nation, corporations benefit from the destruction of national economies via globalization. Portraying nationalism as parochial, ethnic, disruptive, short-sighted and exclusionary, or as 'an exceptional interruption to the anticipated growth of world peace' (Calhoun 1997: 26), confirms the corporate agenda. Anti-nationalism thus empowers corporations. Just as corporations invoke 'feeding the world' to justify monopolistic chemical-intensive monocropping, they invoke 'peace' against locality, cultural claims and autonomy; this is a dominating peace.

Thus at the moment of corporate ascendance to global hegemony, social justice forces are in a quandary. Having embraced critiques of the nation, are we *ready* to lose it? The production of human rights, environmental and other conventions by centralized agencies has been accompanied by a marked lack of interest in implementing and enforcing them. With the FTAs even these liberal national and international reforms are in a very tenuous position. This shift raises difficult and important questions about how well massive centralized civic political formations have done in protecting and expanding human rights etc. and how well positioned they are to defend them now. As Lisa Lowe points out, 'the civil rights project confronts its limits where the pursuit of enfranchisement coincides with a refortification of the state as the guarantor of rights and precludes the necessary critique of the state as the protector of liberal capitalism' (1996: 23–4).

Why do we need the nation? One of the most positive contributions of the nation is its mobilization of epistemology and culture as the basis of law and politics. What the nation adds is the collective *myth* that will inform sovereign refusals; and the more such myths are alive in the world, the more difficult territory and peoples will be to colonize. A proliferation of smaller-scale nations would enable the multiplication of alternative epistemologies, resulting in *less* total homogenization and making life difficult for economic globalization. Wiegandt (*Telos* Staff 1995) and Berman (1995) argue that smaller-scale governments will be *more* vulnerable to corporate predations. But the predation will come in different forms; instead of licensed by comprador politicians it will have to engage in a direct battle with the local community. Exploitation would be less peaceable, raising questions about the cost of what for some of us appears to be peace.

Can we recover nationalism as a project of self-determination, as a community project of sovereignty and territory? What framework of nationalism do we need to recover the analytical clarity of anti-colonialism? Perhaps we need to understand the 'common-sense' Black Power spirit of nationalism that resonated so deeply with African American experience and vision (Gwaltney 1980; Lubiano 1997) – and that of other oppressed peoples of colour around the world? Can civic nationalism rearticulate itself in some way that does not reinforce liberal democracy, bureaucracy and the state? Can we centre native versions of nationalism, which are explicitly anti-patriarchal? Can we imagine a form of nationalism that is comfortable with the use of 'pre-democratic institutions' (Kurzman 1996) as part of the new 'surfaces' of democracy (Laclau and Mouffe 1985)? Can we differentiate between 'ancient nations' and the modern state? (Spretnak).[22]

Leftists, dependent on statist enforcement of social justice, fear autonomous localities. Some of this is fear of the potential for local fascist essentialism, which is a danger that must be carefully assessed in the context of corporate hegemony and its genocidal practices. Another aspect of the fear arises from simplified notions of the meaning of traditionalism. Similarly, the concept of community is used constantly by movements of relocalization and raises fears among many leftists. While these are important concerns, the dangers of community and locality must be considered in the context of the dangers of corporate globalization. Moreover, intolerance appears to be a function of insecurity. If corporate globalization is causing the insecurity, then it – not community – is the enemy of diversity.[23]

'Globalize This!'

In the context of globalization, being clear about the enemy is more possible than it has been in recent decades. With the ascendancy of the World Trade Organization, the enemy ceases to be diffusely everywhere (in a Foucauldian sense), becoming instead hierarchically everywhere through vertical and horizontal integration, and ever more of us are multiply made its victims. Cancelled, along with states' and nations' sovereign rights to regulate, are economic protections that enable the survival of local economic sectors. It is becoming more apparent that first and third world communities may need to employ similar means of struggle against this common enemy if they are to survive. A number of movements, responding to a variety of conditions and emerging from the entire spectrum of political positions, are recognizing corporations as the enemy and mobilizing to change radically the political economy.

Massive and creative movements are afoot and afire. Much of the fieriest footstomping is led from the third and fourth worlds. First worlders may find particular inspiration in the possibility of alliances with third and fourth world activists. Exciting new approaches have been developed, including new techniques of extra-legal confrontation, such as have been used in the anti-genetic engineering mobilizations; alternative forms of democracy, such as the indigenous councils relearned by the Zapatistas; and new ways of thinking about class demonstrated by radical smallholders. These movements are proposing rather surprising visions and going about politics in novel, but not quite postmodern, ways.

These movements are radical and unwilling to compromise. A leader of the indigenous residents' resistance to construction of the Three Gorges dam in China says: 'The highest expression of dignity can be summed up in the single word "No!"' (in Korten 1995: 294). A US worker says: 'Right now, a "radical" is somebody that stands up and says enough's enough, we ain't taking no more' (Brecher 1998: 27).

> the walls of the town hall blazed with slogans and symbols: 'Tierra y Libertad,' 'No to Golf!,' 'No to Bourgeois Caprice!,' and just simply 'No' – the unanimous response of Tepoztecos to national investors ... who were trying to site a very First World golf course on 187 hectares of community land. (Ross 1998: 240)

Perhaps 'no' is also a high expression of political economy. Their enemy is colonialism. Sovereignty is the appropriate political response. 'No' insists on decolonization and re-embedding the economy into a political framework based on community decisions. 'No' claims a place and a moral order over it. These non-negotiable moral positions arise from communities' long-term interdependence with their places and/ or unwillingness to permit outsiders to redefine the most important aspects of life.

These movements say more than 'No'. They propose a quite radical vision, one that has already demonstrated its ability to meet needs while protecting what we call 'diversity'. This vision can best be summarized as agricultural, encompassing first world farmers seeking market protection, farmers resisting genetic engineering, indigenous sovereignty movements seeking to control land and practices, sustainable development, localist economic visions, and third world peasant movements reacting to the failures of urbanization and neoliberalism by insisting on rights to land and subsistence. These movements have a variety of relationships to political economy, formal democracy and existing nations. But none imagines that growth, modernization or technology provide answers to their problems; indeed they see corporate technology as economically and ecologically dangerous. The emergence of a social movement centred on agricultural issues, rather old technology and rurality may come as a surprise to cosmopolitan theorists, particularly when the urban poor organize their politics around rural land rights and self-sufficiency. Such motion is neither postmodern nor socialist nor 'identity-based', but it is radical political economy.

Centring food in economic and community analysis is an important way to get people to deal with environmental and economic issues. In 1906, Peter Kropotkin proposed that 'the question of bread' is the preeminent social question. Settling the question 'in the interests of the people', will mean endorsing 'the principle of equality' (in Bradford 1989: 48). Indigenous people often refer to food as symbol of their relationship with the earth: corn is mother in Aztlán, taro is progenitor of the people of Hawai'i (Trask 1993). Scholars Vandana Shiva and Helena Norberg-Hodge explain that 'shortening food links' can be the first step in building community security in the face of globalization and indeed 'is a way to short circuit globalization'.[24]

How can the 'no' be enforced and the space defended to pursue alternatives? In the context of globalization, decolonization means independence. Any country may choose to defend its laws from WTO-based repeals (and its economy from WTO-facilitated pillage) by choosing to accept trade sanctions. Surviving such sanctions will require reducing dependence on export-based income and on imports of basic needs. Similarly, third world countries can only escape structural adjustment policies by refusing all loans, including those needed to pay existing debt. This situation is survivable by the same means, reduction of dependency on import and export. Cuba has been following this path and offers many examples of national independence in energy, food, agricultural inputs and medicine.

Independence will also require defence. Economic boundaries will be needed to prohibit corporate seductions of consumers and attacks on small producers. Tim Lang and Colin Hines' *The New Protectionism* (1993) explains how trade laws can be redesigned around the goal of protecting and rebuilding local economies. Lang and Hines encourage legislation requiring foreign retailers to 'site [production facilities] here to sell here' and local savings to be used only for local investments. Obviously, protectionism should not be used to further imperialist practices. Surely protectionism in pursuit of the survival of unique places and cosmologies can be disentangled from proto-fascism. Independence also attracts the wrath of predatory extractive economies, which have in the past responded with force. Defence against military pressure will require great coordination between third world nations (or autonomous regions) and solidarity from civil society.

The independence project raises the question of scale. Shall we continue trying to build more liberatory political structures at nation scale? Alternatively, we could follow the lead of Indian tribal areas and declare absolute political and economic sovereignty over fairly small territories. These areas, too, will need to become independent of imports and exports. The logistics of such a transition may be easier on a small scale than on a national one. Bioregionalist analysis has produced viable plans for regional political-economic units. This may be a more highly developed model than anything based on national government, because existing government plans are designed to facilitate corporate business, not to meet needs, and have no relationship to ecosystems. World-historically, we have thousands of models of sustainable, viable economies that did meet human needs. This explains indigenous peoples' and sustainable development activists' total confidence in their abilities to survive without global economies.

It could be read as a hopeful sign that the largest 100,000 corporations employ only 3 per cent of the world's workforce. Elite corporate control covers *only* 40 per cent of world merchandise trade (Hines and Lang 1996: 489). So corporations do *not* monopolize all production of basic needs. They threaten to. If they do, then people will be utterly dependent on corporate jobs and products. Reportage of the 'unemployment rate' in third world countries is constantly interpreted as a need for foreign direct investment (factories), rather than the need for the development of non-job alternatives – or, for that matter, the need for some analysis of what people were doing before they became 'unemployed'. If, instead, people are to have livelihoods that somehow enable them and their neighbours to eat, it is essential that people retain control over the land and natural resources (seeds, land, water, forests).

Some level of local political autonomy will be necessary to exert control over the local economy. We have a history of developed models for democratic relocalization. The oldest and richest Western tradition is anarchism. We can also examine European local democracies, the most famous of which is the Swiss canton system. Indigenous societies' technologies of multiculturalism and of democracy could be models. Alternative institutions (production and consumer cooperatives, social service organizations and some political movements) have extensive experimental experience with structures of participation, inclusion, and diversity. 'Participatory development', hegemonized in development practice during the 1980s (although rarely managing to devolve power) has been established as a model of quasi-democratic secular local governance in localities all over the world. Villages (or bioregions) could be economically autonomous, but allied as federations for some political purposes, like civil and human rights and public health.

Access to and use of alternative epistemology is a great strength for anti-corporate movements not only because we need new spaces for our heads (spaces independent of the globalization episteme), but also because we need models for new economic systems. Alternative values and cultural systems for sharing and celebrating them are being articulated in urban intersections (among other places), where Reclaim the

Streets! and other movements disobediently dance to protest against free trade agreements and take back the commons for human activities.

MOSOP has danced the military guns to silence. Now the Ogoni people will dance Shell's lies and public relations to silence. (Ledum Mittee, Acting President Movement for the Survival of the Ogoni People)

We are dancing on the ruins of multinational corporations! (songwriter K. C. Neal sung by Ramona, activist protecting Headwaters forest)

> Come.
> A name we have.
> Now we will not die.
> Let us dance.
>
> (Zapatistas)[24]

Amid modernization, postmodernization, fragmentation, globalization, technology and trade, we find peoples' movements from first and third and fourth worlds, cities and countryside, cosmopolitan and traditional, confidently naming their world, lovingly embracing agriculture and other local economic traditions, and bravely dancing in defence of their territory and autonomy.

Notes

1. At IFG 1997.

2. Evelyn Iritani, 'S. Korea unions join pact, drop threat to strike', *Los Angeles Times*, 21 January 1998: A1, A10.

3. National Labor Committee, 'An open letter to Walt Disney', 29 May 1996: 1.

4. Both at IFG 1997.

5. IFG 1999.

6. Both from Nick Alexander, 'Missing pieces: how the Nike campaign fails to engage African Americans', *Third Force*, July/August 1997, editing his.

7. Tim Huet, 'Can coops go global?: Mondragón is trying', *Dollars & Sense*, 214 (November/December 1997): 16–19, 41–2.

8. At IFG 1997.

9. At IFG 1997.

10. Jerry Mander, Fritjof Capra, Andrew Kimball (Center for Technology Assessment), David Morris (Institute for Local Self-Reliance), JoLani Hirnaka (Santa Clara Center for Occupational Safety and Health) at IFG 1997.

11. Fritjof Capra, citing Neil Postman at IFG 1997.

12. At IFG 1997.

13. Concerns about the military vulnerability of small nations must be analysed in context of the lack of security (both internal and external) afforded by modern militarized nations.

14. Both at IFG 1997.

15. This is a fascinating set of issues. Is the IFG strategically avoiding Marxist analysis or smartly repackaging Marxism? Of course, American Marxists suddenly jumped on the anti-globalization bandwagon when it became clear that a significant and political economic social movement was really going to do something in Seattle.

16. Community Food Security panel at IFG-3.

17. Permaculture Design Course, Ojai, CA, July 1997.

18. At IFG 1997.

19. Gabriel Metcalf, 'Arguing for decentralization', *Slingshot* (Berkeley, CA), early spring 1997: 14.

20. Anthropologists George Peter Murdoch and microbiologist René Dubos, in Sale 1996: 479.

21. Trask is a leader of the largest Hawaiian Sovereignty organization.

22. IFG 1997.

23. I must thank Colin Hines for reminding me to use this argument here. (Conversation in Seattle, November 1999.)

24. At IFG 1997.

25. Big Noise 1998.

Select List of Organizations

This is a very small listing of some of the organizations discussed in the book. Please be aware that web addresses often change and you may have to do a web search if the address provided here is outdated. Where possible, e-mail and fax addresses are also provided. Please note that some organizations are attempting to exist primarily in cyberspace and it has not been possible to provide a ground address. Finally, some organizations are participants in more than one movement; here they are mentioned only once. No organizations are listed for religious nationalism because this research used secondary texts.

Fighting Structural Adjustment

50 Years Is Enough: 1247 E Street, SE, Washington, DC 20003, USA

Tel: 202-IMF-BANK (202-463-2265) Fax: 202-544-9359
wb50years@igc.org
http://www.50years.org/

Jubilee 2000: 1 Rivington Street, London EC2A 3DT, UK

Tel: +44 (0)20 7739 1000 Fax: +44 (0)20 7739 2300
mail@jubilee2000uk.org
http://www.jubilee2000uk.org/

Bretton Woods Reform Organization: 9 Third Avenue, Subryanville, Georgetown, Guyana

Phone/Fax: 592 2 61420

Green Scissors: c/o Friends of the Earth, 1025 Vermont Avenue, NW, Suite 300, Washington, DC 20005-6303, USA

Tel: 202-783-7400 Fax: 202-783-0444
http://www.foe.org/eco/scissors98/index.html

Peace and Human Rights

Project Underground: Tel +1 510 705 8981 Fax: +1 510 705 8983

project_underground@moles.org
http://www.moles.org/ProjectUnderground/

Free Nigeria Movement: PO Box 441395, Indianapolis, IN 46244, USA

Tel/Fax: (317)216-4590
FNM@ix.netcom.com
http://pw2.netcom.com/~fnm/Main.html

Human Rights Watch: Rue Van Campenhout, 1000 Brussels, Belgium

Tel: (2) 732-2009, Fax: (2) 732-0471
hrwatcheu@gn.apc.org
http://www.hrw.org

Witness for Peace: 1229 15th Street, NW Washington, DC 20005, USA

Tel: (202) 588-1471 Fax: (202) 588-1472
witness@witnessforpeace.org
http://www.witnessforpeace.org/

Sustainable Energy and Anti-Uranium Service: Australia

http://www.sea-us.org.au/

Land Reform

FoodFirst Information and Action Network (FIAN): PO Box 102243 D69012, Heidelberg, Germany

Tel: +49-6221-830620 Fax: +49-6221-830545
fian@fian.org
http://www.fian.org

The Land is Ours: Box E, 111 Magdalen Road, Oxford OX4 1RQ, UK

Tel: 01865 722 016
office@tlio.demon.co.uk
http://www.oneworld.org/tlio/

Via Campesina: Operational Secretariat Consejo Coordinador de Organizaciones Campesinas de Honduras, COCOCH, Rafael Alegria, Barrio La Plazuela, Calle Real de la P.C., Casa No 934 Apdo, C.P. 3628 , Tegucigalpa, Honduras

asocohon@nicarao.apc.org
http://www.virtualsask.com/via/

Greenbelt Alliance: 530 Bush Street, Suite 303, San Francisco, CA 94108, USA

Tel: (415)398-3730 Fax: (415)398-6530
http://www.greenbelt.org/gba/index.html

Homes Not Jails Boston: PO Box 390351, Cambridge, MA 02139 USA.

Tel: 617/ 287-9494
red@iww.org
http://www.geocities.com/CapitolHill/7996/index.html

Movimento dos Trabalhadores Rurais Sem Terra (MST): Alameda Barão de Limeira, 1232 012002-002 – São Paulo – SP Brasil

Tel/Fax: (011)3361-3866
semterra@mst.org.br
http://www.mst.org.br

Confédération Paysanne: 81, avenue de la République – 93170 Bagnolet, France

Tel : 01 43 62 04 04 Fax: 01 43 62 80 03
confpays@globenet.org
http://www.confederationpaysanne.fr/

Kilusang Magbubukid ng Pilipinas (KMP): 69 Maayusin corner Malambing Streets, UP Village, Diliman 1100 Quezon City, Philippines

Tel/Fax: (632) 926-74-49
KMP@info.com.ph or PAMPII.@skyinet.net

The Explicit Anti-Corporate Movements

Council of Canadians: 502-151 Slater Street, Ottawa Ontario K1P 5H3, Canada

inquiries@canadians.org
http://www.canadians.org
Ratical: http://www.ratical.org/corporations/

Corporate Watch (USA): http://www.corpwatch.org/trac/

Corporate Watch (UK): 16b Cherwell St, Oxford OX41BG, UK.

Phone:+44 (0)1865 791 391
mail@corporatewatch.org
http://www.oneworld.org/cw/

Corporate Europe Observatory: Paulus Potterstraat 20, 1071 DA Amsterdam, Netherlands

Phone: +31-20-6127023
ceo@xs4all.nl
http://www.xs4all.nl/~ceo/

Adbusters: 1243 West 7th Avenue Vancouver, BC V6H 1B7, Canada

Phone: (604) 736-9401 Fax: (604) 737-6021
General Inquiries: adbusters@adbusters.org
http://www.adbusters.org

INFACT: 256 Hanover Street Boston, MA, 02113, USA

Tel: 617-742-4583 Fax: 617-367-0191
infact@igc.apc.org
http://www.infact.org/

Essential Action: PO Box 19405 Washington, DC 20036, USA

Tel: 202-387-8030
action@essential.org
http://www.essential.org/

Soil Association: 86 Colston Street, Bristol, BS1 5BB, UK

Tel: +44 (0)117 929 0661
Fax: +44 (0)117 925 2504

Alliance for Democracy: Tel: 781-259-9395

peoplesall@aol.com
http://afd-online.org/

Karnataka State Farmers Association: swamy.krrs@aworld.net

Reclaim the Streets: PO BOX 9656 London N4 4JY, UK

Tel: 020 7281 4621
rts@gn.apc.org
http://www.gn.apc.org/rts/

Cyberpunks

2600: The Hacker Quarterly: PO Box 752 Middle Island, NY 11953, USA

Tel: 516-751-2600 Fax: 516/474-2677
http://www.2600.com/mindex.html

Hackers.com: http://hackers.com/main.htm

Cyberpunk Project: http://project.cyberpunk.ru/

Environmentalism

European Federation of Green Parties: Federation of European Green Parties, EP- LEO 2C85 Rue Wiertz, B-1047 Brussels, Belgium

Tel. 32-2-284.51.35 or 32-2-284.71.35 Fax. 32-2-284.91.35
rmonoe@europarl.eu.int
http://www2.europeangreens.org/europeangreens/

Industrial Shrimp Action Network: 4649 Sunnyside Avenue N #321 Seattle, WA 98103, USA

http://mangroveap@aol.com

Greenpeace International: Keizersgracht 176. 1016 DW Amsterdam, The Netherlands

http://www.greenpeace.org

Global Network for Anti-Golf Course Action: 1047 Naka, Kamogawa, Chiba, Japan 296-01

Tel: (81) 47 097-1011 Fax: (81)47 097-1215

Asia Pacific Peoples Environment Network: 27, Lorong Maktab, 10250 Penang, Malaysia

Tel: (60)4 227-6930 Fax: (60)4 227-5705

Rainforest Action Network: 221 Pine Street Suite 500 San Francisco, CA 94104, USA

Tel: (415) 398-4404 Fax: (415) 398 2732
http://www.ran.org/

Ecodefense!: Moskovsky prospekt 120-34, 236006 Kaliningrad, Russia

http://ecodefense@glas.apc.org

Labour

Korean Confederation of Trade Unions: 4th Fl. Samsun Bldg., 12-1 Samsun-Dong 1 Ga, Sungbuk-Ku, Seoul 130-141, Korea

Tel.: +82-2-765-7269; Fax: +82-2-765-2011;
inter@kctu.org
http://www.kctu.org/

National Labor Committee: 275 Seventh Avenue, 15th Floor, New York, NY 10001, USA

Tel: 212-242-3002
nlc@nlcnet.org
http://www.nlcnet.org/

Industrial Worker Online: http://parsons.iww.org/~iw/

Banana Action Net: http://bananas.agoranet.be

Euro-FIET: Rue Joseph II, 1000 Brussels, Belgium

Tel: +32 2 230 7455 Fax: +32 2 230 7566
hqinfo@fiet.org
http://www.fiet.org/

Socialism

World Socialist Web Site: http://www.wsws.org/

Socialist.org (socialists on the internet): info@socialist.org
http://www.socialist.org/

Socialist International: Maritime House: Old Town, Clapham, London, SW4 0JW, UK

Tel: +44/(0)20 7627 4449 Fax: +44/(0)20 7720 4448
e-mail:secretariat@socialistinternational.org
http://www.socialistinternational.org/

Democratic Socialists of America: 180 Varick St 12th Floor, New York, NY 10014, USA

Tel: (212) 727-8610 Fax: (212) 727-8616
dsa@dsausa.org
http://www.dsausa.org/

International Cooperative Alliance: 15, route des Morillons, 1218 Grand-Saconnex, Geneva, Switzerland

Tel: (+41) 022 929 88 88 Fax: (+41) 022 798 41 22
E-mail: ica@coop.org or treacy@coop.org
http://ica.coop.org/

Coopératives on-line: gnc@cooperatives.org

http://www.cooperatives.org/

Anti-FTA

Third World Network: 228 Macalister Road, 10400 Penang, Malaysia

Tel: 60-4-226 6259 or 226 6728 Fax: 60-4-226 4505
twn@igc.apc.org or twnpen@twn.po.my
http://www.twnside.org.sg/

Peoples' Global Action: info@agp.org

http://www.agp.org/agp/indexen.html

International Forum on Globalization: 1555 Pacific Avenue, San Francisco, CA 94109, USA

Tel: (415) 771-3394 Fax: (415) 771-1121
ifg@ifg.org
http://www.ifg.org

Public Citizen Global Trade Watch: 1600 20th St, NW Washington, DC 20009, USA

Tel: (202) 588-1000
gtwinfo@citizen.org
http://www.citizen.org/pctrade/tradehome.html

Inter-Continental Caravan: gn.apc.org

Zapatismo

Chiapas 95: http://www.eco.utexas.edu/faculty/Cleaver/chiapas95.html
Ejército Zapatista de Liberación Nacional: http://www.ezln.org
Servicio Internacional para la Paz: Box 2415, Santa Cruz, CA 95063, USA

Tel & Fax: int-1-831-425-1257
sipaz@igc.org
http://www.nonviolence.org/sipaz/

Anarchism

Food Not Bombs (first chapter): PO Box 9183 Cambridge, MA 02139, USA

Tel: (617) 864-8786
mgreger@OPAL.TUFTS.EDU
http://www.leftbank.com/FNB/

Workers' Solidarity Movement: PO Box 1528, Dublin 8, Ireland

wsm_ireland@geocities.com

http://flag.blackened.net/revolt/wsm.html

An Anarchist FAQ: http://www.geocities.com/CapitolHill/1931/

International of the Federations of Anarchists (Norway): ifa@anarchy.no

http://www.powertech.no/anarchy/index.html

Anarchist Archives (documents & histories collected worldwide):

http://www.pitzer.edu/~dward/Anarchist_Archives/
worldwidemovements/

Anarchism in Australia: http://www.anarki.net/~huelga/ozanarchy/
index.html

Sustainable Development

City Farmer: Canada's Office of Urban Agriculture

cityfarm@interchange.ubc.ca
http://www.cityfarmer.org/

Toronto Food Policy Council: http://www.city.toronto.on.ca/health/
food_news0601.htm

Planet Drum Foundation (founder of 'bioregionalism'): PO Box 31251, San
Francisco, CA 94131, Shasta Bioregion, USA

Tel: (415) 285-6556 Fax (415)285-6563
planetdrum@igc.org
http://www.planetdrum.org/

AK Bioregionalismus Sauerland: c/o Leif-Thorsten Kramps, Klippchen 8a,
D-58093 Hagen/Westfalen (Bioregion Sauerland), Germany

stachelbeere@web.de

Permaculture Activist: PO Box 1209 Black Mountain, NC 28711, USA

pcactiv@metalab.unc.edu
http://metalab.unc.edu/pc-activist/

Slow Food: http://www.slowfood.com

Schumacher Society: Foxhole, Dartington, Totnes TQ9 6EB, UK

Tel/Fax: 01803 865051
email schumacher@gn.apc.org
http://www.oneworld.org/schumachersoc/

Chefs Collaborative 2000: http://www.cc2m.org/about_us.html

Community Food Security Coalition: PO Box 209 Venice, CA 90294, USA

Tel: 310-822-5410 Fax: 310-822-1440
asfisher@aol.com
http://www.foodsecurity.org/

Small Business

Landsman Community Services Ltd (LETS Community Currency System): 1600 Embleton Crescent Courtenay, BC V9N 6N8, Canada

Tel. (604) 338-0213
lcs@mars.ark.com
http://www.gmlets.u-net.com/ (design manual is on-line at this address)

Ithaca Hours: Box 6578, Ithaca, NY 14851, USA

Tel: 607-272-4330
hours@lightlink.com
http://www.lightlink.com/hours/ithacahours/

Open Air Market Net: http://www.openair.org/

SprawlBusters: 21 Grinnell St, Greenfield, MA 01301, USA

Tel: (413) 772-6289
info@sprawl-busters.com
http://www.sprawl-busters.com/

Angry, Young, & Poor: 140 N. Prince Street, Lancaster, PA 17603

Tel: (717) 397-6116
http://angryyoungandpoor.com/

The Opiate Independent DIY Distribution: links are international
http://members.tripod.lycos.nl/opiate/

Tony Brown Productions: 1501 Broadway, Suite 412, NY, NY 10036, USA

Tel: (212) 575-0876 Fax: (212) 391-4607
http://www.tonybrown.com/

Sovereignty Movements

Unrepresented Nations and Peoples Organization: 40A Javastraat, NL-2585 AP, The Hauge, The Netherlands

http://www.unpo.org *

Center for World Indigenous Studies and Fourth World Documentation Project: 1001 Cooper

Point Road SW, Suite 140-214, Olympia, WA 98502, USA
http://www.halcyon.com/FWDP/

Abya Yala Net: http://abyayala.nativeweb.org/

Bibliography

Adorno, Theodor W. (1951) 'Freudian theory and the pattern of fascist propaganda', in A. Arato and E. Gebhardt, *The Essential Frankfurt Reader*, New York: Continuum.

— (1972) *Aesthetic Theory*, ed. G. Adorno and R. Tiedemann, trans. C. Lenhardt, London: Routledge and Kegan Paul.

Ahmed, Leila (1982) 'Feminism and feminist movements in the Middle East: a preliminary exploration: Turkey, Egypt, Algeria, People's Democratic Republic of Yemen', *Women's Studies International Forum*, 5: 153–68.

Althusser, Louis (1970) 'Ideology and ideological state apparatuses', in L. Althusser, *Essays on Ideology*, New York: Verso.

Amin, Samir (1985) *Delinking: Towards a Polycentric World*, trans. M. Wolfers, London: Zed Books.

Amoore, Louise, Richard Dodgson et al. (1997) 'Overturning "globalization": resisting the teleological, reclaiming the "political"', *New Political Economy*, 2 (March): 181–97.

Anderson, Benedict (1983) *Imagined Communities: Reflections on the Origin and Spread of Nationalism*, New York: Verso.

Andrews, Bruce (1980) 'Criticizing economic democracy', *Monthly Review*, 32 (May): 19–25.

Arendt, Hannah (1958) *The Human Condition*, Garden City, NY: Doubleday Anchor.

Armstrong, Jeanette (1996) '"Sharing one skin": Okanagan community', in J. Mander and E. Goldsmith (eds), *The Case Against the Global Economy*, pp. 460–70.

Aronowitz, Stanley (1992) 'Postmodernism and politics', in S. Aronowitz, *The Politics of Identity: Class, Culture, Social Movements*, New York: Routledge.

— (1996) *The Death and Rebirth of American Radicalism*, New York: Routledge.

Auld, Gary, Amory Starr et al. (1999) 'Sustainable agricultural ecosystems: cultivating local foodlinks', grant proposal (January).

Barber, Benjamin R. (1995) *Jihad vs. McWorld*, New York: Random House.

Barnet, Richard and John Cavanagh (1994) *Global Dreams: Imperial Corporations and the New World Order*, New York: Touchstone.

Barnet, Richard and Ronald E. Müller (1974) *Global Reach: The Power of the Multinational Corporations*, New York: Simon and Schuster.

Basu, Amrita (ed.) (1995) *The Challenge of Local Feminisms: Women's Movements in Global Perspective*, Boulder, CO: Westview Press.

Bellah, Robert N. et al. (1985) *Habits of the Heart: Individualism and Community in American Life*, Berkeley, CA: University of California Press.

Bello, Walden (1993) 'Global economic counterrevolution: the dynamics of impoverishment and marginalization', in R. Hofrichter (ed.), *Toxic Struggles: The Theory and Practice of Environmental Justice*, Philadelphia: New Society, pp. 197–208.

Bello, Walden and Stephanie Rosenfeld (1990) *Dragons in Distress: Asia's Miracle Economies in Crisis*, San Francisco: Food First, The Institute for Food and Development Policy.

Bello, Walden with Shea Cunningham and Bill Rau (1994) *Dark Victory: The United States, Structural Adjustment and Global Poverty*, London: Pluto Press with Food First.

Benjamin, Walter (1940) 'Theses on the philosophy of history', in W. Benjamin, *Illuminations*, New York: Schocken Books.

Berman, Russell A. (1995) 'Beyond localism and universalism: nationalism and solidarity', *Telos*, 105 (Fall): 43–56.

Bernard, Elaine (1993) 'Opposing the new world order in Canada', in J. Brecher, J. B. Childs and J. Cutler (eds), *Global Visions*, pp. 207–11.

Berry, Wendell (1977) *The Unsettling of America: Culture and Agriculture*, San Francisco: Sierra Club.

— (1996) 'Conserving communities', in J. Mander and E. Goldsmith, *The Case Against the Global Economy*.

Bhabha, Homi K. (1990) *Nation and Narration*, London: Routledge.

— (1996) 'Culture's in-between', in S. Hall and P. duGay (eds), *Questions of Cultural Identity*, London: Sage.

Big Noise Films (1998) 'Zapatista communiqué', zapatista@silcom.com

Birkhölzer, Karl (1996) 'Promoting community self-reliance in Europe', *Development*, 3: 60–3.

Boggs, Carl (1986) *Social Movements and Political Power: Emerging Forms of Radicalism in the West*, Philadelphia: Temple University Press.

Boron, Atilio (1995) *State, Capitalism, and Democracy in Latin America*, Boulder, CO: Lynne Reinner.

Bottomore, Tom (1983) *A Dictionary of Marxist Thought*, Cambridge, MA: Harvard University Press.

Boulding, Elise (1993) 'Ethnicity and new constitutive orders', in J. Brecher, J. B. Childs and J. Cutler, *Global Visions*, pp. 213–31.

Boyte, Harry C. (1977) 'The populist challenge: anatomy of an emerging movement', *Socialist Revolution*, 7 (March–April): 39–81.

Bradford, George (1989) *How Deep is Deep Ecology?*, Times Change Press.

Brecher, Jeremy (1998) 'American labor on the eve of the millennium', *Z Magazine*, 11 (October): 25–8.

Brecher, Jeremy, John Brown Childs and Jill Cutler (eds) (1993) *Global Visions: Beyond the New World Order*, Boston, MD: South End Press.

Brecher, Jeremy and Tim Costello (1994) *Global Village or Global Pillage: Economic Reconstruction from the Bottom Up*, Boston, MD: South End Press.

Brown, Richard Harvey (1987) *Society as Text: Essays on Rhetoric, Reason, and Reality*, Chicago: University of Chicago Press.

Brown, Tony (1997) *Black Lies, White Lies: The Truth According to Tony Brown*, New York: William Morrow.

Brubaker, Rogers (1996) 'Nationalizing states in the old "New Europe" and the new', *Ethnic and Racial Studies*, 19: 411–33.

Bullard, Robert D. (ed.) (1993) *Confronting Environmental Racism: Voices from the Grassroots*, Boston, MD: South End Press.

— (ed.) (1994) *Unequal Protection: Environmental Justice and Communities of Color*, San Francisco: Sierra Club Books.

Butler, Judith (1990) *Gender Trouble: Feminism and the Subversion of Identity*, New York: Routledge.

Buttel, Frederick H. (1980) 'Agriculture, environment, and social change: some emergent issues', in F. H. Buttel and H. Newby (eds), *The Rural Sociology of the Advanced Societies*, Montclair: Allenheld Osmun.

Cable, Vincent (1995) 'The diminished nation-state: a study in the loss of economic power', *Daedalus*, 124 (Spring): 23–53.

Calhoun, Craig J. (1982) *The Question of Class Struggle: Social Foundations of Popular Radicalism During the Industrial Revolution*, Chicago: University of Chicago Press.

— (1997) *Nationalism*, Minneapolis: University of Minnesota Press.

Cardoso, Fernando Henrique and Enzo Faletto (1979) *Dependency and Development in Latin America*, Berkeley: University of California Press.

Caufield, Catherine (1997) *Masters of Illusion: The World Bank and the Poverty of Nations*, New York: Henry Holt.

Chatterjee, Partha (1993) *The Nation and its Fragments: Colonial and Postcolonial Histories*, Princeton, NJ: Princeton University Press.

Chayanov, A. V. (1966) *The Theory of Peasant Economy*, ed. D. Thorner, B. Kerblay and R. E. F. Smith, Homewood, IL: American Economics Association/Richard D. Irwin.

Chin, Christine B. N. and James H. Mittelman (1997) 'Conceptualising resistance to globalization', *New Political Economy*, 2: 25–37.

Chowdry, Kamla (1989) 'Poverty, environment, development', *Daedalus*, 118 (Winter): 141–54.

Churchill, Ward (1986) *Pacifism as Pathology: Reflections on the Role of Armed Struggle in North America*, Winnipeg: Arbeiter Ring Publishing.

Clarke, Tony (1996) 'Mechanisms of corporate rule', in J. Mander and E. Goldsmith, *The Case Against the Global Economy*, pp. 297–308.

Clastres, Pierre (1987) *Society Against the State: Essays in Political Anthropology*, trans. R. Hurley and A. Stein, New York: Zone Books.

Cleaver, Harry (1994) 'The Chiapas uprising and the future of class struggle in the new world order', *RIFF-RAFF*, Padova, Italy (February).

Cleveland, David (1991) *Food from Dryland Gardens: An Ecological, Nutritional, and Social Approach to Small-Scale Household Food Production*, Tucson, AZ: Center for People, Food, and Environment.

Collins, Patricia Hill (1991) *Black Feminist Thought: Knowledge, Consciousness, and the Politics of Empowerment*, New York: Routledge.

Commoner, Barry (1971) *The Closing Circle*, New York: Knopf.

Cook, Christopher D. and John Rodgers (1996) 'Community food security: a growing movement', *Food First Backgrounder*, San Francisco: Institute for Food and Development Policy (Spring).

Cornelius, Wayne A. and David Myhre (eds) (1998) *The Transformation of Rural Mexico: Reforming the Ejido Sector*, San Diego/La Jolla: Center for US–Mexican Studies, University of California.

Daly, Herman E. (1993) 'From adjustment to sustainable development: the obstacle of free trade', in R. Nader et al. (eds), *The Case Against Free Trade*, San Francisco: Earth Island Press, pp. 121–32.

Danaher, Kevin (ed.) (1996) *Corporations Are Gonna Get Your Mama*, Monroe, ME: Common Courage Press.

deCerteau, Michel (1984) *The Practice of Everyday Life*, Berkeley: University of California Press.

Deloria, Vine, Jr. (1994) *God is Red: A Native View of Religion*, Golden, CO: Fulcrum Publishing.

D'Emilio, John (1983) *Sexual Politics, Sexual Communities: The Making of a Homosexual Minority in the United States, 1940–1970*, Chicago: University of Chicago Press.

de-Shalit, Avner (1996) 'National self-determination: political, not cultural', *Political Studies*, XLIV: 906–20.

Douglas, Ian R. (1997) 'Globalization and the end of the state?', *New Political Economy*, 2: 165–77.

Douthwaite, Richard (1993) *The Growth Illusion*, Tulsa, OK: Council Oak Books.

— (1996) *Short Circuit: Strengthening Local Economies for Security in an Unstable World*, Foxhole, UK: Green Boooks.

Dragadze, Tamara (1996) 'Self-determination and the politics of exclusion', *Ethnic and Racial Studies*, 19: 341–51.

DuBois, W. E. B. (1940) *Dusk of Dawn: An Essay Toward an Autobiography of a Race Concept*, New York: Schocken Books.

Eagleton, Terry (1991) *Ideology: An Introduction*, New York: Verso.

The Ecologist (1993) *Whose Common Future? Reclaiming the Commons*, Philadelphia, PA: New Society.

Eisinger, Peter K. (1976) *Patterns of Interracial Politics: Conflict and Cooperation in the City*, New York: Academic Press.

Ekins, Paul (1992) *A New World Order: Grassroots Movements for Global Change*, New York: Routledge.

Elgin, Duane (1981) *Voluntary Simplicity: Toward a Way of Life that is Outwardly Simple, Inwardly Rich*, New York: Morrow.

Ertman, Martha M. (2000) 'Oscar Wilde: paradoxical poster child for homosexual and gay identity as well as queer post-identity', *Law and Social Inquiry*.

Etzioni, Amitai (1995) *New Communication Thinking: Persons, Virtues, Institutions, and Communities*, University of Virginia Press.

Faksh, Mahmud A. (1997) *The Future of Islam in the Middle East: Fundamentalism in Egypt, Algeria, and Saudi Arabia*, Westport, CT: Praeger.

Falk, Richard (1993) 'The making of global citizenship', in J. Brecher, J. B. Childs and J. Cutler, *Global Visions*, pp. 39–50.

Fanon, Frantz (1961) *The Wretched of the Earth*, New York: Grove Press.

Field, Patrick (1988) 'The anti-roads movement: the struggle of memory against forgetting', in T. Jordan and A. Lent, *Storming the Millennium: The New Politics of Change*, London: Lawrence and Wishart, pp. 68–79.

Flacks, Richard (1988) *Making History: The American Left and the American Mind*, New York: Columbia University Press.

Flax, Jane (1992) 'The end of innocence', in J. Butler and J. W. Scott (eds), *Feminists Theorize the Political*, New York: Routledge.

Foran, John (1992) 'A historical–sociological framework for the study of long-term transformations in the third world', *Humanity and Society*, 16: 330–49.

— (1993) *Fragile Resistance: Social Transformation in Iran from 1500 to the Revolution*, Boulder, CO: Westview Press.

Foucault, Michel (1976) 'Two lectures', in M. Foucault, ed. C. Gordon, *Power/Knowledge: Selected Interviews and Other Writings*, New York: Pantheon.

— (1982) 'The subject and power', in B. Wallis (ed.), *Art after Modernism: Rethinking Representation*, New York and Boston: New Museum of Contemporary Art in association with David R. Godine.

Franklin, V. P. (1984) *Black Self-Determination: A Cultural History of the Faith of the Fathers*, Westport, CT: Lawrence Hill.

Fraser, Nancy (1989) *Unruly Practices: Power, Discourse, and Gender in Contemporary Social Theory*, Minneapolis: University of Minnesota Press.

Freire, Paulo (1969) *Education for Critical Consciousness*, New York: Continuum.

Friedland, Roger and Richard Hecht (1996) *To Rule Jerusalem*, Cambridge: Cambridge University Press.

Frith, Simon (1996) 'Music and identity', in S. Hall and P. duGay (eds), *Questions of Cultural Identity*, London: Sage.

Fuentes, Marta (1989) 'Ten theses on social movements', *World Development*, 17 (February): 179–91.

Gamson, William A. (1992) *Talking Politics*, Cambridge: Cambridge University Press.

Gandhi, Mahatma (1908) *Hind Swaraj or Indian Home Rule*, Madras: G. A. Natesan.

Gedicks, Al (1993) *The New Resource Wars: Native and Environmental Struggles Against Multinational Corporations*, Boston, MD: South End Press.

Gellner, Ernest (1992) *Postmodernism, Reason and Religion*, London: Routledge.

Getz, Arthur (1991) 'Urban foodsheds', *Permaculture Activist*, VII: 26–7.

Geulen, Eva (1995) 'Nationalisms: old, new and German', *Telos*, 105: 2–21.

Gibson, William (1984) *Neuromancer*, New York: Ace Books.

Gibson-Graham, J. K. (1996/97) 'Querying globalization', *Rethinking Marxism*, 9: 1–27.

Gilroy, Paul (193) *The Black Atlantic: Modernity and Double Consciousness*, Cambridge, MA: Harvard University Press.

Glasberg, Davita Silfen (1990) 'Bank hegemony and class struggle in Cleveland, 1978–79', in M. Davis et al. (eds), *Fire in the Hearth: The Radical Politics of Place in America*, New York: Routledge, pp. 195–218.

Goering, Peter et al. (1993) *From the Ground Up: Rethinking Industrial Agriculture*, London: Zed Books.

Goldblatt, David, David Held, Anthony McGrew and Jonathan Perraton (1997) 'Economic globalization and the nation-state: shifting balances of power', *Alternatives*, 22: 269–85.

Green, Philip (1985) *Retrieving Democracy: In Search of Civic Equality*, Totawa, NJ: Rowman & Allanheld.

Griggs, Richard (1992) 'The meaning of "nation" and "state" in the fourth world', Olympia, WA: Center for World Indigenous Studies.

Grossman, Richard L. and Frank T. Adams (1996) 'Exercising power over corporations through state charters', in J. Mander and E. Goldsmith (eds), *The Case Against the Global Economy*, pp. 374–89.

Gunder-Frank, André (1967) *Capitalism and Underdevelopment in Latin America*, New York: Monthly Review Press.

Gunn Allen, Paula (1986) *The Sacred Hoop: Recovering the Feminine in American Indian Traditions*, Boston, MD: Beacon Press.

Gwaltney, John Langston (1980) *Drylongso: A Self-portrait of Black America*, New York: Random House.

Habermas, Jürgen (1979) *Communication and the Evolution of Society*, ed. T. McCarthy, Boston, MD: Beacon Press.

Hall, Stuart (1980) 'Cultural studies: two paradigms', *Media, Culture and Society*.

— (1996) 'Who needs "identity"?', in S. Hall and P. duGay, *Questions of Cultural Identity*, London: Sage.

Hamilton, Cynthia (1990) 'Women, hope, and community: the struggle in an urban environment', in I. Diamond and G. Orenstein, *Reweaving the World*, San Francisco: Sierra Club Books, pp. 215–22.

— (1993) 'Coping with industrial exploitation', in R. Bullard (ed.), *Confronting Environmental Racism: Voices from the Grassroots*, Boston, MD: South End Press.

Hannum, Hurst (1990) *Autonomy, Sovereignty, and Self-Determination: The Accommodation of Conflicting Rights*, Philadelphia: University of Pennsylvania Press.

Haraway, Donna J. (1983) 'A cyborg manifesto: science, technology, and socialist-feminism in the late twentieth century', in D. J. Haraway, *Simians, Cyborgs, and Women: The Reinvention of Nature*, New York: Routledge.

Harding, Sandra (1986) *The Science Question in Feminism*, Ithaca, NY: Cornell University Press.

Harris, Marvin (1974) *Cows, Pigs, Wars and Witches: The Riddles of Culture*, New York: Random House.

Heilman, Samuel (1992) *Defenders of the Faith: Inside Ultra-Orthodox Jewry*, New York: Schocken Books.

Held, David and Anthony McGrew (1998) 'The end of the old order? Globalization and the prospects for world order', *Review of International Studies*, 24: 219–43.

Hendrickson, J. A. (1993) 'The foodshed: heuristic device and sustainable alternative to the food system', in *Agriculture, Food and Human Values Society*, Association for the Study of Food in Society, and the Pennsylvania State University College of Agricultural Sciences, Pennsylvania: State College.

Henwood, Doug (1996) 'Antiglobalization', *Left Business Observer* (January).

Herman, Edward S. (1999) 'The threat of globalization', *New Politics*, 7: 40–6.

Hines, Colin and Tim Lang (1996) 'In favour of a new protectionism', in J. Mander and E. Goldsmith (eds), *The Case Against the Global Economy*, pp. 485–93.

Hirschman, Albert O. (1991) *The Rhetoric of Reaction: Perversity, Futility, Jeopardy*, Cambridge, MA: Belknap.

Hirst, Paul and Grahame Thompson (1996) *Globalization in Question*, Cambridge: Polity Press.

Hobsbawm, Eric (1990) *Nations and Nationalism Since 1780: Programme, Myth, Reality*, Cambridge: Cambridge University Press.

Hofrichter, Richard (ed.) (1993) *Toxic Struggles: The Theory and Practice of Environmental Justice*, Philadelphia, PA: New Society.

Horkheimer, Max (1947) *Eclipse of Reason*, New York: Continuum.

Ichiyo, Muto (1993) 'For an alliance of hope', in J. Brecher et al. (eds), *Global Visions*, pp. 147–62.

— (1998) 'Ecological perspectives on alternative development: the Rainbow Plan', *Capitalism Nature Socialism*, 9 (March): 3–23.

IFG (International Forum on Globalization) (1997) *Teach-In 3: The Social, Ecological, Cultural, and Political Costs of Economic Globalization*, Berkeley, CA: IFG (April).

— (1999) *Teach-In on Economic Globalization and the Role of the World Trade Organization*, held at Benaroya Symphony Hall, Seattle.

Imbroscio, David L. (1995) 'An alternative approach to urban economic development: exploring the dimensions and prospects of a self-reliance strategy', *Urban Affairs Review*, 30: 840–67.

Imhoff, Daniel (1996) 'Community supported agriculture: farming with a face on it', in J. Mander and E. Goldsmith (eds), *The Case Against the Global Economy*, p. 425–33.

IWGIA (International Work Group for Indigenous Affairs) (1989) *Document No. 63: Indigenous Self-Development in the Americas: Proceedings of the IWGIA Symposium on the Congress of the Americanists, Amsterdam 1988*, Copenhagen: IWGIA.

Jagose, Annamarie (1996) *Queer Theory: An Introduction*, New York: New York University Press.

Jaimes, M. Annette with Theresa Halsey (1992) 'American Indian women: at the center of indigenous resistance in contemporary North America', in A. Jaimes (ed.), *The State of Native America: Genocide, Colonialization, and Resistance*, Boston, MD: South End Press, pp. 311–44.

Jameson, Fredric (1998) *The Cultural Turn: Selected Writings on the Postmodern, 1983–1998*, London: Verso.

Jankowski, Martín Sánchez (1991) *Islands in the Street: Gangs and American Urban Society*, Berkeley: University of California Press.

Johnston, Marie-Josée (1997) 'Defending and reconstructing emancipation: using the Zapatista uprising as a guiding heuristic', MA thesis, Edmonton: Department of Sociology, University of Alberta.

Judis, John (1976) 'California's new new left: Tom Hayden and the CDC', *Socialist Revolution*, 6: 51–63 (July–September).

Juergensmeyer, Mark (1993) *The New Cold War? Religious Nationalism Confronts the Secular State*, Berkeley: University of California Press.

Kelly, Petra (1993) 'A very bad way to enter the next century', in J. Brecher et al. (eds), *Global Visions*, pp. 133–43.

Kemmis, David (1990) *Community and the Politics of Place*, Norman, OK: University of Oklahoma Press.

Kepel, Gilles (1991) *The Revenge of God: The Resurgence of Islam, Christianity, and Judaism in the Modern World*, trans. Alan Braley, University Park, Pennsylvania: Pennsylvania State University Press.

Khor, Martin Khor Kok Peng (1993) 'Economics and environmental justice: rethinking North–South relations', in R. Hofrichter (ed.), *Toxic Struggles*, pp. 219–25.

King, Jonathan and Doreen Stabinsky (1998–99) 'Biotechnology under globalization: the corporate expropriation of plant, animal and microbial species', *Race and Class*, 40 (October–March): 73–90.

King, Mel (1981) *Chain of Change: Struggles for Black Community Development*, Boston, MD: South End Press.

Kofman, Daniel (1998) 'Rights of secession', *Society*, 35: 30–7.

Korten, David (1995) *When Corporations Rule The World*, West Hartford, CT: Kumarian Press.

Kovel, Joel (1998) 'Symposium: John Clarke's "A Social Ecology"', *Capitalism Nature Socialism*, 8 (March): 25–45.

Krauss, Celine (1993) 'Blue-collar women and toxic-waste protests: the process of politicization', in R. Hofrichter (ed.), *Toxic Struggles*, pp. 107–15.

Kumar, Satish (1996) 'Gandhi's Swadeshi: the economics of permanence', in J. Mander and E. Goldsmith (eds), *The Case Against the Global Economy*, pp. 418–24.

Kurzman, Charles (1996) 'How Islamic was the 1979 Islamic Revolution in Iran?', New Orleans: *Social Science Historical Association* (12 October).

Kutty, Omar (1996) 'Sources of intolerance: the modern discourse of the self in the Bharitiya Janata Party', unpublished.

Laclau, Ernesto and Chantal Mouffe (1985) *Hegemony and Socialist Strategy: Towards a Radical Democratic Politics*, London: Verso.

Lacy, Michael G. (1982) 'A model of cooptation applied to the political relations of the United States and American Indians', *Social Science Journal*, 19: 23–36.

Lampkin, Nicolas (1990) *Organic Farming*, New York: Farming Press.

Landau, Saul (1996) 'The Sixth Sun', available from Cinema Guild 800/723.5522.

Lang, Tim and Colin Hines (1993) *The New Protectionism: Protecting the Future Against Free Trade*, New York: New Press.

Latham, Robert (1997) 'Globalization and democratic provisionism: re-reading Polanyi', *New Political Economy*, 2: 53–63.

Lawrence, Bruce (1989) *Defenders of God*, San Francisco: Harper & Row.

Laxer, Gordon (1999) 'Rescuing positive nationalism from the scrap heap of history, or the return of nationalism', submitted to *Studies in Political Economy*.

Lenin, V. I. (1916) *Imperialism: The Highest Stage of Capitalism, A Popular Outline*, New York: International Publishers.

Lévi-Strauss, Claude (1963) *Structural Anthropology*, New York: Basic Books.

Livingston, Donald W. (1998) 'The very idea of secession', *Society*, 35: 38–48.

Logan, John and Harvey Moloch (1987) *Urban Fortunes: The Political Economy of Place*, Berkeley: University of California Press.

Lorde, Audre (1984) *Sister Outsider: Essays and Speeches by Audre Lorde*, Freedom, CA: Crossing Press.

Lowe, Lisa (1996) *Immigrant Acts: On Asian American Cultural Politics*, Durham: Duke University Press.

Lubiano, Wahneema (1997) 'Black nationalism and black common sense: policing ourselves and others', in W. Lubiano, *The House that Race Built: Black Americans, US Terrain*, New York: Pantheon.

Lukács, Georg (1922) *Reification and the Consciousness of the Proletariat*, trans. R. Livingstone, Cambridge, MA: MIT Press.

McKenna, George (ed.) (1974) *American Populism*, New York: Putman.

McKnight, John (1995) *The Careless Society: Community and its Counterfeits*, New York: Basic Books.

Macpherson, C. B. (1977) *The Life and Times of Liberal Democracy*, Oxford: Oxford University Press.

MacShane, Denis (1993) 'Labor standards and double standards in the new world order', in J. Brecher, J. B. Childs and J. Cutler (eds), *Global Visions*, pp. 197–205.

Mander, Jerry (1978) *Four Arguments for the Elimination of Television*, New York: William Morrow & Co.

Mander, Jerry and Edward Goldsmith (eds) (1996) *The Case Against the Global Economy and For a Turn Toward the Local*, San Francisco: Sierra Club Books.

Marcuse, Herbert (1964) *One Dimensional Man*, Boston, MD: Beacon Press.

Marx, Karl (1859) *A Contribution to the Critique of Political Economy*, Berlin: Franz Duncker.

— (1867) *Capital Vol. I*, Chicago: William Benton.

— (1972) *The Ethnological Notebooks of Karl Marx*, trans. and ed. L. Krader, Assen: Van Gorcum.

— (1973) *Grundrisse: Foundation of the Critique of Political Economy*, trans. Martin Nicolaus, Harmondsworth/Baltimore: Penguin Books.

Marx, Karl and Frederick Engels (1846) *The German Ideology*, ed. C. J. Arthur, trans. Lawrence and Wishart 1970, New York: International Publishers.

Mason, Jim and Peter Singer (1980) *Animal Factories*, New York: Harmony Books.

Mattelart, Armand (1993) 'New horizons of communication: the return of culture', *Das Argument*, 35 (September/October): 689–706.

Meeker-Lowry, Susan (1996) 'Community money: the potential of local currency', in J. Mander and E. Goldsmith (eds), *The Case Against the Global Economy*, pp. 446–59.

Mellor, Mary (1998) 'Symposium: John Clark's "A Social Ecology"', *Capitalism Nature Socialism*, 9 (March): 23–45.

Melucci, Alberto (1980) 'The new social movements: a theoretical approach', *Social Science Information*, 19 (2): 199–226.

Mernissi, Fatima (1992) *Islam and Democracy: Fear of the Modern World*, Reading, MA: Addison-Wesley.

Meyer, Christine and Faith Moosang (eds) (1992) *Living with the Land: Communities Restoring the Earth*, Philadelphia, PA: New Society Publishers.

Michan, Ezra J. (1967) *The Costs of Economic Growth*, New York: Praeger.

Mies, Maria and Veronica Bennholdt-Thomsen (1999) *The Subsistence Perspective: Beyond the Globalized Economy*, London: Zed Books.

Mihevc, John (1995) *The Market Tells them So: The World Bank and Economic Fundamentalism in Africa*, London: Zed Books.

Miller, David (1996) *On Nationality*, Oxford: Oxford University Press.

Mills, C. W. (1951) *White Collar*, New York: Oxford University Press.

Mollison, Bill (1990) *The Permaculture Designers Manual*, Tyalgum Australia: Tagari Press.

Mollison, Bill with Rene Mia Slay (1994) *Introduction to Permaculture*, Tyalgum, Australia: Tagari Press.

Molotch, Harvey (1976) 'The city as a growth machine', *American Journal of Sociology*, 82 (2): 309–30.

Moore, Michael (1997) 'Is the left nuts? (Or is it me?)', *The Nation*, 17 January.

Morris, David (1996) 'Communities: building authority, responsibility, and capacity', in J. Mander and E. Goldsmith (eds), *The Case Against the Global Economy*, pp. 434–45.

Morris, Jane Ann (1996) 'Corporate rule', speech for Santa Barbara chapter of the Citizens' Alliance (now Alliance for Democracy), May, Faulkner Library.

Myerson, George (1994) *Rhetoric, Reason and Society*, London: Sage.

Nader, Ralph et al. (1993) *The Case Against Free Trade: GATT, NAFTA, and the Globalization of Corporate Power*, San Francisco: Earth Island Press.

Nandy, Ashis (1983) *The Intimate Enemy: Loss and Recovery of Self Under Colonialism*, Delhi: Oxford University Press.

Nettleford, Rex (1994) Speech at National Symposium on Indigenous Knowledge and Contemporary Social Issues, Tampa, FL.

Niebuhr, Reinhold (1932) *Moral Man and Immoral Society*, New York: Charles Scribner's Sons.

Nomani, Farhad and Ali Rahnema (1994) *Islamic Economic Systems*, London: Zed Books.

Norberg-Hodge, Helena (1991) *Ancient Futures: Learning from Ladakh*, San Francisco: Sierra Club.

— (1996) 'Shifting direction: from global dependence to local interdependence', in J. Mander and E. Goldsmith (eds), *The Case Against the Global Economy*, pp. 393–406.

Nyang, Sulayman (1998) 'Conceptualizing globalization', *American Journal of Islamic Social Sciences*, 15 (Fall): 129–32.

Omi, Michael and Howard Winant (1986) *Racial Formation in the United States: From the 1960s to the 1980s*, New York: Routledge.

Parajuli, Pramod (1991) 'Power and knowledge in development discourse: new social movements and the state in India', *International Social Journal*, 43 (February): 173–90.

Peña, Devon and Joseph Gallegos (1993) 'Nature and Chicanos in Southern Colorado', in R. Hofrichter, *Toxic Struggles*, pp. 141–60.

Petras, James (1998) 'The new revolutionary peasantry', *Z Magazine*, 11 (October), 29–34.

Pfohl, Stephen (1992) *Death at the Parasite Café: Social Science (Fictions) and the Postmodern*, New York: St. Martin's Press.

Piccolomini, Michele (1996) 'Sustainable development, collective action, and new social movements', *Research in Social Movements, Conflict and Change*, 19: 183–208.

Pieterse, Jan Nederveen (1997) 'Globalization and emancipation: from local empowerment to global reform', *New Political Economy*, 2: 79–92.

Piven, Francis Fox and Richard Cloward (1997) *Poor People's Movements*, New York: Pantheon Books.

Plamenatz, John Petrov (1970) *Ideology*, New York: Praeger.

Polanyi, Karl (1944) *The Great Transformation*, Boston, MD: Beacon Press.

Rady, Martyn (1996) 'Self-determination and the dissolution of Yugoslavia', *Ethnic and Racial Studies*, 19: 379–90.

Raghavan, Chakravarthi (1990) *Recolonization: GATT, the Uruguay Round and the Third World*, Penang, Malaysia: Third World Network.

Reagon, Bernice Johnson (1982) 'My black mothers and sisters or on beginning a cultural autobiography', *Feminist Studies*, 8 (Spring): 81–96.

— (1994) 'Keynote address' at National Symposium on Indigenous Knowledge, Tampa, FL.

Renan, Ernest (1990; originally published 1882) 'What is a nation?', in H. K. Bhabha (ed.),*Nation and Narration*, London: Routledge.

Ricardo, David (1817) *Principles of Political Economy and Taxation*.

Riesebrodt, Martin (1990) *Pious Passion: The Emergence of Modern Fundamentalism in the United States and Iran*, trans. D. Reneau, Berkeley: University of California Press.

Rifkin, Jeremy (1885) *The End of Work*, New York: G. P. Putman's Sons.

Ritchie, Mark (1996) 'Cross-border organizing', in J. Mander and E. Goldsmith (eds), *The Case Against the Global Economy*, pp. 494–500.

Robinson, Cedric (1980) *Terms of Order: Political Science and the Myth of Leadership*, Albany, NY: State University of New York Press.

Robinson, William I. (1998/99) 'Latin America and global capitalism', *Race & Class*, 40: 111–31.

Rodney, Walter (1972) *How Europe Underdeveloped Africa*, Washington, DC: Howard University Press.

Rose, Nikolas (1996) 'Identity, genealogy, history', in S. Hall and P. duGay (eds), *Questions of Cultural Identity*, London: Sage.

Ross, John (1998) *The Annexation of Mexico: From the Aztecs to the I.M.F.*, Monroe, ME: Common Courage Press.

Rosset, Peter and Medea Benjamin (1994) *The Greening of Cuba: A National Experiment in Organic Agriculture*, San Francisco: Food First Books.

Rosset, Peter with Shea Cunningham (1994) 'The greening of Cuba: organic farming offers hope in the midst of crisis', *Food First Action Alert*, Spring.

Rotkin, Michael (1977) 'Populist insurgency and socialist submersion: a response to Harry Boyte', *Socialist Revolution*, 7 (March–April): 39–81.

Rupert, Mark (1997) 'Globalization and American common sense: struggling to make sense of a post-hegemonic world', *New Political Economy*, 2: 105–16.

Sadeq, Abul Hasan M. (1996) 'Ethico-Economic Institution of Zakah: an instrument of self-reliance and sustainable grassroots development', *Humanomics*, 12: 47–69.

Said, Edward (1978) *Orientalism*, New York: Vintage.

Sale, Kirkpatrick (1985) *Dwellers in the Land: The Bioregional Vision*, San Francisco: Sierra Club Books.

— (1995) *Rebels Against the Future: The Luddites and Their War on the Industrial Revolution*, Reading, MA: Addison Wesley.

— (1996) 'Principles of bioregionalism', in J. Mander and E. Goldsmith (eds), *The Case Against the Global Economy*, pp. 471–84.

Sandler, Blair (1995) 'Globalization or capitalism?', *Socialist Review*, 25 (December): 13–18.

Shumacher, E. F. (1973) *Small is Beautiful: Economics as if People Mattered*, New York: Harper & Row.

Schwartzman, Kathleen C. (1998) 'Globalization and democracy', *Annual Review of Sociology*, 24: 159–81.

Scott, James C. (1990) *Domination and the Arts of Resistance: Hidden Transcripts*, New Haven, CT: Yale University Press.

Shiva, Vandana (1991) *The Violence of the Green Revolution: Third World Agriculture, Ecology and Politics*, London: Zed Boooks.

— (1997) *Biopiracy*, Boston, MD: South End Press.

Shuman, Michael (1998) *Going Local: Creating Self-reliant Communities in a Global Age*, New York: Free Press.

Sivanandan, A. (1989) 'New circuits of imperialism', *Race and Class*, 30 (April–June): 1–19.

— (1990) *Communities of Resistance: Writings on Black Struggles for Socialism*, London: Verso.

Sivaraksa, Sulak (1989) 'Development and environment in Southeast Asia', *Zygon*, 24 (December): 429–36.

Sklair, Leslie (1998) 'Debate transnational corporations: as political actors', *New Political Economy*, 3: 284–7.

Sklar, Holly (1980) *Trilateralism*, Boston, MD: South End Press.

— (1995) *Chaos or Community: Seeking Solutions, Not Scapegoats for Bad Economics*, Boston, MD: South End Press.

Smith, Adam (1776) *The Wealth of Nations*.

Snow, David A., E. Burke Rochford, Jr, Steven K. Worden and Robert D. Benford (1986) 'Frame alignment processes, micromobilization, and movement participation', *American Sociological Review*, 51 (August): 464–81.

Spivak, Gayatri Chakravorty (1989) 'The political economy of women as seen by a literary critic', in E. Weed (ed.), *Coming to Terms: Feminism, Theory, Politics*, New York: Routledge.

Stan, Adele M. (1995) 'Power preying and a guide to the new right', *Mother Jones*, November–December.

Starr, Amory (1994) 'It takes the whole village: beyond the war on youth in urban communities', unpublished manuscript.

Starr, Amory and John Rodgers (1995) 'On discourses and social movements: traversing the first world/third world development divide', *Journal of Developing Societies*, XI: 74–97.

Starr, Paul (1979) 'Keeping the left alive', *Working Papers for a New Society*, 6 (March/April): 10–11.

Strange, Marty (1988) *Family Farming: A New Economic Vision*, San Francisco: Food First Books.

Strange, Susan (1996) *The Retreat of the State*, Cambridge: Cambridge University Press.

Telos Staff (1995) 'Nationhood, nationalism and identity: a symposium', *Telos*, 105 (Fall): 77–111.

Tickner J. Ann (1986) 'Local self-reliance versus power politics: conflicting priorities of national development', *Alternatives*, XI: 461–83.

Tiryakian, Edward A. (1998) 'Secession, autonomy and modernity', *Society*, 35: 50–8.

Tomlinson, John (1991) *Cultural Imperialism*, Baltimore, MD: Johns Hopkins University Press.

Tovey, Hilary (1997) 'Food, environmentalism and rural sociology: on the organic farming movement in Ireland', *Sociologia Ruralis*, 37: 21–37.

Trainer, F. E. (1989) 'Reconstructing radical development theory', *Alternatives*, 14 (October): 481–515.

Trask, Haunani-Kay (1993) 'Malama 'aina: take care of the land', in J. Brecher, J. B. Childs and J. Cutler (eds), *Global Visions*, pp. 127–31.

UNDP (1997) *Human Development Report 1997*, New York: Oxford University Press.

Vellinga, M. L. (1971) 'On academic colonialism: the case of US–Latin American studies', *Sociologische Gids* (July–August): 338–53.

Vogel, David (1974) 'The politicization of the corporation', *Social Policy*, 5 (May–June): 57–62.

Wallerstein, Immanuel (1976) *The Modern World System: Capitalist Agriculture and the Origins of the European World-Economy in the Sixteenth Century*, New York: Academic Press.

Walton, John and David Seddon (1994) *Free Markets and Food Riots: The Politics of Global Adjustment*, Oxford: Blackwell.

Ward, Colin (1982) *Anarchy in Action*, London: Freedom Press.

WCED (World Commission on Environment and Development) (1987), *Our Common Future* (the Brundtland Report), New York: Oxford University Press.

Weber, Max (1904–5) *The Protestant Ethic and the Spirit of Capitalism*, New York: Scribner's.

Weinberg, Bill (1991) *War on the Land: Ecology and Politics in Central America*, London: Zed Books.

Weissman, Robert (1993) 'Corporate plundering of third-world resources', in R. Hofrichter (ed.), *Toxic Struggles*, pp. 186–96.

Wilkins, Jennifer L. (1995) 'Seasonal and local diets: consumers' role in achieving a sustainable food system', *Research in Rural Sociology and Development*, 6: 149–66.

Williams, Patricia J. (1991) *The Alchemy of Race and Rights: Diary of a Law Professor*, Cambridge, MA: Harvard University Press.

Williams, Walter L. (1986) *The Spirit and the Flesh: Sexual Diversity in American Indian Culture*, Boston, MD: Beacon Press.

Williams, William Appleman (1988) *The Contours of American History*, New York: Norton.

Worms, Jean-Pierre (1982) 'Toward a decentralization of social action', *Futuribles*: 84–9.

Wray, Stefan (1998) 'Electronic civil disobedience and the World Wide Web of Hactivism: a mapping of extraparliamentarian direct action net politics', presented at Contemporary Cultural Theory Conference, Drake University.

Zinn, Howard (1980) *A People's History of the United States*, New York: Harper.

Index

Development Studies Titles from Zed Books

Samir Amin, *Capitalism in the Age of Globalization: The Management of Contemporary Society*

Walden Bello, Nicola Bullard and Kamal Malhotra (eds), *Global Finance: New Thinking on Regulating Speculative Capital Markets*

Robert Biel, *The New Imperialism: Crisis and Contradictions in North/South Relations*

C. M. Correa, *Intellectual Property Rights, the WTO and Developing Countries: The TRIPS Agreement and Policy Options*

Emma Crewe and Elizabeth Harrison, *Whose Development? An Ethnography of Aid*

Bhagirath Lal Das, *An Introduction to the WTO Agreements*

Bhagirath Lal Das, *The WTO Agreements: Deficiencies, Imbalances and Required Changes*

Bhagirath Lal Das, *The World Trade Organization: A Guide to the New Framework for International Trade*

Diplab Dasgupta, *Structural Adjustment, Global Trade and the New Political Economy of Development*

Oswaldo de Rivero, *The Myth of Development: An Emergency Agenda for the Survival of Nations*

Wim Dierckxsens, *The Limits of Capitalism: An Approach to Globalization without Neoliberalism*

Mark Duffield, *Global Governance and the New Wars: The Merging of Development and Security*

Graham Dunkley, *The Free Trade Adventure: The WTO, GATT and Globalism: A Critique*

Terence Hopkins, Immanuel Wallerstein et al., *The Age of Transition: Trajectory of the World-System, 1945–2025*

Arthur MacEwan, *Neo-liberalism or Democracy: Economic Strategy, Markets and Alternatives for the 21st Century*

John Madeley, *Big Business, Poor Peoples: The Impact of Transnational Corporations on the World's Poor*

Hans-Peter Martin and Harald Schumann, *The Global Trap: Globalization and the Assault on Prosperity and Democracy*

James Petras and Henry Veltmeyer, *Globalization: The New Face of Imperialism*

Harry Shutt, *The Trouble with Capitalism: An Enquiry into the Causes of Global Economic Failure*

Kavaljit Singh, *The Globalization of Finance: A Citizen's Guide*

Kavaljit Singh, *Taming Global Financial Flows: Challenges and Alternatives in the Era of Financial Globalization*

Bob Sutcliffe, *A 100 Ways of Seeing an Unequal World*

Oscar Ugarteche, *The False Dilemma: Globalization: Opportunity or Threat?*

David Woodward, *The Next Crisis? Foreign Direct and Equity Investment in Developing Countries*

For full details of this list and Zed's other subject and general catalogues, please write to:

The Marketing Department, Zed Books, 7 Cynthia Street, London N1 9JF, UK or email: sales@zedbooks.demon.co.uk

Visit our website at: http://www.zedbooks.demon.co.uk